P9-AQL-785

Nomadic Voices of Exile

Nomadic Voices of Exile

FEMININE IDENTITY IN FRANCOPHONE
LITERATURE OF THE MAGHREB

Valérie Orlando

OHIO UNIVERSITY PRESS
ATHENS

Ohio University Press, Athens, Ohio 45701
© 1999 by Valérie Orlando
Printed in the United States of America
All rights reserved

Ohio University Press books are printed on acid-free paper.
∞ TM

03 02 01 00 99   5 4 3 2 1

Library of Congress Cataloging-in-Publication Data

Orlando, Valérie Key, 1963-
    Nomadic voices of exile : feminine identity in Franco-
phone literature of the Maghreb / Valérie Orlando.
        p.   cm.
    Includes bibliographical references and index.
    ISBN 0-8214-1262-0 (cloth : alk. paper)
    1. North African literature (French)—History and
criticism. 2. North African literature (French—Women
authors—History and criticism. 3. Women in literature.
4.Women and literature—Africa, North. I. Title.
    PQ3988.5.N6075   1999
    840. 9'9287'0961--dc21   98-32063
                                        CIP

For Martha,
in loving memory

Contents

Acknowledgments

This work is the product of many years of fruitful research as well as many years of graduate school stress and, often, overwhelming professional demands—"pressure makes diamonds," my undergraduate professor Lee Alvis Tinnin used to tell me. Many people throughout these years have supported me emotionally, financially, and intellectually. To these people I owe a great deal and I hope that a few words here can offer some semblance of gratitude. To Réda Bensmaïa, my dissertation director at Brown University, academic advisor, mentor, colleague, and friend, I offer my sincerest thanks for opening up the world of Deleuzo-Guattarian philosophy and Francophone literature for me; to Edward Ahearn, my thanks for your valuable advice in the fickle ways of the academic job market and for your expertise in nineteenth-century French literature, which has helped shape certain portions of this book; to Inge Wimmers, also at Brown University, thanks for your initial editing of my draft dissertation when I took those first wobbly steps. Special thanks to Robyn F. Brothers for her hundreds of hours of phone calls and loving support; Andrea Miller for her friendship and advice over the years; T. Denean Sharpley-Whiting, whose critique of my work has been extremely helpful in fine tuning several projects, particularly my article on Assia Djebar for *Spoils of War: Women of Color, Cultures and Revolutions* (Rowman and Littlefield, 1997); William Haney, mentor and friend, who offered enormous help with certain concepts explored in the present volume; Phyllis Clark, whose feedback on some of my ideas on Francophone literature has been extremely valuable over the years. To the Graduate School at Brown University, particularly Michael Diffily, thanks for finding me funds! A warmhearted thanks to Christine Gaspar, Will

Acknowledgments

Shotwell, Fallon Moursund, Beverly and Edgar Bennett, Kathyrn Holderbaum, Michael Jackson, and Margaret Mutter, dear friends who have always offered their best wishes. All my appreciation to Michael Settles, who told me to "get that Ph.D."; and to my friends and colleagues at Eastern Mediterranean University (Northern Turkish Republic of Cyprus), particularly Daphney Haney, Skip Norman, Andreas Kitzmann, Jeffrey Deshell, and Lisa Sheffield, thanks for listening to my half-baked ideas. I owe many thanks to my colleagues in the Department of Foreign Languages and Literatures at Purdue University—particularly to Becky Brown, Sidney Pellissier, and Christiana Keck who supported my intellectual and professional endeavors through a Visiting Assistant Professorship for the 1997–99 academic years.

I am grateful to the reviewers who read my manuscript for Ohio University Press and for the personal attention I received from Gillian Berchowitz, Senior Editor. She has helped shape this book from beginning to end. Her guidance in its preparation calmed my feelings of being overwhelmed.

Yet none of this would have been possible without the loving support of my family: mom Carolyn, dad Andrew, friend Ann, mother-in-law Thérèse, brother Brandon, sister-in-law Sonja, and Drew, my sister in spirit. Most of all I offer thanks to my husband and best friend, Philippe, who has been with me every step of the way.

Permissions

The author and publisher are grateful for permission to reproduce the following copyrighted material:

Excerpts from Leïla Sebbar's *Le fou de Shérazade* (1991) and *Les carnets de Shérazade* (1985), reproduced with the kind permission of Editions Stock, Paris.

Excerpts from Leïla Sebbar's *Sherazade: Missing, Aged Seventeen, Dark Curly Hair, Green Eyes* (translated by Dorothy S. Blair, 1991), reproduced with the kind permission of Quartet Books, Ltd., London.

Excerpts from Assia Djebar's *Vaste est la prison* (1995), reproduced with the kind permission of Editions Albin Michel, S.A., Paris and Seven Stories Press, New York, which recently bought the rights for the English translation.

Excerpts from Assia Djebar's *Fantasia: An Algerian Cavalcade* (translated by Dorothy S. Blair, 1993), reproduced with the kind permission of Quartet Books, Ltd., London, England.

Excerpts from Tahar Ben Jelloun's *The Sand Child* (1987) and *The Sacred Night* (1989) (both translated by Alan Sheridan), reproduced with the kind permission of Harcourt Brace Publishers, Orlando, Florida.

A version of my article "Assia Djebar's *Vaste est La Prison:* New Feminine Agency for Algeria" (1997), reproduced with the kind permission of the editors of *Paroles Gélées* (UCLA).

A version of my article "A la recherche du 'devenir-femme' dans le troisième espace de culture: *Shérazade: Dix-sept ans, brune, frisée, les yeux verts* de Leïla Sebbar" (1994), reproduced with the kind permission of the editors of *Women in French Studies*.

A version of my article "Women, War, Autobiography, and the

Permissions

Historiographic Metafictional Text: Unveiling the Veiled in Assia Djebar's *L'Amour, la fantasia,* "for *Spoils of War: Women of Color, Cultures, and Revolutions* (1997), reproduced with the kind permission of the editor of the anthology, Professor T. Denean Sharpley-Whiting, and Rowman and Littlefield Publishers, Inc.

Jacket illustration *Femmes des Ouled-Nail, Groupe de trois,* 1857 (photographer: F.J.A. Moulin), courtesy of the Bibliothéque Nationale de Paris.

Introduction

Mediating the Notion of Difference

> Difference is "mediated" to the extent that it is subjected to the fourfold root of identity, opposition, analogy and resemblance. . . . Difference must leave its cave and cease to be a monster.
>
> —Gilles Deleuze, *Difference and Repetition*

B Y THE MID-1870s, the scramble for the African continent led by Britain and France was well underway. While Britain entrenched itself in the deepest realms of the "dark continent" thanks to the efforts of great explorers such as David Livingston and Sir Henry Morton Stanley in the mid 1850s, North Africa was being slowly conquered by the French. Tunisia, Morocco, and Algeria—a vast region known also as the Maghreb, Arabic for "west" (i.e., the direction) and "The West" (the occident)—were continuously invaded by the French in a frenzy of imperial expansion. While Tunisia and Morocco eventually fell under the category of French protectorate in 1881 and 1912, respectively, Algeria was conquered much earlier (in 1830), after a long succession of bloody battles with Algerian rebels (led by 'Abd al-Qādir). Morocco and Tunisia proceeded, without much loss of life, to independence in 1956. Conversely, Algeria became a bloody battleground from 1954 to 1962 in a war of liberation with France. France eventually gave up its former colony; however, Algeria was left with its internal politics in shambles and its resources laid waste.

Introduction

Although France's colonial period officially ended in the Maghreb on 2 July 1962 with the end of the Franco-Algerian War, its legacy has succeed in maintaining concepts of otherness and exclusion that have precluded the stereotyping and marginalizing of France's formerly colonized Maghrebian peoples, even in our present day. The wounds of the Franco-Algerian War remain open, festering on both sides of the Mediterranean. The residue of what has become known as the *refoulement*—denial—of this last colonial war is just one cause among many of the racism that France's immigrant Maghrebian citizens endure. Neo-Orientalism, today's byproduct of the long French Orientalist love affair with all of North Africa cultivated during the nineteenth and early twentieth centuries, has also hindered the process of equality for Maghrebian immigrants residing in France. These two issues—refoulement and neocolonial stereotyping—provide contemporary Francophone authors of the Maghreb with the building blocks for new literary agendas that incorporate sociocultural as well as historical and political issues pertinent to both France and the Maghreb.

In this work the term *postcolonialism* is also discussed with respect to Francophone texts of the Maghreb. Although this term admittedly promotes "literatures, art, and culture of otherness," it has also contributed to the maintenance of neocolonial stereotypes and the *différenciation* or "containment" of the Other as a collectivized group placed in opposition to the West. This opposition has relegated those of the formerly colonized diaspora to an alterity that is recognized by Western culture only for its difference, not for its diversity. It is time to reevaluate the use of *postcolonialism* as a qualifying term for non-Western works of literature. By essentializing this literature under this diminutive term, entire histories, languages, and cultures have been devalued. Our postmodern world promotes the positivity of difference and ethnicity by including all races, literatures, ethnicities, and nationalities on equal terms. Therefore another, more productive term must be found for literary works in our era of sociocultural multiplicity. Postmodernism, in itself, is a celebration of the diversity of all cultures and of "inclusion," the combining of all facets of the political, the artistic, and the literary. As we shall see in subsequent chapters, postmodernism is a concept both diverse in definition and controversial in scope. It is, nevertheless, a positive incorporation of "cultural activity . . . [which] is fundamentally contradictory, resolutely historical, and inescapably political."[1] The postmodern, rather than the postcolonial, promotes nonhegemonic literature—literature that reflects no polar opposition between Us and Them—as a product of *mondialization* (a term borrowed from Edouard Glissant). Tunisian author and poet Abdelwahab Meddeb notes that mondialization, not postcolonialism, should characterize current movements in literature and art because it creates an energy that both decenters the cultural centers that represent former colonial metropolises, and contributes to the recognition of new literary and artistic forms from thinkers of non-Western countries, particularly those of the former colonial world.[2]

The *mondialiste* who professes a global, interlinking view of culture, language, and history inherently promotes the mediating of difference and cultural exclusion. In such a nonessential world of ethnic and cultural diversity all peoples are given equal negotiating power in which to explore colonial history and the ensuing colonial legacy still present in our postmodern world culture. Such a negotiating space is defined as an intersubjective and interstitial milieu—a Third Space (to use Homi K. Bhabha's term)—created between former colonial history and current Western neocolonizing tendencies. It is here that those who have been repeatedly marginalized in Western culture are afforded the power to draw difference, as Gilles Deleuze suggests, "out of its cave." Drawing out difference diminishes its importance as a quantifying quality used in the conceptualization of non-Western literature and culture. Because difference is destabilized, torn down from its oppositional position, it ceases to be thought of as a void—as the blackness of negativity opposite the whiteness of positivity, or as the Other opposite the West. Difference is excised from negativity and, subsequently, brought out into the light of abstraction. It is no longer a mark of representation, but an alternative, empowering, positive trait, countering the universal stereotype of alterity. Difference is reduced to an abstract, fluid line with no oppositional qualities. It becomes simply an "essence."[3] As an essence, difference functions as a means of affirmation.

The metaphysics of difference, a principle theme of Deleuze's *Différence et Répétition* (1968), marked the beginnings of an unorthodox body of philosophy and scholarly undertaking that lasted until his death in November 1995. Representation for Deleuze is "replaced by the expression or actualization of Ideas, where this is understood in terms of the complex notion of 'different/ciation.'"[4] For Deleuze, modern thought is the product of the failure of representation, or the "loss of identities, and of the discovery of all the forces that act under the representation of the identical."[5] Our modern world is thus simply one of simulacra. In the world of simulacra, repetition plays upon repetitions, and difference plays upon differences. However, repetition and difference coexist and are recognized for their similar qualities. Therefore, the task of our world is to create a space in which difference is distributed so as to allow for no opposition between the One and the Other. In such a space the notion of alterity, therefore, is problematicized. This space, or plane, as defined in Gilles Deleuze and Félix Guattari's *Mille plateaux* (1980; translated as *A Thousand Plateaus*, 1987), is the process of absolute deterritorialization, where subjects free themselves to explain other experiences on lines of flight leading to becomings. It is through deterritorializing and reterritorializing along lines of flight from this plane to other planes that we discover new thresholds that lead to the absolute threshold, where the imperceptible at last becomes evident. Imperceptibility is where perception is no longer a necessity for understanding the relation between a subject and an object. Rather, what becomes important is the movement that serves as the limit of that relation. All relationships reside in that simple shifting fluid period where subject and object come together. In other words, all preconceived notions and stereotypes concerning subjectivity are wiped away. There is no dialectic between object and subject, master and slave, Other and colonizer; rather in this interstitial space, perception is confronted by its own limit and is placed in the midst of things. Perception is affirmed as the presence of one movement in another, by passage from one subject to another.[6]

Becoming is a product of the relations resulting from these movements within intersubjective space. All preconceived notions of identity are dissolved into lines of flight, which are productive, leading to new areas of subjectivity. These areas are becomings that both men and women are free to discover, to mobilize, and to transcend. For the Maghrebian Francophone author, movement along these paths leads to another way of thinking or, as Moroccan poet, author, and intellectual Abdelkebir Khatibi suggests, to *une pensée autre*.[7] Pathways to new modes of reflection open up the possibility of new avenues and spaces in the Maghrebian consciousness. These are not preordained by the historic parameters of the French presence in the Maghreb, but rather by a positive *écart*—a disassociating—both textually and thematically from not only Western (French) tradition but also Arab traditionalism. This latter traditionalism, Khatibi states, has done just as much disservice to the modernization of the Maghrebian text as have the influences of the colonizer because of its insistence on the nostalgic and fixed past as its only thematic reference.[8] A becoming philosophy for the Maghrebian author offers flux and change as it constantly evolves in a dynamic manner.[9] Because becoming will always stand in opposition to all that is fixed, canonized, and stagnant, traditionalism is derailed. When studying feminine identity in the works of contemporary Fracophone authors of the Maghreb the issue of becoming is also extremely important as the very concepts of "woman," "femininity," and "identity" are inherently in constant motion and exile.

The concept of the becoming-woman philosophy has been born from a need to change the space of the feminine from one dominated by phallocentricism to that of agency and voice. Throughout the world, woman has been thought of for centuries as opposite man—as an object opposite its subject (stripped of all subjectivity other than what is needed to depend on a masculine standard). Because of her temporal place in the sociocultural milieus of the world, her existence depends more readily on adaptation; she therefore easily embraces a becoming philosophy. For this reason the word *feminine* in this book is defined as a positive space of production promoting new becomings and places of identity that are constantly moving, making connections, and supporting the development of active agency for women. I define active agency as the promoting of women's voices politically, socially, and culturally in order to develop platforms of change in the way women are perceived. It is my objective to demonstrate how the becoming-woman philosophy of Deleuze and Guattari frees woman from a subjugated position as an appendage of man, releasing them to new modes of self discovery and individualism.[10] The feminine space of active agency I am promoting in this book is a milieu liberated from the politics of phallocentrism that have confined women for centuries. The authors of the texts discussed in this work express the feminine as a positive vision of a unique subjectivity in which there is no opposition implied in the definition of woman.[11] Deleuze and Guattari argue that embracing feminine becoming requires a series of steps or "segments." In *A Thousand Plateaus,* they posit "becoming-minority" as a second segment of becoming (following the becoming-woman), and this step is important because it eradicates all opposition based on gendered, racial, or ethnic denominators.

The becoming-woman space of intersubjectivity occurs where past historic experiences meet present events. It is a space that incorporates the social ideals concerning both public and private spheres of agency, and it allows negotiation between social, cultural, and racial issues. Intersubjective space, as a product of deconstructed desire, promotes the dissolution of preordained rhythms and polarities between men and women, West and East, white and black, colonizer and colonized, and subject and object. As we deconstruct rigid, single-subject Western identity, we destabilize old paradigms and subsequently reinscribe new ones for a new unity of women that questions "the couplings which make Man and Woman so problematic [and subvert] the structure of desire, the force imagined to generate language and gender." This subversion in turn derails "the structure and modes of reproduction of Western identity."[12] It is here, in the space of destructured desire, that feminine subjects are placed at a new beginning, where agency is possible.

Placed at "the beginning," a new feminism that is both cultural and global is born. This new cultural feminism constructs an original agenda for women, promoting a feminine community that extends beyond the stifling ideology of sexual desire in order to embrace a public sphere of enunciation that is productive for women. Such a space is made up of layers upon layers of differences that are considered imperative to the global existence of women embodied in a multiplicity of cultures. As we shall see, these new layers of enunciation are particularly essential for Maghrebian authors such as Assia Djebar, who seeks to promote her multicultural background and, at the same time, to reinscribe the lost voices of Algerian women both historically and in the present.

Contemporary authors of Maghrebian Francophone literature are writing of and about feminine identity in the Third Space. This interstitial space is one in which women become socially embodied, enjoying productive agency. Such embodiment allows authors to rewrite former historical paradigms concerning alterity, otherness, feminism, and colonialism. It also aids women to reformulate their position in postrevolutionary societies, where patriarchal systems have often taken the place of colonial regimes, particularly in countries like Algeria. The texts of authors such as Assia Djebar and Malika Mokeddem are especially viewed as subversive because they turn the tables on socioculturally as well as historically determined roles for women. In order to continue their work as promoters of feminine emancipation in the Maghreb, Djebar and many others have preferred exile to the violence of patriarchal and religious fanatical regimes (such as those currently found in Algeria). Exile, therefore, has become a predominant factor in the reformulation of feminine identity of Maghrebian women on both a literary and a cultural level. Authors like Djebar view the identity of Maghrebian women from this perspective of exile. The identity of these women has for centuries been hindered both by colonial, Orientalizing notions of exoticism and by restrictive Muslim laws that have left women with little voice in Maghrebian postrevolutionary societies.

Algeria's Family Code, legislation passed in 1984 that "legally" effaces feminine identity and women's rights in Algerian society, may be considered a direct cause of a failed democratic process that never bore fruit once the revolution of 1954–62 was won. Women's important presence and contributions to independence and the building of the new postcolonial Algerian state have been overlooked—their hopes dashed definitively in the legal strictures of the code. Today, as we witness the closing of the twentieth century, we sadly note that Algerian women have had to explore their feminine identity, their historic roles, and feminism itself beyond the patriarchal political, judicial, and cultural structures of their homeland. Authors, journalists, activists, academics, and intellectuals in Algeria—both men and women—have been forced either into hiding or exile, sometimes even murdered, often for their transgression of sociopolitical "justice." As Réda Bensmaïa explains, these "troublemakers" who disrupt the established "order" find themselves in an abnormal "situation where there cannot be a national dialogue because there has never been a true and clear separation between the executive, legislative, and judicial powers" since independence.[13]

Lack of dialogue between the branches of the so-called democratic government, the rise of Islamism in militant form, and reliance on military power by the Algerian government have all created this abnormal situation and have equally contributed to the symptoms of decay found in present-day Algeria. However, the most odious symptom is the backlash, both socially and culturally, against the rights and freedom of Algerian women. It is this backlash that women authors, scholars, and intellectuals throughout the Maghreb hope to counter in order to create a new feminine discourse for women, one that includes the important realms of the cultural and the political.

Drawing on a philosophical-theoretical base, this book focuses on parameters in contemporary Francophone literature of the Maghreb that have developed because of the upheaval of the sociopolitical and cultural arenas in this region—at the center of which women have found themselves. The question of women's "place" in Maghrebian Francophone texts cannot be considered without viewing feminine identity as linked to these arenas in the postmodern Maghrebian consciousness. Employing Deleuze and Guattari's concepts of the becoming-woman, nomadology, and the plane of consistency and Homi Bhabha's notion of the Third Space of culture, the concept of the feminine in the Maghrebian Francophone novel is explained as a new site of comprehension and knowledge within the realm of a culturally determined, rather than Western or Muslim, stereotyped identity.

These new sites of comprehension are imperative for the development of a new feminism that operates on a politically active platform. Cultural feminists of the Maghreb such as Assia Djebar and Fatima Mernissi define this platform as one that circumvents political, social, and racial divisions throughout the Maghrebian diaspora in order to make way for new agendas promoting a multicultural feminism. Feminism in these terms incorporates gender, difference, race, and culture, redefining contemporary theories on difference and otherness within a more humanist framework.

Once the cultural feminist-humanist goal of sociopolitical equality has been achieved, women are free to establish new inroads toward the refabrication of the Self, one promoting their subjectivity and their own voice. Cultural feminists who strive to create and then maintain their place of empowered political agency, rely on an ideology that preserves continued communicative interaction. That is, a feminist *self* that incorporates an intersubjective world where women negotiate between selfhood and Other in a productive space of communication.

Introduction

The Self as a product of communication promotes the idea of the socially embodied woman; a multisubject that seeks out a "universality, understood as the inclusion of all concerned; and the reciprocity of equal recognition of the claims of each participant by all others."[14] However, we may ask why such social self-construction is important for women, particularly of the Maghreb. One response would be that it moves women out of the private and into the public sphere of negotiation, which, in turn, establishes a woman's active agency within her social environment. When women move into the space of communication they are automatically destroying the private, hermetically sealed world that has been contrived for them by male oppression (disguised in many forms: nationalist, colonialist, Orientalist, or religious-fundamentalist). Movement into the space of agency once and for all deconstructs "the opposition between the private and the public."[15] Gayatri Spivak explains that the public sphere is characterized by all that represents culture and politics, as well as the social, professional, economic, and intellectual. Conversely, the private sphere comprises all that is emotional, sexual, and domestic.[16] When women breach the fine lines that have been drawn between these two spheres they are automatically overturning and displacing all preexisting social constructions. Women who step into the public sphere of agency are essentially stepping into an environment of marginality and of exile where their numbers are few. Once in the sphere of agency (always public) women gain access to the one thing they have always been denied—the right to a voice and to negotiate their identity. Jürgen Habermas describes this place as one where there is "a circular process in which the actor is two things in one: an *initiator* who masters situations through actions of which he [or she] is accountable and a *product* of the traditions surrounding him [or her], of groups whose cohesion is based on solidarity to which he[or she] belongs, and of processes of socialization in which he [or she] is reared."[17] Overstepping boundaries into this realm of public agency in turn frees up women's ability to reinscribe, or *write,* their identity. Such an establishment of identity, or sign, involves a new body of ethics that results in a change of attitude favoring new modes of feminine discourse.

Understanding and having access to the realm of the public is important for all women of the world. Establishing public agency, although it differs in certain aspects, depending on the society and culture, marks a new beginning for women, a new becoming. For women of the postcolonial world the road toward public agency and becoming is longer and more difficult perhaps than that of European or American white women, but they still embrace many of the same processes in order to achieve their objectives. All women, whether white or of color, must step into a public space in order to establish agency and voice. This public sphere is often an exiled space—a place of marginalization on the peripheries of traditional feminine roles. In the case of Assia Djebar and Leïla Sebbar, their socially embodied self is the exiled self; one that embraces new beginnings and becomings because it is constructed within a marginalized place.

This book explores not only feminine identity and the founding of a new Maghrebian feminism as posited in a contemporary framework of Francophone literature, but also the sociocultural, historical, and political events affecting all formerly colonized peoples in our era. It is my objective to focus a critical eye on the debut of postcolonial complexities in France that surfaced primarily in the early 1960s after the Franco-Algerian War. The novels of Tahar Ben Jelloun, Assia Djebar, Leïla Sebbar, Malika Mokeddem, and Hajer Djilani are not only analyzed for their "feminine" themes, but also considered for other important contemporary issues implicating France and the Maghreb. These issues include immigration, marginalization, exile, education, ethnicity, and the legacy of colonialism and how it affects North Africans residing in France.

It is my wish to offer a cogent historio-cultural background as well as a critical analysis of each literary work studied. These novels cannot be considered without also situating historic, cultural, and political parameters of the author's space. The novels of the authors analyzed here reflect our postmodern age—an age, as François Lyotard suggests, that "refines our sensitivity to differences and reinforces our ability to tolerate the incommensurable."[18] This incommensurability extends to all notions of ethnicity, subjectivity, and history. The authors of contemporary Francophone Maghrebian texts search beyond preconceived Western narrative strategies to establish their own notions of subjectivity, freed of debilitating stereotypes. The goals of the contemporary Francophone authors studied here are to reinstall the paradoxical—the Other side of the story—in order to question prevailing norms and to interpret new signifying systems of culture and history.

Chapter 1 focuses on three developmental stages in the thematic treatment of feminine identity in texts written in French by Maghrebian authors of the pre- and postcolonial eras. Particular attention is paid to the changes in how women are perceived in literature by male authors such as Kateb Yacine, Mohammed Dib, and Nabil Farès during the French colonial period and immediately after the Algerian war, which ended French rule in the Maghreb. A subsequent study of the "awakening" of the feminine voice in the Maghreb focuses on the works of female authors who have greatly contributed to the proliferation of feminine texts written in French in the postcolonial period. Much of the "refocusing" of literary study on feminine texts is also reshaping the larger manner in which readers and literary scholars perceive postcolonial novels in general, and Francophone narratives in particular.

In Chapter 2 I suggest that Moroccan-born Tahar Ben Jelloun uses his position as an author to not only explore the feminine side of the self, but also to delve into the world of the marginal. The anomalous space in which his character Zahra wanders throughout the two novels *L'Enfant de sable* and *La Nuit sacrée* is not unlike his own as an author living in exile writing on the dissonant issues taking place in his own country. Through his "becoming-woman" Ben Jelloun delves into a space of otherness that allows him to review the conflicts between male and female, Arab and French, Muslim and Christian, and real and mythical.

Chapter 3 explores the sociopolitical agenda of well-known contemporary Francophone author Assia Djebar. Exile due to the religious fundamentalism currently menacing her literary efforts (as well as those of many intellectuals, authors, journalists, artists, and political activists) and its influence on her writing is the primary focus of this chapter. Djebar writes to create a new space of active agency for herself and all the women of Algeria who have been effaced from history through patriarchial discourse, fundamentalist traditionalism, and French colonialism.

Chapter 4 studies the multifaceted works of Leila Sebbar's trilogy about a young Beur[19] woman's fight to gain identity in a French world of stereotypes and misconceptions concerning the Maghreb. Perhaps in no other collection of works by a Francophone author is Deleuzo-Guattarian philosophy so applicable. Sherazade is young and intrepid, the product of two cultural identities. She seeks to define her individualism by entering a place of negotiation her own Third Space. It is here, in the in-between of cultures, that she finds her becoming-woman.

In the epilogue I offer concluding remarks on future developments of Francophone literature of the Maghreb. Using two very recent works by Algerian author Malika Mokeddem and Tunisian author Hajer Djilani, current sociocultural and political influences on women are explored. Both authors seek to recontextualize the role of women in a space of active agency in the hope of forging new parameters for feminine identity in the Maghreb.

Chapter One

The Francophone Maghrebian Feminine Text

New Problematics of Agency

THROUGH THEIR narratives Maghrebian Francophone authors such as Leïla Sebbar and Assia Djebar have sought to analyze the shortcomings of the complex social and political arena of the Maghrebian woman. Negotiation between social, racial, and gender spheres are a constant battle for the Maghrebian woman, whether she lives in exile or in her home country. It is through writing that these authors study their own history as well as that of hundreds of women who have no voice or sociopolitical recourse in their respective societies. In an interview in *Le monde*, Assia Djebar reiterates her personal feminine duty to all those other women who have been lost because of violence, famine, and neglect. On the bloody events in Algeria she states, "What one expects of me, as a writer, is to take a position, to comment on the present [situation in Algeria]. In reality, the feminine arena can only promote writing that is militant, journalistic, and oriented toward protest."[1] For Djebar and many other women authors of the Maghreb, writing from a militant space has meant stepping into a public sphere of agency. Yet this same agency has isolated and exiled them from the traditional roles they are expected to play. These authors have sought to engage discourse in a space of exile that assures freedom from hierarchical and patriarchal domination. The sphere of agency, which is a new and yet undefined space of freedom, allows exiled women authors to write their own autobiographies as well as those of other women who have been left "out." Their collective autobiographies establish new parameters for feminine becoming. This becoming enables the Maghrebian woman to gain access to a place of feminine commonality that provides a new beginning for innovative feminine sociopolitical and cultural production.

The global-cultural feminist agenda is important for authors like Djebar. Here the author finds a means by which to record her own experiences and autobiography, while at the same time creating a feminine communitarian discourse that favors new agendas in women's language, worldviews, and consciousness. From this empowerment, Djebar reinscribes lost feminine voices from Algerian history. Yet, what are the processes used by authors such as Assia Djebar and Leïla Sebbar to achieve what we may define as a feminine collective autobiography, an autobiography that reinscribes and restores feminine historic agency? Furthermore, how does this reinscription create a new politics of representation for women of the Maghreb?

In seeking answers to these questions such authors employ three succinct strategies (which may be thought of as progressive stages) in their narratives. First there is an awakening of the feminine self, next the writing of a totalized narrative that includes feminine memories never before told, and finally, entrance into a becoming-woman equal to true knowledge and the recognition of the one perfect feminine self.

In her 1949 work *Le deuxième sexe*, Simone de Beauvoir writes: "Thus humanity is male and man defines woman not in herself but as relative to him; she is not regarded as an autonomous being. Michelet writes: 'Woman, the relative being . . .' And Benda is most positive in his *Rapport d'Uriel:* 'The body of man makes sense in itself quite apart from that of woman, whereas the latter seems wanting in significance by itself. . . . Man can think of himself without woman. She cannot think of herself without man.'"² In this passage, Beauvoir exposes the central conflict that all women of the world have experienced since the dawn of their existence: the fact that they have never been considered within a separate subjective sphere apart from that of men. The feminine being dependent on the masculine *sign* is evident in almost all societies and cultures. The key elements of Western logocentrism have been established through the repression of other logoi (such as the feminine-Other) within society. These different logoi are those that run contrary to the paradigm of male domination. God, Truth, Being, and Reason —the essentials in Western metaphysical philosophy—are represented as unequivocal male ideals to be appropriated by the passive, female half of society. Through these philosophical realities all other oppositions, such as difference (otherness), have been conveniently repressed. Woman has been throughout the ages the prime representative of difference. She has been "theoretically subordinated to the concept of masculinity . . . viewed by the man as *his* opposite, that is to say, as *his* other, the negative of the positive, and not, in her own right, different, other, otherness itself." Therefore, women's speech, like identity, has been conceived solely as a masculine "sameness, apprehended as *male* self-presence and consciousness-to-itself."³ Women, for centuries, have thus been speaking through the thoughts and speech of men—dictated to by a male conception of the world that has always dispossessed womanhood and feminine agency. It is, therefore, imperative that women learn to develop a theoretical discourse through which to voice their own identity.

However, it is not enough simply to break the silence and speak as women. The female author must move outside the masculine-feminine dialectical framework of established notions of subjectivity in order to eradicate the male model and in its place set up her own modes of identity. It is here that the Deleuzo-Guattarian theory of the becoming-woman becomes so important. By embracing their marginal position, women recontextualize feminine difference. Difference now is no longer viewed as being a subordinated, dominated, or sexually determined trait. It is rather positively considered as acentered to polar oppositions. Subsequently, feminine autobiography takes on an entirely new meaning. The woman who steps outside the normalized feminine identity codes ordained by men will not only tell her own story, but recontextualize former masculine historic representations of herself. It is here that stepping into the public sphere of agency becomes so important. Establishing a voice gives women the power of totalizing their own narrative in order to exert their being within a feminine sphere of identity.

What is a totalizing narrative? It is a literary process of our postmodern era by which "writers of history, fiction, or even theory render their materials coherent, continuous, unified—but always with an eye to the control and mastery of those materials, even at the risk of doing violence to them."[4] This process is a recontextualization of text and history in true terms (i.e., women's history according to a woman's point of view). Within the totalizing paradigm, women *write* their history by mastering it and freeing it of male domination, thus positing total control. Women and minorities, in terms of postmodernism, gain their voices back and therefore provide readers with "the histories (in the plural) of the losers as well as the winners, of the regional (and colonial) as well as the centrists, of the unsung many as well as the much sung few, and . . . of women as well as men."[5] Historic events within the postmodern framework are thus no longer hidden. Assia Djebar, in particular, demonstrates the importance of recontextualizing Algerian history within the boundaries of a totalized narrative. Both her novels, *Vaste est la prison* (1995) and *L'amour, la fantasia* (1985), provide crucial examples of recontextualized historic narratives concerning women who had little or no voice throughout Algerian history during both colonial and postcolonial periods. By mixing autobiography and historic accounts with her hypotheses about women's roles in pre- and postcolonial times (for the most part women's accounts were not set down in Algerian history books), Djebar writes a historiographic metafiction that reviews Algerian history—seen from the vantage points of Maghrebian women.

Defining historiographic metafiction calls upon the postmodern phenomenon of combining history with probability, or possibility, in order to recontextualize what was ignored by the dominating phallocentrism, colonialism, and Western logocentrism. Historiographic metafiction emphasizes not only the recontextualization of history, but also an enunciative process of "production, reception, historical and social contexts" that reinstall "a kind of . . . communal project"[6] that includes all possible facets (social, cultural, and traditional) of women's agency. A communal feminine project under these terms involves contemporary theories and discourses in communication and ethics. As Habermas suggests, it is through the active process of communication that "a change of attitude" takes place,[7] with the end result of affording women new modes of discourse.

The feminine communal project is not, however, limited to historiographic biography. Leïla Sebbar's novel *Fatima ou les Algériennes au square* (1981) reviews empowered feminized modes of enunciation within the immigrant community in France. Particularly in this novel, Sebbar's women take on a communal project to establish women's voices and agency. By reuniting Maghrebian women in the public squares of France's immigrant ghettos, Sebbar (herself the daughter of an Algerian father and a French mother) allows her readers to witness both the voices and physical presence of these usually silent, effaced women. The determination of a voice is imperative because (as the author explains) most of these women are illiterate in their own language as well as in French and thus have no means by which to contextualize their existence or express themselves through writing. Physical presence, forming a collective bond with other women in the square, is essential because most of the women must constantly fight against strict Muslim traditions that dictate a sequestered life within the confines of home and domestic responsibility. Sebbar reiterates the division between Muslim public and private space in Muslim society in terms of gender as her heroines constantly seek to break down masculine domains where women are not allowed.[8]

Breaking free of confining traditions, male domination, and a life of marginalization in the ghettos of France are themes repeated throughout Sebbar's novels to describe the evolving situation of the Beur community.[9] The author's feminine space is made up of both older transplanted Algerian women who have followed their immigrant husbands to France and daughters from the second and third generations, who have no direct memory of their parents' country. Sebbar's younger protagonists seek more than what can be found within the walls of the ghetto. For these women, flight from the confines of their immigrant prison becomes the only option by which to break free from lives of delinquency and a male-dominated home. These women follow lines of flight in order to seek new roads to a feminine identity that will assure them new modes of agency and subjectivity on their own terms. Once a woman embarks on a different road she is free to embrace her becoming and her feminine agency. In no other place is Simone de Beauvoir's well-known statement, "One is not born, but rather becomes, a woman," more applicable.[10] Women, as Sebbar's work attests, must discover what it is to be female while at the same time breaking the mold that male society has fashioned for them.

Sebbar's protagonists—Fatima, Shérazade, Dalila, and so many others—are prime examples of women who cross over the barrier between feminine passivity and active agency. Often they carve out their own becoming-woman from the liberty they discover in the margins between the Muslim immigrant world and the alien French culture. Therefore Sebbar's protagonists find their active agency exists neither totally within French nor Maghrebian worlds, but interstitially, between the French Orientalist and exotic sexualized images that stereotyped the Maghrebian woman during colonial times (and which persist today predominantly encouraged by the French media, as Sebbar describes in her *Shérazade* trilogy), and another, more traditional sphere, where Muslim culture insists that women live under a watchful masculine eye.

Seeking such liberty often means a total break with family, tradition, and cultural ties, as Sebbar's various female protagonists, or *fugueuses* (runaways), find out once they succeed in breaking free of the confines of their HLM[11] ghettos. Ruptures, such as those that young Beur women face, are often violent because of the strict male-dominated microsociety in which they have grown up. These women want to reformulate and merge their Arab heritage and identity with that of their French assimilated culture, while embarking on new roads that will lead them to their own independence. In most of Sebbar's novels the author suggests that rupture offers young women only two roads: either homelessness, which often includes destitution and prostitution, or the discovery of a new, open-ended freedom leading them down paths to unknown territories. Rupture as a positive experience, furnishing a means by which to harmoniously fuse young Beur women's French and Arab identities, is often Sebbar's central message. In many of her works she leaves the road open to her female protagonists because the author herself is unsure of where the actions of young Beur women today will take them in the future. Her novels evoke for us the question, Is this second generation of young Maghrebian-French women destined to be marginalized forever, or will they succeed in establishing their own identity as multiculturally embodied feminine subjects who have discovered a true becoming-woman? Sebbar, like all cultural feminists, awaits the answer and the outcome of entering this unexplored sphere of subjectivity.

Contemporary Francophone literature of the Maghreb offers a panoply of diverse views on feminism, agency, alterity, subjectivity, and identity. It is through the analysis of these views that a cogent recontextualization of the Maghrebian feminine protagonist is being forged by such authors as Tahar Ben Jelloun, Assia Djebar, Leïla Sebbar, Malika Mokeddem, and Hajer Djilani. The Maghrebian feminine subject has entered a new phase of identity—one in which she alone is master of her actions and representation, both historically (as she rewrites the annals of history) and in the present. She is striving to create a new feminine collective sphere in which all women enjoy the right to speak, to shape their subjectivity, and to reformulate their identities. These identities are freed from colonizing and Orientalizing processes, as well as from the phallocentric dictate under which they have been oppressed since the end of colonial rule. The themes presented in the works of the aforementioned authors refocus our thoughts on identity and feminine subjectivity within the larger scope of non-Western literature written in French, as well as questions concerning the concept of "postcolonial" and what that term means for the literature of non-Western populations.

In order to consider the works of the contemporary Francophone authors of Algeria, Tunisia, and Morocco, we must first properly contextualize the parameters within which they are working. These parameters have remained elusive and ill-defined since the first appearance of Maghrebian literature written in French.[12] Pertinent questions include, Should we simply designate Maghrebian Francophone literature as postcolonial literature, or is it something more? Should all literatures produced in former imperial colonies in the languages of the former colonizers (British, French, Dutch, Portuguese, etc.) be considered under the same postcolonial heading? Moreover, what is the significance of the term *postcolonialism* today? Current debates concerning the ideology behind postcolonial theory have further complicated the analytical study of non-Western literatures. In this chapter, not only will Western ideologies that have been used to form postcolonial theories be considered, but also their impact on the development of other literatures. More often than not Western postcolonial theories have hindered the acceptance of literature written by those of the former colonies as equally important contributions to the world's literary collection. This problem leads to questions of definition for the contemporary Francophone text. For example, how should we define the place of contemporary Francophone literature of the Maghreb within the scope of other postcolonial literatures? Certainly it is necessary to consider the following three essential components that lie within the framework of today's definition of non-Western texts.[13]

The first component involves reviewing and clarifying existing dilemmas associated with the term *postcolonialism*. Many postcolonial critics and theorists accurately suggest that the very use of the word *postcolonial* is problematic and has been manipulated in order to accommodate varying themes, theories, and hypotheses that often have brought about confusion and misinterpretation concerning emerging literatures[14] of the formerly colonized diaspora.

The second component studies the transition of Francophone Maghrebian texts from themes of nationalism to those drawing on more contemporary sociocultural issues important to the postcolonial diaspora. Historically, such literature has been associated with resistance and revolution. Often it is still interpreted as having only a political agenda. Today, although some texts do have political leanings, it is inappropriate to place all contemporary Francophone Maghrebian texts in a militant-nationalist category. Revolutionary texts written in the late 1950s and early 1960s by Frantz Fanon, Albert Memmi, Kateb Yacine, Mohammed Dib, and Aimé Césaire among others, established the ideals behind nationalist movements in the Maghreb and in other colonized countries. However, long after struggles for independence have been won, militancy is of less importance to authors seeking to forge new paradigms for Maghrebian literature. It is widely accepted that once decolonization had been achieved, these revolutionary texts fell short of aiding the newly emerging independent populations to develop and implement cohesive structures on which to found progressive social programs. Therefore, many contemporary authors have sought to disassociate themselves from revolutionary polemics popular in the 1950s and 1960s, but today viewed as too narrowly militant and idealistic. These former militant discourses have been overtaxed and attenuated by the sociopolitical problems that arose between the uneducated masses and the intellectual native elite at the end of the colonial era.[15]

A third component of this chapter examines the role of women in postcolonial ideology. Newly independent governments of decolonized nations instigated few social changes favoring the improvement of the status of women and of other marginalized groups within their respective societies.[16] Postcolonial nationalism from its earliest origins favored an educated male elite and the reshaping and empowerment of the colonial man, or what Fanon represented as "[t]he existence of a new type of man . . . revealed to the public."[17] This "new man" persona is both a historical and a "psychosexual phenomenon" which, after years of oppression under colonialism, is freed both physically and psychologically, attaining "full manhood or 'wholeness' through revolutionary solidarity and the violent overcoming and expulsion of the colonizer."[18] The new man is posited as a whole man, and thus a "humanized" being, who has shrugged off the bonds of slavery and the "animalization" of colonialism. In his *Discours sur le colonialisme* (1955), Aimé Césaire outlines the steps that must be taken to de-animalize the colonist perception of the Other. If the colonizer were to at last visualize the Other as human (and therefore individualized as a person), the less-than status applied to the colonized-Other by Europeans would be eradicated. This in turn would efface what Albert Memmi termed the "mark of the plural," the European stereotype noted for hindering the acceptance of the "colored man" as having anything other than a collectivized identity.[19] Unfortunately, such militant male nationalism in favor of the Whole New Man shrouded in the progressive guise of postcolonial democracy (particularly in countries such as Algeria) reinstated patriarchal institutions, leaving women with little representation or voice in social or political circles. Women of the Maghreb may be considered prime examples of a marginalized group that has seen its political and social situation grow increasingly worse since decolonization began. Therefore, with so many women of the Maghreb writing today in exile, should the term *postcolonial* be used to designate their contributions to contemporary literature? Although providing an avenue for the Francophone elite to voice their revolutionary-nationalist ideology in favor of independence, the ensuing postcolonial rhetoric has produced little development of a contemporary voice from the feminine sphere in the Maghreb.

Postcolonial vs. Post-Colonial: Defining the Term

Over the years since Algeria's 1962 independence, themes of contemporary Maghrebian Francophone literature have extended beyond the political dichotomy of Fanon's discourse, seeking out new sociocultural agendas that were not characteristic of earlier postcolonial texts. Because of the uniqueness of today's literary themes, such as feminine identity in Muslim society, Arab identity in France, and current sociocultural conflicts within the Maghreb, a new literary category must be created in order to study contemporary Maghrebian narratives written in French. Recent works by such authors as Assia Djebar (Algeria), Albert Memmi (Tunisia), Nabile Farès (Algeria), Leïla Sebbar (France/Algeria), Malika Mokeddem (Algeria), Tahar Ben Jelloun (Morocco), and Hajer Djilani (Tunisia) reflect more than a revolutionary past. These authors seek to write a new future for emerging independent Maghrebian identity, one that incorporates all facets of Maghrebian society (such as gender, race, ethnicity, language, and human rights) while favoring the recontextualization of historic French depictions that contribute to Western Orientalist stereotypes.

In recent years confusion has resulted over the term *postcolonial* although it has existed since 1959.[20] The word *post-colonialism* was not given a hyphenated form in its 1989 Oxford English Dictionary entry. However, in the OED the compound exists alongside other compounds such as *post-adolescent* and *post-cognitive*. Therefore, the concept of "postcolonialism" is still "a compound in which the 'post-' is a prefix which governs the subsequent element. 'Post-colonial' thus becomes something which is 'post' or after colonial."[21]

There is at present a debate centered around to what exactly the "post" in "postcolonial" should refer. It is widely agreed on by postcolonial scholars that literature written in the first few years of the postcolonial era (1960s to 1970s—there are different dates for every formerly colonized country) differed in thematic scope from later works of the 1980s and 1990s. Militant nationalism was a thematic rallying point for Maghrebian authors seeking to define new voices of the decolonized Maghreb. However, three decades of evolving themes have led Francophone authors in new directions away from original messages full of nationalist rhetoric. Scholars wonder if such a static term should be used to define contemporary literature of the formerly colonized Diaspora. After all, as noted in succeeding chapters, authors in regions such as the Maghreb have sought out other themes and topics than those originally associated with the postcolonial/revolutionary era. Contemporary discussions tend to contemplate sociocultural subjects that are much more important to these authors' developing homelands. To "cover all the culture affected by the imperial process from the moment of colonization to the present day"[22] without any regard for nuances, thematic development, new political agendas, and socioeconomic policies of importance to authors in regions such as the Maghreb needs to be rethought. This globalized term has propped up and hemmed in emerging Anglophone and Francophone literatures of African countries, as well as those of Asia, Australia, Bangladesh, India, the South Pacific, Malta, Pakistan, and Canada (among others). However, the only commonality between these countries' literatures is that they "emerged in their present form out of the experience of colonization and asserted themselves by foregrounding the tension with the imperial power."[23] The insistence on keeping the baggage of "colonialism" in the term used to describe this literature has for too long grounded authors of the former colonial diaspora in the quagmire of a temporal field, thus denying any further development beyond this stagnant state.

Western literary critics and theorists' relegation of these works to a category such as "postcolonial" has succeeded in reducing the importance of this literature within academic and scholarly circles. Too often *postcolonial* has stood for "Third-World," which brings to mind more Western connotations alluding to the realm of inferior, lesser, or not as good. The West has conveniently created discourses concerning the Third World in order to maintain a balance between "Us" and "the oppressed and exploited," who have been left "outside civilization," locked into a cavernous "heart of darkness."[24] By using such discourse critics have succeeded in banishing the Other and his or her literature to an isolated area of lesser literary importance. Regardless of the usage of terms, more appropriate, positive headings need to be created for non-Western literature. This of course will entail upsetting the West's intricate balance of Us versus Other.

In order to resist locking non-Western literature into a diminished genre, the notion of "postcolonial" would be better used to refer only to a mere stage in the development of the emerging literature of the formerly colonized diaspora. Perhaps postcolonialism should be considered as an enigmatic time frame through which Other literatures have passed and are now ready to move onward toward a more multicultural, universal, and less marginalized status. Such a multicultural state renounces the notion of colonialism altogether in order to form its own independent basis for existence. Anne McClintock suggests that postcolonialism should only has to "invite you through a slightly larger door into the next stage of history, after which you emerge, fully erect, into the brightly lit and noisy HYBRID STATE." McClintock's hypothesis is applicable to this study. Her suggestion that postcolonialism has been achieved through the transgression of a series of states is significant. In her analysis, colonial discourse is a passage in which time is space and history "is shaped around two, necessary movements: the 'progress' forward of humanity from slouching deprivation to erect, enlightened reason . . . [and] the reverse: regression backwards from (white, male) adulthood to a primordial, black 'degeneracy.'"[25] This primordial degeneracy includes women, minorities and the colonized. If the term *postcolonial* was indeed created with helpful Western intentions to ensure emerging literatures a voice, it failed to open up any innovative literary possibilities for culturally based discourses free of colonial associations for former colonized peoples. Because non-Western discourse sought to challenge the weight of Western historicism, the end result has been the creation of a series of binary opposites. These oppositions include self-other, metropolis-colony, center-periphery, among others,[26] and stem internally from one dialectical pull; that of the colonial-postcolonial, which has neither furthered the independence of emerging literatures nor created new bodies of literary theory that enlighten or promote the non-Western voice.

In order to scrutinize the problems associated with the term *postcolonial*, let us first review the connotation the prefix *post-* generates. Using a hyphen in the word *postcolonial*, some theorists argue, has provided the West with a convenient means by which to relegate entire populations back to what McClintock perceives as being "prepositional time." The prefix *post-* invariably locks the non-Western formerly colonized text into a preordained, "ahistorical" time frame that cannot be altered. The term's continued reference to "colonial" automatically confers "colonialism . . . [as] the determining marker of history" for a given literature. Defining cultures and their literature in this manner marks them not by "what positively distinguishes them, but by a subordinate, retrospective relation to linear, European time."[27]

In light of the above arguments, new agendas for postcolonial literatures must be sought. The effect of the prefix *post-* must be mitigated by writing *postcolonial* without a hyphen. Nevertheless, that deletion does not change the colonial half of the term and the derogatory connotations it still evokes. But would the term *hybrid*

be any better? After all, hybridity effaces the implications of subor-
dinating prefixes and it is the last stage of stages on the postcolonial
time line, according to McClintock. Yet, I argue that *hybridity* has
become a postmodern buzzword too often erroneously associated
with emerging literatures and hypocritically viewed in a positive
sense by Western literary theorists. It surreptitiously marginalizes
literature of the formerly colonized diaspora because it relies on
maintaining an ideology that places the Other in a split position—
half European and half Other—instead of granting any unique
cultural identity. Moreover (and more detrimental to non-Western
authors), these same Western literary theorists view hybridity as
the only means by which the Other-author may obtain the feeling
that he or she is incorporating past colonial experience while at the
same time including new cultural aspects unique to his or her own
identity. Homi K. Bhabha, in *The Location of Culture,* argues that
"hybridization" is the result of "an unresolved contradiction between culture and class; from deep within the struggle of psychic
representation and social reality."[28] When studied within the
scheme of Bhabha's logic, hybridization becomes both affirmation
of Self and the Self of the former colonizer, a sort of Lacanian
twist to the mirror identification of Self. Hybridity, therefore, is no
better than a form of mimicry because the Other has been forced
into accepting appendages of his/her former colonized status. As
Bhabha affirms, "the *menace* of mimicry is its *double* vision." Split
vision only allows the non-Western author "partial representation"
and thus still insures "a colonialist chain of command." This de
facto brand of representation thus grants these authors the only
"authorized versions" for their identity.[29]

Essentially hybridity plays the postcolonial game of positioning
the formerly colonized diaspora on the borders of two worlds—
that of the former colonizer and that of the neocolonial, play-our-
way Western literary theorist. Relegated to the peripheries of these
two worlds, the hybridized subject is rendered mute; no longer colonized but not yet totally free of the Western patriarchial grasp. He

or she is thus destined to remain in the postcolonial state. An applicable metaphor for the debilitating position hybridity causes the Other is reified in the terminology of the deconstructionist. Jacques Derrida's metonymical *a* in his theory of *différance* represents the "neutering" of the Other or forced existence in the in-between of a silenced space: "this graphic difference ('a' instead of 'e'), this marked difference between two apparently vocal notations, between two vowels, remains purely graphic: it is read, or it is written, but it cannot be heard. It cannot be apprehended in speech. . . . It is offered by a mute mark, by a tacit monument. . . . The *a* of *différance*, this is not heard; it remains silent, secret and discreet as a tomb."[30]

Deconstructionists' discussion of racial-cultural-historical otherness has inaccurately appropriated terms such as *différance* to interpret literary theoretics in non-Western texts. This reveals the refusal of Western critics to call on non-Western modes of theory to explore the texts produced by authors of the non-Western diaspora. Theories such as Derrida's différance, although groundbreaking in their hypotheses concerning the genesis of a space for Other texts, do not create significant "modes of representation of otherness."[31] Whether expressed as différance, hybridity, or syncretism, and although they promote the study of varying forms of alterity, these terms have marginalized the Other within an ahistorical (abstracted from history) context. Différance and hybridity have furnished the West with further means by which to relegate the Other's literatures to an inferior status, thus relativizing the fact that, "hybridity . . . [will always be] the primary characteristic of all post-colonial texts, whatever their source."[32]

We may conclude from the issues already mentioned that presently there is extensive debate over the terminology used within postcolonial discourse. Some deconstructionist and postcolonial theorists argue that fusing together the *post* and the *colonial*, and thus writing *postcolonial*, would alleviate prepositionalized associations and delineate the vacuum caused by the juxtaposition of two dialectical words that seem incongruous. Yet as previously mentioned, deleting a mere hyphen in the term *postcolonialism* still does not erase the colonial overtones that come to mind when the term is used in conjunction with the decolonized world. The term *postcolonial* does not do justice to contemporary Francophone literature, which incorporates so much more than the simple dialectic of its former colonial past and its decolonized present.

The nationalist themes of revolutionary discourse have disappeared in contemporary Francophone texts of the Maghreb. The concept of "post" no longer situates itself with regard to past, present, or future time, but has been integrated into a massive amalgam of events, histories, cultures, traditions, and languages that characterize the contemporary Francophone text of the Maghreb. Such a body of literature extends its themes beyond the West's preconceived notions concerning its meaning. Instead, the contemporary texts of the Maghreb incorporate both European and Arabic traditions while seeking to explore new textualities that view colonial history according to a non-Western perspective. Thirty-two years after the last bastion of colonialism was dismantled in Algeria, for example, the idea of "post" today seems irrelevant and outdated. Issues other than the colonial past are important to the Maghreb and thus need to be addressed.

After Nationalism: The Postcolonial Contemporary Francophone Text

The narrative analyses in this book explore the paths taken by both Maghrebian female and male authors toward a becoming-woman and the new questions concerning subjectivity they have raised as being important to the new postcolonial consciousness of the Maghreb. How will postrevolution feminine identity affect social and cultural issues in the Maghreb? What will be the results of exploring both a French and an Arab heritage? What impact are the works of these authors having on women's present political position within Muslim culture? Will there be change, or will women like Assia Djebar be forced to live forever in exile in order to continue a feminine dissident discourse? Ben Jelloun, Djebar, Sebbar, Mokeddem, and Djilani all search for different forms of feminine identity through transcendence to a new space of agency—the place of the becoming-woman. In order to subvert the continuing threats made against women in the Maghreb and elsewhere, these authors realize that a new sphere of agency for the emancipation of feminine identity must be defined. As for all women, the task of the Maghrebian woman and author is to embrace a new space of negotiation in which all points of difference and diversity are challenged. It is only through this negotiation that new empowered, feminine-communitarian agency may be formed, thus promoting a new global "womanism."[33]

Unfortunately, in the Maghreb the postrevolutionary nationalism of the 1960s has often led to patriarchial governments that, certainly in the case of Algeria, have presented insurmountable obstacles for the development of programs favoring social and cultural change, including those associated with the emancipation of women. Consequently, Francophone literature has born the brunt of the polarity that nationalist movements caused. As Abdelkebir Khatibi explains in *Le roman maghrébin* (1968), from 1962 onward "the Maghrebian author is henceforth confronted with the problems of his society."[34]

The struggle against colonial oppression gave the Maghrebian Francophone author an opportunity to voice his or her opinion through a new venue in the Maghreb as well as abroad. The diffusion of their texts granted these authors a certain amount of autonomy and universalism. However, once independence was achieved Maghrebian authors more often than not were denied artistic freedom. In many cases an officially imposed "authorized" ideology set in motion the debate, For whom and about what should we write? Reflecting on this debate in *Le roman maghrébin*, Khatibi ponders the duty of the author and how much he or she should be "engaged" with the public, society, and culture in this new postrevolutionary era: "The author must write for his public. . . . he must necessarily treat the questions which interest this public. . . . the work must express the profound realities of a people. This is the only condition by which the author can effectively contribute to a work which is national and modern. . . . To be revolutionary, our culture must be national. . . . This liberty must be inscribed in this national, revolutionary framework; only the engaged author—in the sense of history—can truly shoulder [the responsibility]."[35]

Their refusal to wave the nationalist banner and their continued use of French resulted in the subsequent isolation of Francophone authors in the postrevolutionary Maghreb. Postrevolutionary governments in all three Maghrebian countries unfavorably viewed the authors' insistence on using French as subversive to newly constructed scholastic systems favoring Arabization programs (begun immediately following independence). Countering these accusations, Francophone Maghrebian authors argued that they were using the French language in a universalist context that would assure new modern and multicultural texts appealing to not only the Maghreb but also the European reading public.

In 1954 Tunisian Albert Memmi, favoring multiculturalism, evoked the idea of the French-Arab dialectic as a mixed marriage: "Every marriage is a difficult enterprise, but a mixed marriage is the most difficult."[36] Today the debate concerning literature written in French by Maghrebian authors is no less problematic. As recent as 1997, Assia Djebar's novel *Oran, langue morte,* calls our attention to this difficult "marriage" that still haunts the Francophone author's pen. She observes that the marriage is born from "two countries, France and Algeria, that history has for so long linked together in confrontation in coupling?—torn with passion, desire and violence."[37]

Djebar, Memmi, and others believe that although difficult, restitution of the novel as a means of communicating history, intrigue, and form is more important than the language in which it is rendered. If a body of literature can incorporate "political liberation ... a radical separation of the secular and the religious [and] the end of feminine slavery" then a mixed marriage is possible and valid.[38] However, it is necessary to find a balance between postcolonial Arab identity and acceptance of the "Frenchness" that today is still inherent in the Maghreb. After all, as Khatibi has affirmed, "bilingualism and plurilingualism are not, in these regions, recent phenomena. The Maghrebian linguistic landscape is still plurilinguistic; diglossia (between Arabic and the dialectical), Berber, French [and] Spanish" are the norm.[39] Thus it may be said that all languages and cultures are part of the multiplicity of social and linguistic strata that constitute the very inner fabric of the Maghreb.

Francophone literature of the Maghreb has undergone three stages of development since the first novella written by an Algerian appeared at the end of the nineteenth century. The first stage, beginning in 1891 with the first French novellas written by Algerians and lasting until the end of the 1930s, reflects some nationalistic writing but is more profoundly characterized by Algerian writers who attempted to assimilate and mimic the literary style of the colonizer. This mimeticism stems partly from the process of indoctrination forged by French culture and language (most specifically from the French school system), which had been set definitely into place by the 1880s. Jean Déjeux states that it is ironic, however, that mimicry of the French novel was necessary in order for the Francophone Maghrebian author to later turn the colonial language against the colonizer as a means of investigating the past and forging a conquest of knowledge and liberation.[40]

The second stage of writing in the Francophone Maghreb reflects a militant nationalist influence. The massacres at Sétif, Algeria, on 8 May 1945[41] set off a wave of anticolonial literature, thus commencing the resistance era during which novels such as Algerian Kateb Yacine's *Nedjma* and Mohammed Dib's *L'incendie* made their first impact. New, young, politically charged authors

Mohammed Dib, Malek Haddad, Kateb Yacine, and Mouloud Mammeri published their works in numerous *revues culturelles* such as *Simoun, Forge, Terrasses, Soleil, Progrès,* and *Consciences maghrébines.* As their articles attest, these authors did not seek to hide their political and anticolonial agendas and thus openly fueled the rhetoric of the revolutionary process.[42]

Nedjma, Yacine's 1956 novel, foregrounds a definite thematic rupture with former Maghrebian novels written in French. Yacine's novel is filled with allusions to the social struggle going on in Algeria at the time. *Nedjma* is not only the name of the elusive female figure who is a constant object of desire for the four male protagonists, but is also the word for "star," the principal emblem for the *étoile nord-africaine,* the nonsecular symbol of Algerian independence.[43] The novel is historically depictive, centering on the riots and violence stemming from the massacre at Sétif on Armistice Day as well as reports of torture and abuse by the French in the early years of the revolution. Indeed violence, repression, and dispersion are constant factors for Lakhdar, Rachid, and the other key male figures in the novel as they seek to escape the turmoil of their native country.

Nedjma raises crucial questions about the identity of the Algerian people; at the same time it evokes both hope in the possibility of a people emerging from the bondage of colonialism and the despair of characters caught in an endless spiral of failures (exile, violence, torture, and death).[44]

Perhaps the most interesting aspect of *Nedjma* is Yacine's manipulation of the unreal and the mythic as means of escaping endless circles of violence. It is important to point out that the use of myth is an essential dimension in the historic construction of nationalism. *Nedjma* both incited revolutionary anticolonial discourse and augmented an ideal of "nation" among Algerian nationalists. The author's reference to nationalist uprisings and repression of the Algerian people by the French promotes both the ideology of independence and the will of the people to throw off the shackles of colonialism. The author transforms the written word into a voice for the people representing, therefore, the power of the collective will for independence. This voice opens up an entire memory of life burdened by the traditions of colonialism.[45] Kateb's novel reinstalls the memory of the people, granting a space of dialogue to a voiceless nation. Alluding to the independence movement as a collective force of resistance, Kateb plants the seeds that will later lead to revolution and the regaining of lost memory and a sense of identity. Incorporating the textual style of Algerian myths, the author creates a powerful symbol an entire people can understand. The symbolism prevalent in *Nedjma*, inspired by ancestral myth, is the centering force that drives Yacine's narrative toward its nationalist sentiment, promoting a unifying ideal for a colonized people.

The blending of myth and Algerian history in *Nedjma* bridges the gaps between the past, present, and future. Although years away from independence, the author is able to foresee the emergence of a new decolonized nation. In some respects, Kateb's novel is a precursor to Algerian Francophone postrevolutionary writing. While purely nationalistic, Kateb does touch upon a larger objective that propels the collective conscience of a people toward an individualized multicultural identity. By evoking both ancestral myth and the brutal reality of colonialism, Kateb is able to explore French and Arab identity—clearly demonstrating to his people that these two realities will forever make up the Algerian modern world. Unfortunately, as previously explained, Kateb's nationalist novel speaks only for the collective, leaving individual needs unattended. This is clearly evident in the portrayal of Nedjma, an elusive collectivized symbol of femininity. She is rarely seen and hardly ever heard. Her body is a metaphor for a nation in turmoil. As Rachid, the central protagonist clearly indicates, Nedjma is little more than a mythical form standing for "blood" and "country."[46] Her body is transposed or metamorphosed into a symbol for a violated nation. Devoid of any positive feminine subjectivity, Nedjma is considered only as a sexual object that drives the four male protagonists who desire her to madness and even death. Born as the offspring of "death and revenge," her identity is encased in the shell of an "ogress" who "ate her three brothers." Her blood lines are "obscure"; she is a woman with no human qualities, "who no spouse could tame."[47]

As the symbol for a country in turmoil, Nedjma cannot represent anything but militancy and nationalism. The only glimpse of femininity the reader obtains is when she is objectivized through the male protagonists' discourse. She is reduced to a femme sauvage, a "complex figure embodying volatile forces that resist incorporation into any fixed configuration of gender." Nedjma's role of femme fatale is also a unifying metaphor that brings together "disparate peoples who comprise Algeria while simultaneously opening the national configuration to ever-renewable forms and meanings."[48] The novel *Nedjma,* when considered in these collective terms, achieves its goal as representative of the militant nationalist struggle of an entire people. However, Nedjma as a woman fails to realize any form of individuality.

Kateb Yacine's 1957 novel, despite its masculine collectivized overtones, aided in enlarging the scope of contemporary Maghrebian literature written in French. Although rooted in nationalist rhetoric, *Nedjma* broke ground for the later emergence of postrevolutionary novels by drawing attention to issues such as alterity and identity within the French-Maghrebian dialectic. These same issues were later used to reformulate literary agendas concerning Franco-Arab relations, human rights, and women's status in the postcolonial Maghreb.

Postrevolutionary Space, Women,
Social Issues: New Themes of the
Maghrebian Francophone Text

I have suggested that themes reflecting concerns associated with feminine identity, immigration, and exile in Francophone texts of the Maghreb began to proliferate after 1962, immediately following the end of the Franco-Algerian War. Authors writing during this time seek to define the parameters of a much more socioculturally based literature that extends its themes into areas other than those of nationalism and revolution, which were prevalent in the 1950s. As previously noted, these postrevolutionary texts mark a definite thematic shift to topics that explore formation of new emerging identities of the postcolonial Maghreb.

Contemporary Maghrebian authors writing in French develop themes beyond the former colonizer-colonized dialectic as well as those centered on war, revolution, and nationalism. One of the reasons for this expansion is that more and more Maghrebian writers began writing after decolonization. Postrevolutionary narratives are centered less on the duality between the worlds of the colonizer and the colonized, and more around questions of individualism and how to cope with living between two histories, two cultures, and two identities.

Nabile Farès's *Yahia, pas de chance* (1970) and Albert Memmi's *Le scorpion* (1969) seek not only to explore the historical legacy of colonialism and militancy, but also to cope with issues (such as identity) inherently important to recently independent nations. These issues also grapple with the complications associated with the use and place of the French language and the heritage of French culture in postrevolutionary societies. Francophone Maghrebian authors were therefore forced to ask themselves such critical questions as, What is my identity as an immigrant in France? and How do I live in two worlds, juggle two conflicting political spheres— one secular and one Muslim?[49] These questions become even more complex when considering the Beur authors. This second generation, more often than not erroneously categorized as immigrants, has found integration into the French system virtually impossible. Because they are so far removed from either French or Arab cultures, they remain in an isolated world caught between two societies, religions, and traditions. Their fate has become ambiguous as they revolve on the liminal edges around two very different cultures.

The Beurs are often depicted in the French press or by the French government as one of those "precarious and fragile groups" whose destiny within the social order of France is still unknown. Some gains in their political, economic, and social status have been made in recent years with the aid of organizations, such as SOS-Racisme and France Plus, which have sought out various means of integration into French society for young Beurs. However, the gains made have been limited due to the overwhelming and diverse problems of each Beur community in France.[50] In recent years, more and more Beur writing, by authors such as Leïla Sebbar (*Shérazade;* 1982) and Azouz Begag (*Béni, ou, le paradis privé;* 1989), has drawn the French reading public's attention to the deplorable plight of a lost generation that has found it impossible to fit into French society.[51] Questions concerning Arab identity and community within France emerged when the parents of this second generation first immigrated to France at the end of the Franco-Algerian War (2 July 1962). Termination of the war also set in motion a new era of Francophone literature within the Maghreb, thus marking a definite rupture with the more militant, male nationalist character previously discussed.

Women within the space of the postrevolutionary Francophone Maghrebian novel also take on new contours, identity, and sexuality. Works such as Assia Djebar's *Les enfants du nouveau monde* (1962) and *Les alouettes naïves* (1967) posit feminine presence and sexuality in a unique light. Traditional Muslim culture versus encroaching European modernization and the debates concerning their ramifications for women are constant areas of sociocultural discourse within the author's texts. Therefore, it is no surprise that feminine sexuality and the identity of the modern Algerian woman are central forces within Djebar's postcolonial narrative.

Acknowledgment by the French of Djebar's contribution to Algerian literature in the early 1960s marks a shift in how the Franco-Algerian War was perceived in France. This shift is due mainly to the different publishers who contracted Algerian authors' works during the 1950s and 1960s. Prior to the war, the French publishing house Éditions du Seuil published the works of Mohammed Dib and Kateb Yacine in order to highlight the authors' nationalist militant view and to create a certain sensibility in France for the pos-sibility of war and the inevitability of Algerian independence. In contrast, the publishing house Julliard used Assia Djebar's work to counter the militaristic-nationalist reputation many Algerian authors had gained. In the late 1950s, the editors at Julliard sought to emphasize Djebar's *"écriture féminine"* with the publication of *La soif* (1958) and thus to play down the escalation of the French-Algerian conflict. In 1962, when the war finally became a reality and France's imminent defeat was evident, Assia Djebar's *Les enfants du nouveau monde* was published. It was hoped that the novel would cause more sympathy among the French public for the sociocultural realities and dilemmas of the former colonies, generating sentiment for the fate of the young, postwar generation on both sides of the Mediterranean.[52]

La génération de 1962—avant-garde Algerian authors such as Assia Djebar, Albert Memmi, and Nabile Farès who wrote with the future of Algeria in mind—were groomed by sympathizers in France and publishers like Julliard to create a new range of literature. By providing alternative views of the conflict, this literature aimed to counter the negative press that the Algerian War generated in France. The goal of these postrevolutionary novels was to first explain; that is, to serve a cause by discursively illustrating what had happened and was happening in an understandable literary language.[53]

Djebar's three early important works—*Les impatients* (1958), *Les enfants du nouveau monde* (1962) and *Les allouettes naïves* (1967)—all favor a feminine perspective. Engagement, sexuality, and marriage contrasted with the everyday reality of war, poverty, death, as well as the subsequent, postrevolutionary uncertainty concerning the role of women in a new independent society, are prevalent themes in all these texts. Of equal importance is the author's reflection on the conflicts that arise between Algerian traditions and encroaching Western values (which the author notes pose greater difficulties for women than for men). Past tradition, as opposite future modernity, and its effect on women is the most notable theme in Djebar's *Les enfants du nouveau monde*.

For this revolutionary novel's female characters, the choice between modernity and tradition involves a complicated process, as Djebar demonstrates through the different situations she creates for them. Not only does this process entail facing the turmoil of war that threatens to fragment, and even annihilate their families, but also the resulting changes in Muslim traditions. These particular changes are the direct result of women's participation in the revolutionary struggle. Djebar describes feminine militant participation on four levels: (1) the traditional role in which women stay at home with the children, cloistered, silenced, and sequestered from direct contact with the conflict (these women are victims of loneliness and isolation while their husbands are absent); (2) a modern role where women live by themselves, participating somewhat in revolutionary endeavors, but not totally involved in the conflict itself; (3) a militant role where women are actively participating in battles against the French; and (4) women as traitors, manipulated as victims of both French and Algerian violence.

However, all these different roles involve to some extent the struggle of the Algerian population with a world caught between modernity and traditionalism. This duality constantly plagues the Algerian revolutionary woman in 1962. In all of Djebar's examples, women walk a tightrope between unveiled Western decadence and cloistered, passive Muslim traditionalism. Walking this thin line means that the author's protagonists must struggle against issues involving traditional Algerian family values, while at the same time seek to adhere to strong modern revolutionary ideals.[54]

In *Les enfants* Djebar not only presents the tough choices women face between modernism and traditionalism, but also choices on a larger, humanist scale. These roles implicate all who live in Algeria and in France. Reworking the formerly canonized Other-Us dialectic traditionally drawn within colonial space, Djebar formulates a third space of dialogue and negotiation within her text. This space is an intersubjective area situated between French and Algerian worlds. In such a space, polar opposition is erased, as well as any central protagonist or discourse. Between these two opposing spheres of colonized and colonizer, Djebar's characters disregard their "expected" roles, instead taking on new traits such as humanism and compassion. Certain white European males are perceived as being sympathetic to the rebels of the Algerian forces, while some native Algerians are depicted as wanting to remain French. Djebar thus destabilizes the accepted colonizer-colonized polemic in order to study the possibility that the lines between forces were not always distinctively marked during the colonial era as well as during the struggle for independence. Studying both the sympathetic and the demonic values of a society formed between two cultures exposes Djebar's larger social message. This message is one of hope for the young 1960s generation of Algeria and its future ability to come to terms with both sides of history—the colonial and the revolutionary.

Assia Djebar's images of youth, freedom, and the unstereotyped characters portrayed in *Les enfants* take the modern-day reader by surprise, as does the abrupt ending, which leaves one lone rebel standing on a hillside watching a little girl run away into the sunset. The uncertainty of the child's fate (and, perhaps, the fate of all women in Algeria) metaphorically evokes the larger uncertainty associated with Algeria's future one that neither the Algerian people nor Djebar could predict in 1962.

Assia Djebar's uncertainty about her country's future remains a central theme in her later works.[55] Such uncertainty is also a prevalent theme in the novels of other Algerian, Moroccan, and Tunisian authors of the late 1960s and early 1970s. Consequently, most of these postrevolutionary literary works center on the importance of forging new noncolonized identities that promote positive solutions for social change within postrevolutionary cultures of the Maghreb.

Other predominant themes of this era are growing Western racism and the marginalization of the formerly colonized immediately following the Franco-Algerian War. These dilemmas were acerbated by the ensuing social upheavals caused by both immigration and emigration between France and the Maghreb.

Francophone Maghrebian authors writing in the late 1960s and early 1970s built upon postrevolutionary agendas such as exile, Franco-Arab relations, immigration, identity, marginalization, and the new place of Maghrebian women both at home and in France. Nabile Farès and Albert Memmi explore the emerging freedom of the postcolonial world and the uncertainties associated with the creation of innovative empowered identities for men and women that grew out of the fight against colonization. As a result of their efforts to mediate between French and Arab cultures, these authors formulated new hypotheses for, and solutions to, social problems in their respective countries. These solutions reflected both Western and Maghrebian ideologies concerning feminine emancipation, identity, language, culture, and society.

Following the period of revolutionary nationalism, relationships between men and women of the Maghreb took on new contours. Whether influenced by the revolutionary duties women were forced to embrace out of necessity during the Algerian War or by the Western sexual revolution of the late 1960s,[56] it is clear that many male Maghrebian authors in the early 1970s considered women's roles differently than during the revolution and preceding colonial era. The precarious situation of women within Muslim postcolonial societies in the 1970s was synonymous with the traumatic changes each country endured during the brief transformation from colonialism to independence. It is therefore not surprising that at this time the literature of the three formerly colonized Maghrebian countries—Tunisia, Algeria and Morocco—echoes the authors' own misgivings concerning the reliability of postcolonial governments to assure a new life and some form of equality for women in their newly reconstructed countries.

On a larger scale, Maghrebian peoples were faced with a new dialectical pull that risked jeopardizing the fragile independence for which they had so diligently struggled. The dialectic between integrity and national specificity further divided postrevolutionary societies (including intellectuals and authors) over the ever present conflict between traditionalism and modernism.[57] Should writers seek to posit a return to traditional Islamic sources for inspiration because Islam, for newly formed revolutionary governments, had become an all encompassing force synonymous with dogma, cult, country, nationality, religion, state, spirituality, and action? Or, in the name of progress, should traditions be denied in order to embrace new social modes favoring a more modern Westernized culture? During the 1970s these themes, as well as finding a place somewhere between the modern and the traditional, the French and the Arab, were incessantly explored.

Faced with modernity and political turmoil within their newly decolonized country, the intellectuals and authors of the Maghreb asked themselves, Where am I at home? The fact that Algeria had been for so long considered an immense extension of the French state[58] made doing away with all Frenchness practically impossible for native Algerians. Ties with Algeria as well as Tunisia and Morocco were also difficult to sever on the French side, since the wheels of modernization pushed French factories to search for more cheap labor. Algerian immigration was particularly encouraged, thus making the divorce between the two countries impossible. The bitter marriage, "with its history of dirty family secrets,"[59] remained, assuring a long and painful future together.

The marriage metaphor once again was implanted and subsequently intertwined forever in the very tissue of the Franco-Maghrebian polemic. Unfortunately, in the late 1960s the metaphor reified predominant colonial discourse, placing Algeria in a state of economic dependence on France. France was thus slow to admit it had been defeated by its former colony. The Algerian revolution had been for France a "destruction of the household,"[60] a divorce that, once set in motion, left little room for amends. Immigration further encouraged a form of pseudocolonialism which, although purely economic, nevertheless was detrimental to building a new Algerian nation. As France sought to modernize her still decrepit post World War II urban infrastructure, immigrants from the Maghreb, economically disillusioned by ineffective postcolonial nationalist governments, poured into that country, providing cheap labor.[61] French urban renovation thus was built on the backs of African immigration.[62] Immigrants saw themselves slowly pushed out to urban *banlieues*, or ghettos, for the economically disadvantaged. Consequently, Maghrebians residing in France once again found themselves in a "colonized" predicament. Since immigrants were forced to live on the margins of French society, an unprecedented type of neocolonial dialectic between French and Arab social spheres was fashioned. Such a dialectic depended entirely on Western capitalism and economic hierarchy where the the Maghrebian immigrant would be forever at a disadvantage. Moroccan-born Driss Chraïbi, in his 1955 novel *Les boucs*, describes this desperate plight of Algerian workers living on the margins of French society, isolated from their families. *Les boucs*, a term that means both "billy goats," and "scapegoats," for Chraïbi represents "the 300,000 Arabs in France who were [considered] to be the residuals, the pariahs."[63] Maghrebian men in France struggled to keep some semblance of their own tradition while facing the inevitable effacement of their identity as outcasts on the fringes of French society. The danger of living on the edges of an alien society and culture over a long period of time, Chraïbi and other authors point out, is that it eventually erases the immigrant's memories of his or her home country and its traditions. Tahar Ben Jelloun supports Chraïbi's observations in *Hospitalité française* (1984) as he points out that "having come for a few years, . . . Arabs find themselves old and without hope at the end of a long period of exile."[64] In the late 1960s and early 1970s the culture of the immigrant became slowly absorbed into the shantytowns *(bidonvilles)* of Paris. Marginalized in public housing projects, on the peripheries of French society, the Algerian immigrant watched, waited, and simply existed. Considered neither Algerian nor French, the immigrant resided in an enigmatic temporal state caught between "two universes which are confronted by their stereotypes; this gives an image of inferior cultures face to face," leading authors like Ben Jelloun to ask, "What will happen?"[65] The futility of the plight of the Arab immigrant continues to dominate the themes of Maghrebian authors writing in French even today. As Driss Chraïbi states, this unfortunate situation continues because in the last thirty-five years very little has changed with regard to the plight of the immigrant population in France. In his preface of the 1989 edition of *Les boucs*, Chraïbi explains that the deplorable social situation of the Arab worker and his children residing in France is still due to racism, isolation, and misunderstanding: "Someone asked me, Am I still capable, after thirty-five years, of writing such a disturbing book? It is difficult to answer, except with other questions: Thirty-five years later, does racism still exist in France? Are immigrants and their children who are born in this 'highly civilized' country still relegated to the edge of a society and of humanity? Is it still true, according to my Master, Albert Camus, that the bacillus of the plague does not die nor does it disappear?"[66]

Like Chraïbi, Nabile Farès in the early 1970s struggled with the feeling of futility at being caught between these two divergent worlds. His works consider the consequences of his "split" being as he seeks to turn the void of exile into a positive negotiating space of new multicultural identity. Through his inheritance of the French language and culture, Farès creates a modern postrevolutionary Algerian identity, "outside," in the margins. The concept of bordering or living between the liminal peripheries of various identities is thus a primary theme in Farès's works.

By linking the pieces of his disjunctive history and by dismantling the past, Farès formulates a new and individualized identity. He achieves his objective through the manipulation of modes of deviant writing. Transgression is also a primary characteristic of his protagonists, who live by straying from established norms, seeking other possible identities through endless migration between French and Arab, Western and Eastern spheres. The textual form of novels such as *Le champ des oliviers* (1972) and *Mémoire de l'absent* (1974) also exemplifies transience, living on the margins, and the need to break away and migrate in order to define oneself apart from established molds and stereotypes. Farès continues to write against the established paradigms of language. His own writing fragments phrases and employs nonsensical terms that undermine images and preconceived literary notions concerning the French language.

Reformulating a space in the margins where the immigrant Algerian can negotiate identity within the country of his former colonizer is the central theme of *Yahia, pas de chance* (1970). Yahia, Farès's young protagonist, leaves his native region of Kabylia (Algeria) to escape the war of independence, as well as "these days of men [toiling] in the soil of Kabylia, in the anonymity of gunfire, . . . [and] the disappearances during the night."[67] Yahia hopes that France will provide a safe haven where he can continue some semblance of teenage life in high school. His dreams of going to medical school also force the young student into exile, away from war-torn Algeria. For this displaced adolescent, leaving Akbou, his native village, means a definitive rupture with the past and certain isolation in his new home.

In his 1971 novel *Un passager de l'occident,* as in *Yahia,* Farès skips across borders, linking a plurality of cultures, traditions, languages, and peoples. Each protagonist he creates represents not only a unique man or woman, but also a different ideal. James Baldwin, the American black writer exiled in France, embodies the struggle for civil and human rights, while Conchita, the narrator's beautiful Spanish lover, exemplifies a newfound feminine freedom dominated neither by cultural mores nor masculine oppression. All Farès's characters are in constant transition; they reappear and fade away in an endless quest for identity. His principal protagonist, Ali-Saïd (alias Brandy Fax), breaks with the past in order to seek a new future bound not to a single language, culture, or ideal, but a multiplicity of differences that are characteristics of the only world he will ever know—that of exile.

Like Farès, Tunisian author Albert Memmi (most noted for *Portrait du colonisateur;* 1957; transl. 1965) is concerned with the problematics of identity in postcolonial modern Muslim society, as well as the identity of the exiled Arab community in France. The idea of a split identity, inherent in the duality the author experiences as he writes within two languages, is of particular importance in Memmi's works. For Memmi the principal conflict facing the Francophone Maghrebian is rooted in his or her use of two languages. Originally in 1957 he believed that coexistence was impossible and that eventually Francophone narratives would give way to new discourses reflecting the Arabization of emancipated Maghrebian authors. Memmi once stated that "the next generations born in freedom will write spontaneously in their rediscovered language."[68] However, contrary to his predictions, Arabization programs initiated in the Maghreb in the 1970s and 1980s did not succeed in changing Maghrebian authors' preference for French as their language of discourse. Memmi himself changed his views, opting to use French for most of his novels. Like Farès, Memmi manipulated French to create original, more positive discourses for the exiled and the marginalized.

Not unlike Farès, Memmi in *Le scorpion, ou, la confession imaginaire* (1969) endeavors first to deconstruct the French language and then to reuse it, creating his own individual narrative form. In reference to the novel, he states, "I want to break away from the traditional narrative."[69] One method that Memmi uses to achieve that break is the use of different typefaces, evoking colors and wordplay and thereby redefining the established narrative parameters of the French novel and language.[70] In a note to his readers in the closing pages of *Le scorpion,* Memmi states that his purpose for manipulating the French language is to invite the reader into unexplored regions of the imagination evoked by different typefaces.[71] Dividing texts into colors or differing typographies metaphorically alludes to

Memmi's self-exploration and his attempt to collate the conflicting spheres of his Jewish-Tunisian-French-Arab identity. Much like Memmi's own fragmented self, *Le scorpion* incorporates the fragmented lives of a polyphony of various people who, in turn, are depicted through a panoply of presentations. Each individual is accorded a different typeface as well as varying modes of writing. Characters in *Le scorpion*, along with the author himself, moderate debates and heated arguments among themselves in order to carry out a dialogue on the uncertainty and precarious position of Maghrebian identity in France, a country synonymous for exile and isolation: "this double truth . . . this country, outside of which no matter where I am I will be in exile, and this country in which I have never ceased to be in exile."[72] Memmi's double bind cultivates the image of a desert that for so many Maghrebian immigrants isolated in France can only mean a permanent expression of anguish.[73]

Memmi's *Scorpion* not only breaks apart previously established narrative forms like Farès's *Passager de l'occident*, but also provides a mediating space for the exiled. Writing from this space these authors send a cultural message that goes beyond the implications of immigration and the hostilities between France and the Maghreb to "appeal to all nations of the world to show more understanding and tolerance . . . to combine their efforts and pool their resources to combat human suffering."[74] Although foreboding, in many respects Memmi's and Farès's works exemplify typical themes of Maghrebian authors writing in French in the late 1960s and early 1970s. Memmi's rejection of a narrative focused on a unique protagonist or individual subject paved the road for later Maghrebian authors of the late 1970s and 1980s who wished to explore the multifaceted Self that characterized life in exile. In more recent years, exile and the notion of a fragmented Arab identity have also been the object of acute study in works by women Francophone Maghrebian authors such as Leïla Sebbar. Sebbar's novels, in particular her *Shérazade* trilogy, explain the complicated areas of existence in which her protagonists constantly find themselves. She traces the multiple connections of young, marginalized, multiethnic individuals as they set out on quests to know their pasts while fighting to establish an identity of their own in the liminal peripheries of French society.[75] These youths act like agents making connections in a multiethnic culture instead of succumbing to the ready-made exotic or delinquent stereotypes often given them by the French. In order to inscribe their own subjectivity in the French world, Sebbar's characters migrate as nomads to various milieus, building a multiethnic niche where they will no longer be outcasts, but rather accepted for who they are. This nomadism requires breaking the barriers of cultural boundaries in order to establish new ones. New boundaries of agency allow new systems of translation to be installed within the sphere of the marginalized individual, or as Michel de Certeau has indicated, a new system in which "immigrants are the pioneers of civilization founded on the mixing of cultures."[76]

Her breaking of barriers reflects Leïla Sebbar's own views on cultural identity. Writing of herself from an exiled point of view, she upholds that she belongs to no singular essentialist world, but is rather an amalgam of many. Sebbar claims French nationality while retaining her father's Algerian name and heritage. The author refers to herself, however, as a Maghrebian intellectual fighting for human rights in Algeria.[77] Indications of this multitude of diversity within her own identity is found in Sebbar's *Lettres parisiennes: Autopsie de l'exil*, where she writes: "I am not who you think I am, who you seek, who you wish for . . . because it is a question of my books and because I am here as a writer and a person: I am neither an immigrant, nor a child of immigration . . . I am not a Maghrebian Francophone author . . . I am not of native French origin . . . my mother tongue is not Arabic." [78]

Balancing such a precarious existence within a sphere of exile where one is not from one world but from many, implicates a constant negotiation between home country and adopted country, old and new traditions, and cultural diversities. These points of negotiation for Sebbar are crossroads that must intersect so that she can, as she states, "explain quickly what I still can not clarify for myself." Exile, she points out, "is the only place where I can enunciate the contradictions, the division. . . . If I speak of exile, I speak also of cultural crossings; it is at these points of junction or of disjunction where I am, that I see, that I write."[79] Reading and articulating exile are important actions that must be employed by immigrant writers to combat the marginalizing process that occurs within the immigrant communities in France. Sebbar focuses on the social upheaval in the Beur community by studying it through her young protagonists. The author's message is always clear: if children are pushed to the margins of society the only thing that awaits them is delinquency, violence, and death.

From 1945 to 1962, the Maghrebian Francophone novel evolved within a sphere of resistance influenced by the writings of Kateb Yacine and Albert Memmi. Also during this time new inroads were being laid toward a modern multicultural intellectualism (one that incorporated both Western and Maghrebian postrevolutionary views) for the Maghreb and its Francophone authors. Because of its struggle against the colonial presence, the Maghreb was transformed. Authors writing in both French and Arabic embraced new themes including revolt, French acculturation, split identity, exile, and feminine emancipation. There is perhaps no better example of feminine emancipation and resistance in Maghrebian Francophone literature of the 1970s than Driss Chraïbi's *La Civilisation, ma mère . . . !* (1972). This novel marks the transition of one woman from a sequestered child-bride to self-educated feminine activist. Parallel to her story are Chraïbi's observations about the changing political and social climate in Morocco before, during, and after independence. The transformation of woman and country are noted by a man who has seen his wife challenge her veiled, passive, and dominated existence to become an enlightened and active participant in a changing society. He, too, finally sees that the future of his country must include the equal participation of women: "Before [the prosperous] petroleum [era], there was something else—I realize this now. The community is the foundation of all society. And the heart of the community is the family. If the wife is held prisoner at the core of this family, veiled, sequestered as has been the practice for centuries, if she has no opening to the outside world, no active role, the whole society is fatally affected, closes down on itself, and has nothing more to give to itself or to the rest of the world" (173). Confronted with transformations within traditional Muslim society, authors of the Maghreb searched for a means by which to interpret these diverse fluctuations. Abdelkebir Khatibi, in his 1968 essay *Le roman maghrébin,* states that for the first time independent authors of the Maghreb asked themselves, "What does the novel represent for us Maghrebians, now in 1968?"[80] However, answers were not always forthcoming. Authors tended to divide themselves into two camps: those favoring continuing nationalist tendencies and those who embarked on new roads toward a multicultural universalism expressed through the French language.

Putting aside their nationalist-militant agenda of the 1950s and 1960s, contemporary Francophone Maghrebian authors endeavor to interpret a new relationship of literature to society, culture, and history. This relationship links the Maghreb to other literatures and seeks an equal place among them. These authors hope to bridge the gap between two different cultures—Arab and French—while studying the legacy of colonial history and its repression. This shift toward favoring a sociocultural universalism is a direct product of the Algerian revolution as well as of the social complexities associated with the modern decolonized world. These complexities create an unending series of questions for Maghrebian Francophone authors, who must find solutions in order to overcome the problems caused by exile, social changes within their native country, loss of identity, self-determination, and deterritorialization. As Khatibi remarks, it is the "separation [from one's country], loss of identity, [and] deculturation" that have led to "themes to which Francophone writers refer voluntarily when they analyze their situation."[81]

Contemporary Francophone authors of the Maghreb do not draw from French or Arab cultures alone to write their narratives. Their literary force is a multiplicity that includes interaction between the two. It is within these margins (or the intersubjective space between these two identities) that these men and women gather together and explore new themes of subjectivity. Francophone authors of the Maghreb follow nomadic and multicultural paths to embrace and traverse cultures, traditions, languages, and sexuality—all of which are important, not only in Western, but also in non-Western postmodern societies and cultures as well. Traveling beyond canonized Western values implicates the contemporary Maghrebian author in a nomadic journey through an intersubjective space of negotiation—a Third Space—where he or she forms multiple connections with other peoples, ethnicities, and languages as well as diverse notions of becoming and being. This space lies between the former Westernized colonial world, and the new, unexplored space of texts written by the Other. Within this space, contemporary Francophone authors mediate the opposition between Western stereotypes congenial to colonial and current postcolonial texts and their own literary domain of diversity and ethnicity.

The Third Space is a place not only of negotiation but also of enunciation—most significantly of women, minorities, and the formerly oppressed. It is an ambivalent space because it forsakes all preconceived notions concerning stereotypes that have formed Western canonized modes of enunciation and textuality for the Other. It equally destroys all preconceived "mirrors of representation"[82] that constitute structures of meaning and reference as construed by established Western philosophy. By destroying the mirrors of mimetic representation—that is, the Other represented as an ideal formed by Western colonial process and practice—new textualities that "challenge our sense of the historical identity of culture" are brought about,[83] leading to new areas of subjectivity.

But how does one go "beyond" to discover new symbols of culture and subjectivity? Why is nomadism so pertinent to the contemporary Francophone Maghrebian author? How does one arrive at the Third Space? And once there, what are the processes of communication that lead to what is beyond this space? The answers to these questions are crucial since they are imperative to understanding the current literary situation and identity of Francophone Maghrebian culture, literature, and identity, as well as women's positions therein. Therefore the remaining portion of this chapter addresses two theoretical components that I feel are imperative in defining Francophone "feminine" literature of the Maghreb and to answering the above-mentioned questions. The first explores a culturally universal, or *mondialiste,* view of identity as being the key to women's empowerment and embrace of voice and agency. The mondialiste characteristic of contemporary Francophone literature of the Maghreb is one that is connected to many sociocultural political arenas. The mondialiste author follows three steps in constructing his or her rhizome of connections between these areas. These steps involve movement, followed by interaction, which in the end results in subjectivity. In short, they are steps that define presence, agency, and voice. We may designate these steps as nomadology, Third Space, and becoming. They are also processes useful in the development of new literary critical analyses that define and situate themes such as the dissolute or fragmented subject-identity, exile, and duality. As mentioned previously, these themes are prevalent in contemporary Maghrebian Francophone literature. The concepts mentioned above provide innovative paths that aid the author in developing original modes of thinking and ways of being that run contrary to the established single subject (i.e., the Western, white, male-centered subject) and norms inherent in Western colonial discourse. Within these innovative concepts, the Other is posited not as being opposite the Western single subject, but rather as coexisting with it on a socially and culturally diverse plateau.

The literature of the Francophone Maghrebian author promotes the ideal decenteredness (defined here as a subjectivity that is fragmented, yet positively and multiply connected) that subsequently produces a new configuration of the subject. Because it revolves around the "decentered" Franco-Maghrebian subject, contemporary Francophone literature of the Maghreb assumes a multiple view of identity favoring new inscriptions of that identity in history. These texts thus favor a polyphonic textuality that promotes different languages, cultures, and ethnicities within one sphere.

Contemporary works of literature by Tahar Ben Jelloun, Assia Djebar, Leïla Sebbar, Malika Mokeddem, and Hajer Djilani have turned the tables on established Western, French, and Arabic literary norms in order to extend their themes beyond the original paradigms of postcolonial narratives. These authors seek something original to construct new modes of thinking that will lead the author and reader through bypasses and inroads to a multicultural, twenty-first century of literary production. In his essay *Maghreb pluriel*, Abdelkebir Khatibi, forerunner in defining contemporary Maghrebian Francophone literary theory, states that one must "find something else, situate oneself according to a thinking-other, an unprecedented thinking perhaps of difference." His "thinking other" allows one to think only in terms of "plurality and diversity." He posits as important the rethinking and reconnecting "not only of specific margins (Berber, Copt, Kurdish . . . and the margin of margins: the feminine), but also [of the] division of the Arab world by country, people, sect, and class." It is only through such a "thinking plural," Khatibi suggests, that all opposing poles may be linked. It is, he maintains, "only the risk of a thinking plural (of many poles of civilization, language, of many technical and scientific elaborations)" that can "assure the turning of this century on the planetary scene. . . . there is no choice, for anyone." It is a "transmutation of a world with no return on its entropic foundations."[84]

The second theoretical component unique to Francophone literature of the Maghreb is the displacement of the patriarchal Western subject as a defining term in its conceptualization. Authors writing in the Francophone sphere advocate the reinstallation of alternative voices inclusive of women as well as nontraditional themes. As previously mentioned, in general these qualities reflect the multicultural diverse platform of the non-Western diaspora. In the case of the Maghreb, overturning preconceived Western symbols such as Orientalism, has led the formerly colonized to new discourses that recontextualize history as never before. Likewise, contemporary authors of the Maghreb have equally sought to move beyond the more male-centered narratives of the revolutionary era (such as Kateb Yacine's *Nedjma*) that have effaced women's subjectivity. These narratives did serve a valid purpose, that of cultivating a collective movement to fight against colonialism. Yet, in their collective nationalist efforts, they left no place for individual groups' specificity. Certainly issues pertaining to women took a backseat to the revolutionary dialogue of the era.

Today, women and men authors of the Maghreb enter into an intersubjective Third Space of negotiation to write of a new mode of feminine identity. This intersubjective realm affords women an opportunity to reinscribe their own identity; they *become*, in Deleuzo-Guattarian terms, aware of a new feminine agency that allows for a dialogue with the stereotypical, the mimetic, and the oppressive discourses of domination to which they have historically been victims. Feminine being, essentially, is rewritten into the history of the past and the present.

Because feminine becoming includes a wide variety of processes drawing on the historic, the literary, and the cultural areas of the author's environment, a politics promoting a new arena of social feminism that reaches beyond the gender-based rhetorics of earlier Western feminist movements is privileged. Liberation from oppression, even though it be in exile, as Assia Djebar has attested, affords a new space of enunciation for Maghrebian women authors to construct an all-encompassing consciousness as never before depicted. Exile, although difficult, does allow women like Djebar to contribute to the formulation of a worldwide feminism. Maghrebian women authors in this acentered space of negotiation are free to dissolve preconstructed historical processes (such as Orientalism) and subsequently rewrite history and Western notions pertaining to her own subjectivity. Such a space destabilizes and then rebuilds identity, as Donna Haraway suggests: "As orientalism is deconstructed politically and semiotically, the identities of the occident destabilize, including those of feminists. . . . 'Women of color' have a chance to build an effective unity that does not replicate the imperializing, totalizing revolutionary subjects of previous Marxisms and feminisms which had not faced the consequences of the disorderly polyphony emerging from decolonization."[85]

Mondialisme: The Culturally Universal View of Identity

Choosing certain contemporary Western philosophies in order to contextualize and critically consider current Francophone literature of the Maghreb is a very delicate process. The Western literary critic strives for interpretation yet wants to resist recolonizing the foreign text with European misconceptions and thus, once again, devalue the non-Western voice.[86] It is my objective, therefore, to formulate a new theory by which to interpret the contemporary Francophone Maghrebian text within the scope of mondialisme, one that is all encompassing rather than limited by purely Western deconstructionist conceptions of ethnicity, gender, and identity. Such conceptions attempt to recontextualize and give voice back to the Other, however, only according to Westernized paradigms. These paradigms are too often steeped in neocolonizing theories of what the Other ought to do and be.[87] Rather, with regard to the Francophone Maghrebian text, viewing subjectivity through a kaleidoscope of diversity aids the author in the evaluation of his or her dual identity—an identity that reflects two cultures (Arab and French) as well as two traditions, religions, languages, and nationalities.

Contemporary Western literary theory and criticism should do justice to non-Western texts by including them in a more universal, cultural, postmodern context, one that encompasses new areas in both Western and non-Western philosophies. Through a cogent mixture of Western postmodern philosophy and literary criticism from Maghrebian, postcolonial, and Western authors, we may develop comprehensive theories through which contemporary Francophone texts of the Maghreb may be interpreted. These theories will favor the creation of a culturalism that is nonessentialist (defined here as not being determined by gender, race, or ethnicity) and open equally to both men and women.

Contructing a non-essentialist agenda is the object of the contemporary Maghrebian Francophone author. These writers, intellectuals, and academics are shifting toward a nomadic philosophy that promotes the annihilation of borders and frontiers, causing "a total dissolution of the notion of a center and consequently of originary sites or authentic identities of *any kind*."[88] This new nonfixed notion of identity creates a unique sense of consciousness, combining coherence with mobility. Such consciousness enables us to think of the subject without the interference of gendered dualisms or preconceived norms of gender politics that belittle the independence of the female subject. New terms of consciousness link body and mind in an original set of intensive transitions toward a multicultural sense of subjectivity.

Linking segments and fragments (or spheres) of Being in order to extend beyond the many opposing poles of identities and notions of ethnicity constitutes the key elements of nomadism. It is a process of "transmutation," as Deleuze and Guattari explain, where one is obliged to escape "the force of gravity" in order to enter a field of "celerity," where there is a "continuous variation of variables . . . [where] the meaning of Earth completely changes."[89] These changes occur because one is constantly reterritorializing and deterritorializing to extend the territory of relations, points of view, and domains in which he or she constitutes Being. But why does one deterritorialize in search of other territories? And what, or who, is following these nomadic de/reterritorializing paths?

The nomad is the loner, the exiled, the minority, the Other, the "exceptional individual" who has many possible positions, but who never stabilizes in one.[90] He or she exists on the borders or the peripheries of the pack, or of the tribe or the society. The nomad is neither inside nor outside the group or the collectivity but is *anomalous*.[91] The anomal is neither abnormal nor an anomaly, but rather one who is in a position or set of positions in relation to a multiplicity of other entities, ideals, or concepts. Being anomalous for an entity means living and existing on the peripheries. One crosses dimensions and travels across borders, through tribes and into collectivities to incorporate all, or none, or everything into an original identity. The anomal author forms alliances with others through a process of deterritorialization and reterritorialization that guides him or her to other frontiers. Because of this ceaseless movement and constant contact with Others, being anomal can only entail thinking in the plural, which as Khatibi suggests, allows "others (societies and individuals)" to avoid being trapped in a mere sphere of "autosufficiency."[92]

The anomal haunts the fringes while existing between the normal and the abnormal. Leïla Sebbar's Shérazade moves on the fringes of a band of young people.[93] She follows connections between cultures, races, ethnicities, and histories—from Paris to Algiers to the Middle East. Shérazade deterritorializes from one social sphere, follows a line of flight to reterritorialize for a moment in another, only to once again take off, following another path, to another place. This young woman is the Outsider who borders one alliance and subsequently becomes familiar with it because it offers a temporary stage of stability—however, the stability is only fleeting. She must move on further, to other borders, crossings, and multiplicities. Multiplicities are pluralities of experiences, identities, ethnicities, and cultures that have "no relation to the One as subject or object, natural or spiritual reality . . . but [are] an assemblage of dimensions and points."[94]

Shérazade, like the one who is anomal, is a nomad but not a migrant. The migrant travels from one point to another "out of necessity, or for economic benefit." The nomad, on the other hand, moves as a consequence of diverse actions and connections. The nomad is guided by "a territorial principle" that allows for a "distribution of her/himself in a smooth space that he/she occupies, inhabits and holds," if only for a fleeting moment.[95] Thus, the nomadic existence is determined by movement and intensity irrespective of speed. Voyages dictated by movement and intensity may take many different forms. Spiritual voyages may be effected with relatively little movement. Moroccan-born Tahar Ben Jelloun's "*écrivain public*" travels to other borders and lands without ever leaving his writing table. He forms assemblages with faces and bodies he has never seen before by writing to others for others; his life becomes the lives of others and their dreams become his: "An assorted and agitated [group] gathers. Friends with severe faces, old classmates, masked strangers, intense images on a dead sky. A man approaches me and says that he is an actor. He tells me the story of a film in which he acted. Colored images flow out of his mouth. On a wide screen I see the shots he describes to me. I don't hear the words. I try to follow the rhythm of the images, which flow at high speed. He begins to tell me another story, with other characters. On the same screen brief, but different, images are superimposed."[96]

The nomad in his or her anomal state, even though occupying temporal spaces, always seeks to travel beyond stereotypical norms in order to multiply his or her contacts. This beyond is "neither a new horizon, nor a leaving behind of the past." What is the nomad's definition of beyond? It is the disorientation of the normal or the embrace of the *au-delà*, which, as cultural theorist Homi Bhabha explains, is "here and there, on all sides . . . hither and thither, back and forth."[97] The move away from singularities of class, gender, race or ethnicity (as primordial conceptual categories of classification) is inherent in the nomad's search to recontextualize Being within a multicultural, multiconnected world. The nomad-Francophone-Maghrebian author thinks beyond narratives of these categories in order to articulate cultural differences that reside in the spaces between diverse identities. Within the in-between, or the intersubjective, the nomad moves through the interstices (the overlap and displacement of domains of difference).[98] Traveling in the in-between derails barriers of essentialism. Barriers and boundaries are redefined or undefined because the very act of going beyond entails embracing the unknown, or the unrepresentable.

Traveling to existences further out (beyond preconceived notions regarding ethnicity and difference) interrupts the spacial significance of former cultural stereotypes, or as Bhabha suggests, our "collusive sense of cultural contemporaneity."[99] Because of this disjointedness, the nomad who travels within intersubjective space is compelled to reconceptualize notions of past, present, and future time (fashioned always according to the didactic West) in a completely different manner. The reconstituted yet new time frame of history reveals age-old discontinuities and inequalities pertaining to the once colonized other.

The boundaries of enunciation of the nomad are synonymous with the discontinuous and the dissonant. In this space of flux the subject becomes a dissident. His or her history is a dissident history representing voices of those who have never been heard (such as women, the colonized, and minority groups) who have fought against oppressive authority. The boundaries of the outside of the colonized/authoritative space become the places of these Others who seek to begin their subjectivity and the processes of redefinition and recontextualization of their own histories. Therefore, the author who is in the margins or "completely outside his or her fragile community" is all the more likely to "express another possible community and to forge the means for another consciousness and another sensibility."[100]

Forging an-Other sensibility—one free of stereotypes for example—is most important in contemporary Francophone Maghrebian literature. Orientalist stereotypes created by the West as a means of defense against the encroaching power of Islam have fundamentally been the most damaging for Maghrebian peoples.[101] Orientalist stereotypes have succeeded for centuries in insidiously reducing the Arab to a series of standards and conceptions within literature, art, economics, and world politics. These formulas have evolved over the years, but still continue to be posited in our postmodern era. The roots of Orientalism itself reach to the first vestiges of colonization. Popular anti-Arab sentiment prevalent today in the West directly reflects the influence of colonial Oriental history, a legacy of French and British colonial missions, whose oppression throughout North Africa was particularly significant.

The nomad-exiled-Francophone-Maghrebian writer has to contend with the Oriental stereotype. In her trilogy *Shérazade*, Leïla Sebbar's protagonist questions the legacy of the Oriental *monde imaginaire* created by nineteenth-century French painters, exclaiming that "the odalisques are always lying down, listless, blankly staring, almost asleep. For Western painters they stand for nonchalance, lustfulness, the perverse seduction of North African women."[102] Even today the Orientalist wall, one of the last remaining remnants of colonialism, is difficult to tear down. As Tahar Ben Jelloun explains in *Hospitalité française*, "Medieval prejudices are insinuated in the collective unconscious of the West at such a profound level that one can ask, with alarm, if they will ever be eradicated."[103] Effacing the Orientalist stereotype has become a prime objective for contemporary Maghrebian Francophone authors. It is hoped that breaking Orientalist bonds will afford the possibility of engaging the West in a dialogue of comprehension.

The goal of these authors is to develop comprehension and knowledge within the ideal of a culturally differenced, rather than stereotyped, identity. The development of this knowledge will finally assure the benefits of positive connections and the movement of peoples in a space of enunciation that favors promoting all social, cultural, and literary discourses. Arriving at the edge of such a space of multiple ethnicity will mark the completion of the first step of the voyage on the way to the au-delà—the multicultural sphere of a new literature for contemporary Francophone authors of the Maghreb.

The mondialiste concept decenters the centuries-old Western-ized singular subject of canonized narratives. Overturning the Western ideal of single-centered identity entails interconnections between nomads in order to form a collectivity of connected yet different and diverse entities. These are beings and independent bodies that exist within a nondetermined space, one not defined by essentialist paradigms. It is through these connections that a decen-tered yet multicultural universality will codevelop at last, positively affirming the Other's presence as nondetermined by the Western world. Such multicultural mondialisme forms a rhizome of connec-tions that become synonymous for decenteredness because they have no end or beginning, only middleness.[104] They are the prod-uct of both an alliance of difference and of diversity, which guards against the domination of any single entity, event, culture, or ethnicity over another. Such a web of connections extends across a space of negotiation and enunciation[105] or, as Deleuze and Guat-tari suggest, a plane of consistency, upon which all entities may coexist in "any number of multiplicities, with any number of di-mensions. The plane of consistency is the intersection of all con-crete forms."[106]

On such a plane, cultural enunciation collides with predefined Western postcolonial rhetoric (previously construed in order to represent the non-Western subject) in order to form a new, multi-faceted center of meaning for the marginalized of Western society. The intervention of a Third Space, as Bhabha suggests, "makes the structure of meaning and reference an ambivalent process." It de-stroys what he defines as a "mirror of representation" that has "guided the discourse of the world."[107] By turning the tables and destabilizing established modes of representation, Others now are free to negotiate and translate their cultural identities in a discontin-uous intertextual time frame of cultural difference.[108] In other words, Western theoretical, essentialized, postcolonial depictions of the Other, such as Derrida's différance, are no longer the sole means of representing him or her. These depictions coexist with all

other representations that afford the Other a new means of mediation, allowing for the review of both cultural and historical dimensions pertaining to his or her subjectivity.

But how is negotiation defined within this enunciative sphere of
the in-between? And why is this negotiation characteristic of the
narratives of the contemporary Francophone author in this study?
These questions will be answered more extensively later, in my
analyses of the literary works of several prominent contemporary
Francophone authors. It is first pertinent to note the thematic development of contemporary Francophone texts of the Maghreb
that aid in the study of the intersubjective space of enunciation outlined above. Let us begin with two repetitive themes found in this
literature that necessitate the use of the Third Space of enunciation
and negotiation. The first theme is the affirmation of a rupture
(with the colonizer, home country, traditions, family, etc.) that subsequently alienates the author or his or her protagonist from the rest
of his or her social group. Second, the author or protagonist seeks
recognition of his or her position of exile resulting from the rupture. Both these themes are the cause of a larger conflict—a feeling
of duality that plagues either the author's or the protagonist's existence. Dualities such as French-Arab, traditional-modern, or femi-
nine-masculine must be reconciled, or at least studied, to try and
bridge the gap between knowledge of the Self and the Other.

Reconciliation of the dialectic pull between male and female is
one of the principal themes addressed by Tahar Ben Jelloun in his
space of negotiation. In *L'enfant de sable* and *La nuit sacrée*, the author seeks to know the sphere of the other—to explore the realm of
the feminine. He enters a feminine negotiating process in order to
delve into the Other's psyche and soul: "Who am I? And who is the
Other?"[109] These questions are the driving forces to which both author and protagonist seek answers. Crossing the line of sexuality to
explore the Other within the Self is also a theme found in Assia
Djebar's *Vaste est la prison*. The narrator finds herself not only fan-
tasizing about appropriating the body of a young man, but also

about stepping beyond sexual boundaries to an asexual, or androgynous, form:

> He affirmed, seeing me from afar, that I was a young man
> (my hair was very short, my white pants narrow).
> At thirty-seven, I seemed probably younger than thirty:
> slim hips, hair like a boy's, flat buttocks; that day [I was] so
> proud of my androgynous figure.[110]

Building a bridge between the polarities of Self and Other, in order to abolish duality and thus find a new voice, is the task of the nomadic author writing in exile within the sphere of negotiation. Because there is no dialectic polarity within this sphere, negotiation takes place evenly, rhizomatically. The absence of the dialectic between self and other than self results in an otherness that promotes an open-ended selfhood, or a "fused" sense of being that redefines the idea of "self" as both otherness and self-ness at the same time. The exiled subject is at once both subject and object; "one passes into the other."[111]

A further example of this fusing of the self with the Other is depicted most poignantly in Abdelkebir Khatibi's *Amour bilingue*. Seeking to confront the dialectic tension between French and Arab linguistic adversaries, Khatibi reflects on his world of duality and the constant negotiation into which he is forced in the bilingual world: "The bilingual? My chance, my individual abyss." Am I French? Am I Moroccan? he asks, or "some sort of mutant from one language to another[?]"[112] In Khatibi's fused language sphere, difference is overshadowed by his new discourse, one he reinscribes like a palimpsest over former French and Arab fields. Consequently, he finds himself in a new sphere of being, writing in a third, negotiated text in-between French and Arab worlds. By negotiating between these two identities, Khatibi creates a third identity constructed from both spheres of "self and other": "my chance in the bilingual is double: I don't lose, I don't gain anything. The calculation, in its complication, offers me the incalculable. What I can give is pure gratuitousness, selflessness without exchange, [this is] the freedom of the Other in me."[113]

It is the realization and acknowledgment of this fused duality as well as the freedom found through exploration of one's otherness that assure a catalyst reaction by which the Maghrebian Francophone author is drawn into the realm of the Third Space. Within this space he or she is empowered with the force to "become"—that is, to enter into another identity (inclusive of me and the Other) that is the product of many differing and various entities that form multiple connections.

The absence of binarisms, dualities, and dialectical poles within the Third Space opens up an imminent gulf that pulls into itself all bodies, whether animate or inanimate; all genders, whether male, female, or homosexual; all identities, whether Arab or French. These bodies, or elements, move and collide through energy and dynamics fusing into a new entity that constitutes a becoming. A becoming is neither the imitation of a subject nor the proportionality of a form it "possesses," according to Deleuze and Guattari: "becoming is not to imitate or identify with something or someone. Nor is it to proportion formal relations."[114] It is rather, made up mainly of molecular movement and energy that are pushed by the desire for knowledge—to know the Other as part of the Self. Such a desire for the interlocking of self and other eradicates opposition and leads to new configurations of the Self. Desire, in Deleuzo-Guattarian terms, is what pushes all beings to communicate and form connections. Becoming functions, in a sense, as a molecular grouping where the "particles" of one self relate and move with other particles, bonding to form new molecular groups.[115]

All becomings are molecular, whether inanimate or animate, plants, animals, or humans. All these subjectivities have the ability to enter into a becoming. There is a becoming-woman and a becoming-child. However, entering into a becoming-woman does not mean imitating or transforming oneself into a woman. It means simply, "emitting particles that enter the relation of movement and rest, or the zone of proximity, of a microfemininity . . . that produce in us a molecular woman."[116] The molecule of womanness, like the molecule of childness or otherness, is in all forms of being. A becoming-woman, a becoming-child, and a becoming-animal are all segments in a molecular chain through which entities pass, collide, form relationships, and move on. These segments also are minoritarian. Such segments have been overshadowed and dominated by colonialism or phallocentrism. This fact, of course, explains why the Deleuzo-Guattarian philosophy of becoming is so important to the Francophone Maghrebian author; such a philosophy favors the Other—the minority. The idea of "minority" encompasses all that is Other—women, the colonized, the oppressed, the exiled. In the case of the Francophone text, the majoritarian opposing force to the minority is the European, white, adult-male narrative, fashioned from the legacy of domination par excellence. A majoritarian position always implies a state of power, and contrarily, the majority in the universe "assumes as pregiven the right and power of man. In this sense women, children, but also animals, plants and molecules, are minoritarian."[117] Thus the situation of women, or what Deleuze and Guattari designate as being a situation in relation to the man-standard (that is, subservient to men), is similar to the colonized in relation to the colonizer or the nomadic-decentered-exiled author in relation to the Western single-subject canonized literary figure. Therefore, becoming can only be achieved if one first passes through a minority stage, or through a minoritarian position.

Becoming means deterritorializing oneself. One cannot enter into a becoming until he or she first ruptures the ties with the world of oppression. Becoming-woman implies such a break and then passage from one stage to another. A woman must become woman, a child must become child, blacks must become black because "only a minority is capable of serving as the active medium of becoming."[118] Such becoming implies two functions of movement or energy of desire—first the subject is withdrawn from the majority, and then it is deterritorialized to rise up through the act of being minority—to posit itself by its minoritarian subjectivity, or its otherness. Deterritorialization and becoming-minoritarian is "a political affair and necessitates a labor of power, an active micropolitics."[119]

For the contemporary Francophone author of the Maghreb, deterritorializing into a becoming implicates the discovery of a new genre of politics situated between domination (old colonial rule) and the ever-present power of the majority. This old guard insists on prolonging its power. Majoritarianism is the central point that organizes the binary oppositions between Us and Them, Self and Other, colonized and colonizer, French and Arab, woman and man. The majority is built on the weakness of its other, on the pulling of dominated links to its centered point. White European Man is always at the center. His position in literature is also that of the dominant figure—the subject at the center of the canonized text. Since the centered white European male is the dominator of all lines of subjectivity to other points, the Other-author has been locked into a subservient position with no room to move.

The Francophone contemporary author of the Maghreb who enters into a becoming and succeeds in negotiating new orders for his or her existence within a nondetermined cultural sphere—a Third Intersubjective Space—passes between points rather than going from dictated or already plotted ones. Within the in-between of these points or on the margins, in a no-man's-land of intersubjectivity, becomings are formed. But where does becoming lead and to what end does it bring the non-Western author? In Deleuzo-Guattarian terms, all becomings reach imperceptibility. The imperceptible is the immanent end of becoming, which signifies the end of all relations, such as those of the asignifying and indiscernible. As noted in chapter 2, imperceptibility for Ben Jelloun's protagonist, Ahmed/Zahra, also means the end to all difference, duality, and otherness. Such space of imperceptibility is where the subject can go unnoticed, lost in the mass of a becoming of everybody in a cosmos of interlinking connections.

The cosmos, therefore, is the place where all subjects are reduced to only movement and desire or pure forces of embodied being that depend on a collection of differences and diversities. Everything within the sphere of the cosmos exists on an equalized plane; thus, there is no dialectic opposition between Other and Self, black and white, male and female, or any other preconceived notion of otherness—there remains only movement and rest, deterritorialization and reterritorialization between diverse entities, ethnicities, and cultures.

Reinstalling Alternative Voices: Feminine Becoming in the Francophone Maghrebian Text

Feminists today widely agree that while economically emancipating women in the 1960s and 1970s, Western feminism did little to adapt to women's changing needs in the 1980s and 1990s.[120] It is also generally noted that the feminist movement did little for those women outside the white, heterosexual, upper-middle-class echelons of society. As African American feminist bell hooks remarks, "feminism . . . has never emerged from the women who are most victimized by sexist oppression; women who are daily beaten down, mentally, physically, and spiritually—women who are powerless to change their condition in life. They are a silent majority."[121]

During the 1970s and 1980s, fighting their way out of ghettos, poverty, and social conflict was not (and in most respects still is not) an option for a majority of women of color in America, the Maghreb, or anywhere in the world. Many women of color have remarked that for the most part the idea of feminism has been the privilege of their white sisters. Until the 1990s the misassumption of Western feminists had been that all women's oppression was identical and therefore all women shared a common lot implicating common denominators of class, race, religion, and sexual preference. Further, these denominators consequently divided women because they fell secondary to the central issue of sexism—the absolute determining contributor to the oppressive forces that controlled women's lives.[122] Feminists today are seeking new inroads to circumvent the political, social, and racial divisions between them in order to conceptualize new agendas promoting a multicultural feminism—one that incorporates gender, difference, race, and culture. This new agenda marks the impact of poststructuralist and postmodern perspectives, which are constantly redefining contemporary theories on difference and otherness. Some feminists and poststructuralists, such as Luce Irigaray, define modern-day feminine as an "otherness . . . which is not yet represented" because it "remains unrepresentable."[123] If we follow Irigaray's hypothesis, feminism has yet to come into being. Therefore, if we have yet to come into being then we are free to plot points for a more global and relative feminism that will include not only Western white women, but all women of all ethnicities, nations, religions, and cultures.

It is Deleuze and Guattari's nomadic subject that best defines and formulates the new paradigms of the feminine subject—or, as Rosi Braidotti puts it, a "multiple embodied subject." Braidotti maintains that the multiembodied subject has its origins in the Foucauldian concept of materiality, which is "materialism of the flesh. This notion defines the embodied subject as the material concrete effect, that is to say, as one of the terms in a process of which knowledge and power are the main poles."[124] Instead of essentializing the feminine body in terms of sexual desire, the nomadic-multiembodied subject embraces a subjectivity that extends beyond paradigms of gender dualism. This in turn privileges new views of the self as a multiple body espousing an interrelatedness of diverse properties that includes feminine emancipation and agency within society (both Western and Maghrebian). Identity thus becomes a site of differences demonstrating that a subject may include a variety of contrasting positions such as sex, race, class, age, and lifestyle that are modified according to the constantly changing constructions of the self. Such a construction of selfhood is pertinent to Maghrebian women because it extends beyond phallocentric and patriarchal paradigms dictated by males. Within the new paradigms of socially embodied selfhood, Maghrebian women are able to form new conceptions never before envisaged concerning feminine identity in the Maghreb.

It is only through the multicultural, multifaceted subject that women of the Maghreb are at last empowered to write themselves into the history of the world. On the whole, Maghrebian feminism has evolved very slowly because of several factors. Individual feminine identity has gained little ground in a phallocentric world where women have been the victims of male persecution, and where history has left them little room in which to construct a feminist platform. As Moroccan sociologist-feminist Fatima Mernissi points out in *The Forgotten Queens of Islam,* throughout history masculine oppression has left women with little, if any, political representation within Muslim spheres of power: "There is no feminine form of the words *imam* or *caliph,* the two words that embody the concept of power in the Arabic language, the language in which the Qur'an was revealed. The *Lisan al-Arab* dictionary informs us without qualifications that *'al-khalifatu la yakunu illa li al-dhakr'* (*caliph* is used only in the masculine). In such a context, where the principle is exclusion, any infiltration into the realm of political decision-making by women, even under the cloak of and in the corridors of the harem, even behind dozens of curtains, veils, and latticed windows, is an utterly laudable and heroic adventure."[125]

Feminine subjectivity in the Maghreb has had to resist threats of erasure for centuries. A paucity of reference to women's roles in the annals of Islamic history, the Oriental stereotype generated out of the French colonizing process, and women's domination under modern-day patriarchal or nationalist governments have all threatened feminine subjectivity, identity, and sexuality.[126] Today, more than ever, women must continue to resist. Unfortunately, more often than not they have had to forge their own identity from an exiled position—that is, outside the Maghreb. By stepping into another space—an intersubjective domain—women find access to paths of negotiation. These paths lead them to new areas where authors such as Assia Djebar find they are able to recontextualize Maghrebian feminine historical representation as well as conceptualize new feminine political and social roles in the present. Maghrebian feminine identity, therefore, is reinvented from outside the age-old forces that have hindered women's independence in the Maghreb.

Perhaps to no other group of women has the analogy of the nomad been so pertinent. Today, not only is the Maghrebian Francophone woman following lines of flight from and out of oppressive, phallocentric, postrevolutionary regimes or Muslim fundamentalist persecution (or both), she is also seeking to make contact and build bridges between her present and her past. For those Maghrebian women such as Leïla Sebbar, Assia Djebar, Malika Mokeddem, and Hajer Djilani, how to recontextualize past colonial French domination and present-day persecution at home (most notably in Algeria) with the freedom they find in a multicultural world of exile constantly reinforces the image of the nomad.

The literature considered in this book offers a panoply of diverse views on femininism, agency, alterity, subjectivity, and identity. It is through the analysis of these views that a cogent recontextualization of the Maghrebian feminine protagonist is being forged by authors such as Ben Jelloun, Sebbar, Djebar, Mokeddem, and Djilani. The Maghrebian feminine subject has entered into a new phase of identity—one in which she alone is master of her actions and representation, both historically (as she rewrites the annals of history) and in the present. She is striving to create a new feminine collective sphere in which all women enjoy the right to speak, to shape their subjectivity, and to reformulate their identity. These identities are freed from colonizing and Orientalizing processes, as well as from the phallocentric dictate under which they have been oppressed since the end of colonial rule.

In the following literary analyses the paths taken by Maghrebian women and men toward a becoming-woman and new paradigms of subjectivity are explored. How will a becoming-woman affect their social and cultural Muslim Maghrebian ties? What will be the results of accepting both their French and Arab heritage? What impact are their works having on women's political position today within Muslim culture? Will there be change, or will women such as Assia Djebar be forced to live forever in exile in order to continue a feminine dissident discourse? In each of the following analytical chapters Ben Jelloun, Sebbar, Djebar, Mokeddem, and Djilani all search for different forms of feminine identity through transcendence to a new space of agency—the place of the becoming-woman. It is in this active space of agency that women of the Maghreb will subvert the continuing threats against them. Agency and voice in sociopolitical and cultural forms will assure the emancipation of women. The task of the Maghrebian woman and author is to embrace the negotiation of difference and diversity and thus construct a platform of new feminist discourse. It is only through dialogue that new empowered, feminine-communitarian agency may be formed, thus promoting a new global womanism for all women of the world.

Chapter Two

Being Anomalous

Tahar Ben Jelloun's Self-Projecting
Metaphors of Marginality in
L'enfant de sable and *La nuit sacrée*

M OROCCAN-BORN Tahar Ben Jelloun, by writing in
French, has set himself in an anomalous or "ex-centric"
position. Writing from two perspectives—one French
and one Moroccan—he is forced to the peripheries of both Western
and Maghrebian narrative traditions. In order to look into both narrative spheres, Ben Jelloun creates a third space—a space of mediation—from which to write. In weaving his narratives in this
outside peripheral space, he is inscribing the subjectivity of all who
are anomal; those who represent the marginalized, lost, repudiated,
weak, handicapped, and different. Ben Jelloun projects himself
through his protagonist Ahmed/Zahra to call attention to his
agenda. Her confusion, lack of status as a woman in a phallocratic
society, vulnerability, and fear all allude to the author's own con-
fused, complicated, unstable universe.

Ben Jelloun's two novels *L'enfant de sable* and *La nuit sacrée* are
blends of self-projecting metaphors he creates to describe what
may be viewed as his own space of marginality.[1] This analysis of
the two novels demonstrates how both stories about Ahmed/Zahra
are spaces of inscription (planes of consistency), on which Ben Jelloun seeks to justify and subsequently to inscribe his *own* place in

the world. That place is an-Other space that is constructed from exile, difference, and subversion. Within it, Ben Jelloun draws a map he uses to navigate and to travel beyond the limits of stereotyped identity in order to reach a place of imperceptibility—the open, smooth plane of all possibilities. The place of the imperceptible marks the end of all difference, duality, and otherness. It is the place where an entity can go unnoticed, unhampered by gender, deformity, or handicap: "The imperceptible is the immanent end of becoming, its cosmic formula."[2] It is what awaits at the end of a nomadic journey. Becoming imperceptible is the last state of becoming, the last stage where everything that is made to resemble something else terminates.

Ben Jelloun's universe, although seemingly unstable, does open up to this new space of the imperceptible—a space of positive agency. At the crossroads of two cultures in his mediating space, where he subverts established norms (such as linear narrative structure), he inscribes a new method of narration that mixes literary practices from both the West and the Maghreb on all levels: cultural, linguistic, and social.[3] His constant oscillation between the real and the imaginary draws on rich, centuries-old Maghrebian oral storytelling traditions reminiscent of *A Thousand and One Nights*. This borrowing from his traditional culture is a trait characteristic of all Ben Jelloun's novels. Through his retextualization of past tradition with modern literary technique, the author shows that the construction of narrative is more a montage of fiction than a linear development.[4]

Amplifying his own marginal space, Ben Jelloun takes his narrative voice further—into the realm of the feminine Other—a space that is new and uncharted. Why does Ben Jelloun choose to cross the border into this unknown feminine sphere? This unfamiliar domain is a smooth surface on which "multiplicities, lines, strata and segmentarities, lines of flight and intensities, machinic assemblages and their various types," may be inscribed.[5] It is a place of beginning—of commencement—that leads eventually to a becoming-woman, a transcended position of identity, the place of true subjectivity where opposition and difference are eradicated. Feminine subjectivity, or womanness, represents two dimensions for the author. First it signifies complete otherness (an unexplored and unhindered sphere of being). Second, it represents a site of victimization and exploitation. Ben Jelloun appropriates these two dimensions in order to weave his story and define his own marginality, place of exile, and the unknown of the literary imagination that he wants to explore. Writing as a woman he also demonstrates his empathy for women's paltry political and social status in his own country. The author's own exploration of the feminine side of himself is, in part, an effort to understand and to make some sense of a nonsensical and unequal society. As he states in an interview in *Jeune Afrique,* representing himself and others who are marginalized through his protagonist Ahmed/Zahra is an act of solidarity, an alliance with all those who have no voice: "The tests that Zahra faces could very well be those of a people struggling for their liberation. It is the battle of one woman to become what she would have been if she had not been a victim of aggression against her sexuality and her being."[6]

The author's ultimate goal is to find a space of empowerment for himself and his feminine character, something he does achieve at the end of his second novel, *La nuit sacrée*. Ben Jelloun's protagonist enters into a becoming-woman; that is, she realizes her self-affirmation as a subject after going through several stages—different becomings—which ultimately lead her to her *wijdanha* or true being.[7] By entering into a becoming-woman, Ben Jelloun metaphorically opens up a new politics of the body for oppressed women; at the same time he combats his own misgivings concerning his identity as an exiled Francophone Maghrebian author writing in France.

For Ben Jelloun, crossing the gender line also aids in metaphorically mediating the fine line between reality and the imaginary, or between the modern Western world and the Moroccan world of legend and myth. Both these worlds constantly push at the author's pen, forcing him to negotiate between two very different spaces. Ben Jelloun's protagonist Ahmed/Zahra is his mediating point. She is left in the in-between of exile to search for her identity. The real and the unreal are of little consequence because, like the duality of masculine-feminine or French-Moroccan arenas, the author's task is simply to negotiate a milieu where opposition may be united in order to craft his story and his sense of place.

L'enfant de sable and *La nuit sacrée* depict the painful struggle of one woman to gain access to her identity, sexuality, and femininity. Born as the eighth girl child to a wealthy Moroccan merchant in the first novel, *L'enfant de sable,* Ahmed is forced by her father to "become" a boy in order to provide an heir to the family's fortune: "the child to be born was to be male even if it was a girl." Her masculine role condemns her to an existence pulled between both the masculine and the feminine. Under her male mask, she is never quite man, nor can she ever be totally woman. The desire to discover her true femininity and to shed her masculine mask eventually force her to embark on a quest to the outside.

La nuit sacrée follows the first novel's theme of dual identity; however, the female protagonist's name is now Zahra. Upon the death of her father, Zahra flees. She is resigned to follow what she feels is her destiny, but is constantly pursued by her past and by family members who seek to destroy or mutilate her. *La nuit sacrée* is Ben Jelloun's metaphoric plane of consistency—a surface on which he explores the mythical, the real, and the unreal of one woman's quest to establish her own subjectivity. In the final pages his protagonist at last succeeds in transcending the material world when she enters an illuminated paradise of true feminine identity.

Ben Jelloun's metaphoric introspection and projection through his character, Ahmed/Zahra, throughout the two novels follows three successive steps that in the end lead both author and protagonist to construct subjectivity from marginality. These three steps may be defined as recognition, inscription, and perception. Through this progression in which author and protagonist are fused as one defines an intellectual-cultural-social space that does not depend on the specificity of any camp whether it be Muslim or Christian, female or male, Oriental or Occidental, or French or Arab. Ben Jelloun's intellectual, anomal space is not conceptualized in terms of collective passions, preordained identity, or stereotype, but rather concentrates on transcendental values that are applicable to all nations, peoples, and ethnicities.

L'enfant de sable: Recognizing Oneself as Another

L'enfant de sable is a study of the politics of the body and of the hermetically sealed roles of gender within the parameters of Muslim society.[8] As the author indicates in his novel, gender politics defines and shapes every aspect of feminine and masculine space within Moroccan culture. Therefore, how one defines oneself individually as a woman or as a man depends very much on one's predefined space within the larger social whole. These spaces are concretely indicated and leave no room for transgression. But what if the lines are erased? Ben Jelloun's character, Ahmed, is a site of confusion because she is neither totally man nor woman, but a body where two genders overlap, yet are never individually defined: "Who am I now? I dare not look at myself in the mirror. What is the state of my skin, my facade, my appearance? Too much solitude and silence have exhausted me. I have surrounded myself with books and secrecy. Today I am trying to deliver myself. From what, exactly? From the fear that I have piled up? From that layer of mist that served me as a veil? From that relationship with the other in myself[?]" (83).

Because Ahmed is kept from acknowledging her feminine self by her false maleness, her body is reduced to nothing more than a series of relationships. Between these are pulled sites of masculine and feminine sexuality, pain, excess, decadence, and desire. Traits of gender are dissolved to such a degree that Ahmed's body becomes an androgynous, shapeless figure defined by only the social and political power wielding factors of her father's milieu. Because

79

of the "politicization" of Ahmed's body (her father's rule over her and the traditions of the controlling community), the idea of self as woman cannot exist. Her feminine body is abstracted from her Self in order to play a role reflecting a mere set of infinitely disciplined relationships. Ahmed is thus the victim of a political field of power where sociocultural elements have a hold on her body, investing, marketing, training, torturing, and forcing it to carry out tasks over which she has no control.

Ahmed's vacillation between the two gender poles signifies Ben Jelloun's larger critique of the unjust divisions between Muslim masculine outside and feminine inside space. Fatima Mernissi and many other Muslim sociologists, authors, literary critics, and feminists agree that Islamic tradition and religion use space as a device for sexual control. Masculine Muslim ideology concerning sexualized space is constructed upon the notion of women as active monsters who must be contained. As Mernissi states, "In societies in which seclusion and surveillance of women prevail, the implicit concept of female sexuality is active";[9] therefore it is thought that in order to keep men free of harm, women must be contained. Policies of female containment lead to cloistering, veiling, and surveillance of women. Women are thus relegated to the interior, dominated spaces of Muslim society such as home, marriage, children, and the *hammamat*.[10] Ben Jelloun describes this interiority vividly through Ahmed's (male) eyes. At one moment "he" remarks, "for all those women, life was limited. It did not amount to much more than cooking, housework, waiting around, and, once a week, a restful afternoon in the hammam. I was secretly pleased that I did not belong to that limited world" (23).

Ben Jelloun's gendered division of space reflects a world where women are considered the root of chaos and disorder. Mernissi explains that the Arabic word W *tna* has for centuries been used synonymously for women in order to assure ample reason for masculine domination and ultimate rule over what is considered the evil temptations women cause.[11] Azouz Begag and Abdellatif Chaouite further explain that this concept of the feminine as a site of chaos has formed a universal notion in Muslim society that, although symbolic, dictates the roles of women and men: "The Maghrebian space is sexualized according to a universal principle of symbolization: all closed space, determining the 'inside,' falls under feminine domain (home); woman is the true mistress of the house. Contrastingly, all space outside falls under masculine control; man makes his law. This is a general representation, the minimum code by which generations have lived. The woman wears the veil to go out (thus she places herself 'outside' in masculine space) and man discreetly treads when he is inside (he thus stays at the limits of feminine space)."[12]

Hermetically sealed gendered spaces are domains ruled by codes defined by either their respective masculine or feminine functions. In the case of Ahmed, codified Muslim feminine interior and masculine exterior spaces are subverted; she has access to both. However, she/he is never fully able to enter either. In a sense Ahmed is rendered "neuter," caught in the middle and unable to trace her identity or to deterritorialize to new experiences. Ben Jelloun's character exemplifies her own need to find a place of mediation, or an exterior space that will aid in her emergence from the stagnation of her father's false world.

Ahmed's exterior world, ruled by Muslim masculine ideology, hones her body and soul. The author's exploitation of this overdetermined masculine world is undeniable. In both novels, Ahmed/Zahra is constantly confronted with the twisted views of this super-phallocratic/centric world. Although perhaps at times Ben Jelloun's depictions are excessive, he nevertheless exposes certain traditions in Muslim society that have been created, and remain constant barriers, to shut women out, condemning them to a life of sequestration, domesticity, and oppression.

Encouraged by her father, Ahmed forces herself to accept the harshness of the overdetermined Muslim male persona. She becomes so engulfed in the lie that she totally represses her feminine self, denying the very essence of her identity as a woman. When her mind and body do depart from the designated role she must play, she severely chastises herself. Discipline of both body and mind manipulate Ahmed's appearance and train "his" mind to shut itself off from feminine fragility. He convinces himself to view women as frail and "so fat and ugly," stating defiantly, "I would never be like them. . . . An unacceptable ugliness" (24). When Ahmed's chest starts to form breasts, her body is once again disciplined into submission, bandaged with white linen that Ahmed's mother tightens so tightly that she can barely breath (24). Her body becomes a battlefield on which the feminine Other is mutilated, contained, and denied.

Ahmed succeeds, for a short time, in suppressing her inner feminine Other from coming out by embracing the masculine destiny her father has created for her. Ironically, she becomes even more masculine than her role requires. Turning the tables in the domination game, she tells her father that through the hardening of her masculine shell she has "shed the other bark" that made her weak (36). The protagonist realizes that the toughness and virility of the masculine world contain the keys to all that equates institutions of power in her community: mosque, work, and schooling. As a male who is afforded the luxury of learning to read and write, Ahmed is given the power of words, which curiously becomes the sole means of expressing her hidden femininity. Writing becomes an important element in the protagonist's quest for identity and her reinscription in social space as a woman. The writing process affords her several contacts that become important in her refeminization and the subsequent acquisition of her lost feminine Self. Most significant is her correspondence with a figure whose identity remains unknown and speculative throughout the novel. Ben Jelloun's insertion of this unidentified figure is curious. It is this unknown he who at last convinces the protagonist to set out on her quest for feminine identity and knowledge of her Self. The anonymous correspondent becomes Ahmed's confident and conscience, urging her to free herself of the mask she has been forced to wear. It is to him that she first confesses her false identity. Who is this anonymous entity who becomes her only ally? *Entity* seems the only applicable term because "he" is never revealed as either man or woman. Perhaps it is more pertinent to view this unidentified "conscience" as Ben Jelloun's own Third Space of negotiation; the anomalous space in which identity may be mediated. A place where he holds a conversation with his protagonist and his readers. This space of mediation allows Ahmed to begin her feminine metamorphosis and to embark on a nomadic quest of self-discovery. For Ben Jelloun, the anomalous narrative space in which he has chosen to craft his story contains no judgment and no forced rules. The narrative freedom established in *L'enfant de sable* generates a significant amount of intellectual questioning. This freedom is the author's manner of tackling the fundamental problem of how to reconcile his identity and status with regards to his culture, society, and history. Ben Jelloun's definite engagement in his own quest for identity is projected through his character as *she* emerges from her male mask: "To go out. To emerge from underground. My body would raise the heavy stones from that destiny and stand like a new thing on the ground. Ah! The idea of subtracting myself from that memory brings me joy. I had forgotten what joy is! What relief, what pleasure in thinking that it would be my own hands that would mark out the route of a street that might lead to a mountain! It has taken me a long time to reach this window. I feel light" (83).

Ahmed throws off her male mask just as Ben Jelloun seeks to free himself from any preordained narrative strategies—be they French or Arabic. Not only does his narrative space promote the real, the unreal, and the imaginaire, it also helps the author reconcile a void of uncertainty over being a Moroccan author living in France writing a narrative in French through a feminine voice.

On a larger scale, the idea of going out, may be viewed metaphorically as opening up other alternatives for Ben Jelloun's narrative space. Using a traditional oral Arabic storytelling style to narrate Ahmed's quest in the French language, the author constructs an articulation of political and theoretical space reflecting two worlds combined in his own original narrative conception.[13] The fusion of Arabic and French narrative traditions places Ahmed at the crossroads of identity, on the margins of not one place but many, freeing her to seek out her becoming-woman.

The Labyrinth of Ahmed's Manuscript and Inscribing New Parameters of Identity

Once Ben Jelloun establishes his nonfixed space of articulation he places himself in front of a vast narrative plane on which he must inscribe not only his character's path toward identity, but also his own. The storyteller ponders how to map his own lines on the smooth surface of literary space despite the many interruptions throughout the novel. These interruptions are set in a metaphorical labyrinth of walls, passages, and doors that are allusions to the hurdles Ben Jelloun faces, such as his ever-impending doubt about achieving a nontraditional (Western-style?) narrative in French that incorporates dreams and visions.

Ahmed/Zahra fights her battles to inscribe on her newly found femininity what she envisages to be the markings of womanness. In *L'enfant de sable* she sheds her masculine garb and embarks on her quest to begin again in feminine space only after many threats of annihilation to her feminine core. In *La nuit sacrée,* the protagonist undertakes a quest that leads to a continuous series of developments that promotes her ever-changing femininity.

The storyteller, who finds Ahmed's manuscript and subsequently reads it throughout the novel, begins by summoning his listeners together to create his *ḥalqa* (storytelling circle). Ben Jelloun uses the storyteller as an emissary of the rich Moroccan folktale tradition. The storyteller is spurred on to embellish his narrative by the audience's desire to be entertained.[14] He does not just read Ahmed's diary but elaborates on it by playing the role of storyteller and author. Ben Jelloun is therefore allowed to freely weave his tale through an oral narrative tradition that draws upon the use of both the mythical and the real.

However, maintaining the interest of the audience or the readers in a story, whether oral or written, is not easy. In the second part of the novel the disappearance of the storyteller along with Ahmed's notebook risks the entire narrative. Ben Jelloun is perhaps alluding to his own frustration at the possibility of not finishing his narrative. Is writing too daunting a task? The author's story often seems as if it will consume him completely, threatening to lead him down a booby-trapped path, full of pitfalls and dead ends. When five more storytellers offer their own narrative versions to take up where the first storyteller left off, Ben Jelloun's story becomes complicated and his narrator's control seems lost. Yet, if we view this narrative tactic as an inscription toward the writing of a new narrative identity, it makes sense. As if to remind his audience of the very non-Western aspects of his writing, Ben Jelloun chooses to collectivize his story in a traditional oral storytelling manner characteristic of the Maghreb. Such a collectivization bridges the gap between Arab folktale and French narrative. By tying together both these seemingly incompatible elements, Ben Jelloun answers the question, Is this the real me? and, subsequently, affirms that he is a fusion of two worlds. It is through a series of hurdles, multiple characters, and deviations in the narrative of Ahmed that Ben Jelloun joins these worlds together. It is also through this process of fusion that the author defines a space of inscription where an identity for his protagonist and himself is possible.

This path is, however, arduous. All the contributors to Ahmed's story agree; defining her true identity is not easy. First, she must get past a labyrinth of confusion that hinders her quest of self-discovery. These hindrances once again reflect Ben Jelloun's own reservations concerning the roads his feminine voice will lead him down. Will his conceptual space (that of Ahmed) lead him out of the labyrinth of his own reservations to the outside, a place of signification? As Homi K. Bhabha states, the place of signification is the "depth" that "provides the language of Identity with its sense of reality—a measurement of 'me,' which emerges from an acknowledgment of my inwardness, the depth of my character, the profundity of my person."[15]

According to the first storyteller, Ahmed's childhood and adolescence is represented in a series of stages, or as a maze of "gates." These gates open and close at different intervals of her life as her male mask is formed and ingrained progressively into the persona her father has created. Ahmed begins her life at the first door, the Thursday Gate. Why Thursday, the fifth day of the week? The storyteller informs his audience that Thursday is the "day of exchange" or "market day"—a day of beginning (8). This gate is followed by six more doors that plot the life of Ahmed up to the moment her manuscript is lost and the storyteller disappears. From the first disciplining stages of her male body to the final discovery of her femininity the doors open and close as the storyteller weaves his tale.

It is the Friday Gate, "the one that brings people together, for the repose of the body, the recollection of the soul, and the celebration of the day" that marks the final development in her male mask (18). It is also the stage at which Ahmed's femininity is fully repressed. This repression is instigated by two definitive masculine events: circumcision and, subsequently, admittance to male society.

The first narrator tells us that the Saturday Gate "corresponds to the stage of adolescence, a very obscure period" (27). This stage is the most sinister for Ahmed, for it represents the masculine quagmire in which she is engulfed. It is during this stage that the protagonist first notices her femininity, only to see it immediately repressed. A"truth," she says, that retreats into exile (30).

The Saturday Gate, the narrator concludes, closes on Ahmed's adolescence and on any possibility of maintaining some semblance of her femininity (at least for the present). Ben Jelloun reiterates that Ahmed now must concede that her life depends on "keeping up appearances" (34). Achieving this status means winning a game. Constructing the walls of a glass cage of fabricated identity again alludes to the author's own marginality. Ben Jelloun metaphorically asks, What are the consequences of creating a false identity and of denying one's own marginality in order to adhere to accepted norms of Western culture? Or, to adhere to "the ideological construction of otherness," which the West expects of its formerly colonized?[16]

As if to ponder these questions, the author halts Ahmed's story at the gates of the fourth door, Bab El Had, which is at the edge of the unknown, a frontier of uncertainty. Here, the storyteller declares that this is the most critical stage in Ahmed's development. This door provides just a glimpse of femininity: "A tiny gate. One has to stoop to go through it" (33). The audience infers that the door of Bab El Had represents the possibility of leaving and entering— the link between the outside and the inside—or metaphorically, the threshold between femininity and masculinity. It is here that Ahmed chooses to totally enter her masculinity. In order to entirely live up to his persona, "he" takes a wife, Fatima. She helps him seal the lie he has begun and the mask his father fabricated. Ironically, according to the first storyteller, although it represents the summit of masculine perfection, Bab El Had also is the place of a beginning, an initial spark of Ahmed's feminine self assertion. This transformation begins upon the death of her father. The threshold of Bab El Had also marks a point of confusion for the storyteller. He seems to waver on how to continue his narrative. Is it because Ahmed's own narrative is unclear (her manuscript has fallen apart and is hard to read), or is this just some oral technique to regain the admiration of his listeners, who seem to be losing interest? He confusedly proceeds, stating, "I do not know where the story is leading. It does not stop at this gate, but it will go around and around a circular street, and we will have to follow it with ever more attention" (44). According to her manuscript Ahmed is freed of her masculine mask once her father dies. However, instead of continuing on beyond the door of Bab El Had our storyteller prefers to explore "the forgotten openings," which are obscure holes in his narrative

(45). Interestingly, when Ben Jelloun halts his storyteller his narrative stops. This rupture causes confusion for the reader and the listeners of Ahmed's tales in the storytelling circle.

However, the rupture is soon rectified and the storyteller's rambling monologue both regains the attention of his audience and provides the excuse for any further manipulations of Ahmed's story that he might be inclined to make in the name of what he defines as "adventure" and entertainment. This lapse in the story also demonstrates another of Ben Jelloun's self-projecting metaphors. The author, through the storyteller, voices his quest for identity on the peripheries of literary space. Both the fifth and the sixth doors indicate not only traps for the protagonist but allude to the greater complications a storyteller-author has in maintaining his story. The next gate is "walled up," stopping abruptly at the end of what the storyteller calls "the circular street" (44). Is the possibility of the total annihilation of all ideas, or, worse still, of creating a story that cannot be finished, what the author contends with when engaged in a narrative process? Is the possibility of writing in a social space of repressive norms equated with the mask Ahmed must wear? Must the author first throw off the mask in order to establish lines of flight to true identity? Ben Jelloun, like his feminine protagonist, must tear down the walls to gain access to the outside or else risk a life of stagnation under a mask of nonrepresentation.

Not only does Ben Jelloun show the traps an oral story may encounter, he also studies scriptural ones as well. Narrative pitfalls are also metaphors for the author's misgivings over his own marginality. As an exiled Moroccan writer writing in French, will a Moroccan folktale transfer and appeal to Western readers? Although he seems unsure in *L'enfant de sable*, Ben Jelloun, albeit haltingly, does create what Pierre Bourdieu calls a linguistic field. This field is a "space of expressive styles [that] reproduces in its own terms the structure of the differences which objectively separate conditions of existence."[17] By constructing his linguistic field, Ben Jelloun finds a means to continue his story and to inscribe it in another way, even though his first attempt (and that of the principle storyteller) seems doomed.

Ahmed emerges from her masculine prison with the aid of the Anonymous Correspondent, "that distant voice, never named" that "helped him to live and reflect upon his condition" (62–63). This unknown person provides both strength and motivation for the protagonist: to leave, to begin again, and to write. The Anonymous Correspondent leads the protagonist to the unknown and to the possibility of the outward demonstration of a feminine identity.

In the eighth chapter of *L'enfant de Sable*, Ahmed begins her feminine "reconstruction." This chapter, "The Houseless Woman," marks the beginning of the long road toward Ahmed's emergence—the reanimation of her true self. The following chapters are told for the most part in Ahmed's own words (read, of course, by the story-teller). The storyteller seems to have had a change of heart, claiming that he is committed to properly reading the auto-biography even if he is unsure of the outcome or its interest potential (70).

Once Ahmed defines her true feminine self the slow process by which she sheds her masculine persona is explained. This process is detailed from day to day by her diary entries, which are curious because they denote a short period (a matter of weeks) in the in-between space of Ahmed's gender struggle, where both masculine and feminine overlap, each fighting to engulf the protagonist's body and soul. Her fight is a gamble, "an act of violence that requires no justification" (70). She is not thoroughly convinced that the transformation process, or the possibility of viewing herself as a woman will, or can, ever be achieved. This condemnation of both spheres of being on the part of Ben Jelloun alludes to his hesitancy to enter into any prefabricated identity. It is as if the author is asking, Is it not better to rest on the outside, to simply look in and critique? Staying outside grants the possibility of constructing something new—an original Other—without entering into normalized sociocultural political games, Moroccan or French, Eastern or Western. Situating the self outside all spheres of identity represents a new subject, one that acts as an agent articulated in a doubled dimension of identity. In this doubled dimension Ben Jelloun reconciles difference both for his protagonist and himself.

Ahmed starts her identity quest from this acentered space. She begins from ground zero to construct her new body—to inscribe her new set of values, "mapping" her feminine surface. During this period of mapping feminine lines and building feminine foundations, Ahmed discovers the importance of relearning the intricacies of her feminine body, soul, and voice. To reconstruct means turning back to review time, the era of her childhood, before the onslaught of masks and roles that formed her adult life: "For some time I have felt liberated, yes, ready to be a woman. But I am told, I tell myself, that before that I must go back to childhood, become a little girl, an adolescent girl, a girl in love, a woman. . . . What a long path, I shall never get there" (73).

However, just when Ben Jelloun's protagonist seems to have successfully begun a feminization process, she is once again stopped. Faced with diminishing numbers in his circle of listeners, the storyteller is "devoured by his words" (80). The very narrative he had hoped would entertain and bring him success is abruptly halted, leaving his protagonist halfway between her feminine and masculine self. He uses the crumbling state of the manuscript as an excuse for his inability to finish the story, stating, "The manuscript I wanted to read to you falls to pieces whenever I try to open it and free its words, which poison so many birds, insects, and images" (81). Is the narrator's hesitancy a mirrored image of Ben Jelloun's own fear? Is it fear of the total dismantling of his text, or of passing through an unknown space to construct something else on the other side? This unknown is perhaps constituted from the uncertainty created when an author decides to leap off to another plane and follow another line of flight, to make "a landscape, which is not just a milieu but a deterritorialized world."[18]

As if seeking revenge for his demise and for his disappointment at the loss of interest in his story, the storyteller leaves his audience in the lurch, depriving them of the outcome of Ahmed's new state. This rupture in the author-storyteller's story leads us to ask the following questions: Has Ben Jelloun lost his anonymous space, the profitable in-between that allows for mediation and negotiation? Is the fear of constructing another identity by writing in the margins of acceptable norms too great? In the following pages of his tale Ben Jelloun seeks to answer these questions.

As if to reorient his own identity search, the author resuscitates his protagonist. Instead of the storyteller's narrative, Ahmed intervenes, confidently, in her own words, stating that her "retirement has lasted long enough. I must have gone beyond the limits that I imposed upon myself" (83). Limits imposed by whom? Do they represent Ben Jelloun's own self doubts in the validity of continuing his own narrative through the feminine voice of Ahmed? As if haunted by his bad conscience Ben Jelloun effaces the manipulative storyteller, leaving Ahmed once again to begin narrating her own story.

When she finally emerges on the other side of her mask, Ahmed finds that being a woman places her in a vulnerable and precarious situation. She is threatened both mentally and physically by several odious characters. Oum Abbas, an old crone and the codirector of a traveling circus, convinces Ahmed to come to work for her offering an appealing role as a female/male impersonator and dancer. She is once again forced into a dual gender role. Curiously, the prospect of the double-sided persona intrigues the protagonist. She exclaims, "I was fascinated. . . . I was beginning to realize what kind of person I should become. . . . the emotion of a body summoned by another life, new adventures" (92). Ahmed becomes Princess of Love, or The Man with a Woman's Breasts. If viewed as yet another metamorphosis (the becoming-Zahra of Ahmed) she has traveled one more step closer to her final destination, the becoming-woman of Ahmed/Zahra.

Although cast part of the time in a male role, she at least is sometimes acknowledged by others in the circus (this family of artists) as a woman. The opportunities seem to outweigh the disadvantages for Ahmed, as performing half-time as a woman brings her closer to the truth and her real feminine self (94). Yet, once again being in the middle, in such a gender "half" state, confuses her narrative. Although she is somewhat appreciated for her femininity, she is still an object of male oppression. Her manuscript becomes dust, thus providing no further clues to the outcome of her story. The crumbling manuscript provides a metaphor for the storyteller (recently reinstated), who reminds his listeners of how temporal and fleeting self-representation, narrative processes, and identity really are: "Companions! The stage is made of paper! The story that I am telling you is an old piece of wrapping paper. It will need only a match, a torch, to confine everything to nothingness" (96).

The storyteller offers no insight into Zahra's own feelings about her becoming-Zahra. He seems to struggle to keep her in a dual role, as if he were afraid of her potential wholeness. Achieving total feminine form would upset the intrigue and adventure he has promised his audience. Again Ben Jelloun is faced with an apparent dead end in Ahmed's story. He therefore breaks apart the limits of her half-man-half-woman persona, releasing her out into an infinite immanent space (a Night without Escape) in which he attempts to "put some order back into this story" (99). Ahmed again is allowed to take hold of her destiny and her identity quest, just as Ben Jelloun (or the narrator, who could be considered as the spokesman of the author's predicament) allows himself to remain marginalized and therefore open to mediating his own identity further.

The disappearance of the principal storyteller, who was reading Ahmed's story (we are told in chapter 14 that he dies), along with her manuscript, further complicates the novel by leaving the audience without an ending to her tale. The subsequent introduction of five new storytellers, who also offer versions of Ahmed's story, obscures the protagonist's autobiography even more. Salem, Amar, Fatuma, the Blind Troubadour, and the Man with the Blue Turban confuse the conclusion by providing their own variations of her demise. Perhaps the most difficult aspect of Ben Jelloun's novel is determining the significance of these storytellers who finish the story of Ahmed in *L'enfant de sable*.

It is interesting to note that the first four storytellers, Salem, Amar, Fatuma, and the Blind Troubadour, constitute a minoritarian group, each a marginalized figure in Moroccan society: Salem is black, Amar is a heretic, Fatuma is an old woman who never married nor bore children, and the Troubadour is blind. In evoking such a variety of misfits, Ben Jelloun once again creates a metaphor in order to prove a point: to reinscribe the lost voices of the marginalized they too must be given a place of enunciation—a Third Space—in order to mediate their individual identities. Ben Jelloun tells his readers that those relegated to the peripheries of a society that is blocked by its own dogmatic rhetoric will never be guaranteed freedom of expression. These misfits are the victims to whom he alludes in the *Jeune Afrique* interview cited at the beginning of this chapter (note 6). They have been the bearers of aggression and injustice in a society that has been formed out of imperialism, religious dogma, ancient tradition, and sexual taboos. Marginalized because of difference in the same way as Ahmed and Ben Jelloun himself, these four storytellers seek to justify their own identities in a society that has shut them out. They too have had to become anomalous—existing on the fringes—in order to speak out against those who overlook them. The Halqa becomes their space of enunciation.

The storyteller uses the prefabricated story of Ahmed, as begun by the original storyteller, in order to fabricate other endings to her life. Ahmed's story thus becomes a much more communal project, spreading out on all edges of the vast plane Ben Jelloun has created. There is now a web, or a rhizome, of desire, to conclude Ahmed's story. That desire encompasses the audience, the storytellers, and Ben Jelloun. Narration becomes a communal project—a site of active agency in which all participants have equal say. No single storyteller's story is given more weight than the others, they are merely versions of the same theme. Curiously, they all have the identical objective of ending the tragic story of Ahmed and establishing once and for all her true identity as a woman.

We are informed that eighty-four days have passed since the first storyteller disappeared along with Ahmed's manuscript (104). Salem, Amar, and Fatuma, the first three new narrators, decide to take up Ahmed's narrative in a small café at the edge of the Halqa because "they found it hard to accept that everything had suddenly come to an end" (104). Salem, a Senegalese, proposes his version of the story first because, he says, "I've lived and worked in a big house like the one described by the storyteller. There were only girls" (105). His story provides anything but a happy ending for the protagonist. In Salem's version, Ahmed/Zahra is beaten, caged, and raped by Abbas, the circus owner. Salem claims that in order to end the vicious circle of brutality in which she is forced to live Zahra decides to end her life by an act of vengeance against the evil circus owner. Her vengeance leads to her suicide: "She undressed and put the two blades in a rag, which she placed between her buttocks; lying on her belly, she awaited the brute's visit. She had read in an old magazine that during the Indochinese war women had used this method to kill enemy soldiers who raped them. It was also a form of suicide." Salem concludes, "when I found out about it, I was so overcome that I looked everywhere for someone to tell it to, so I wouldn't be the sole witness of such a tragedy. Now I feel better. I feel relieved" (110-11). He confesses that by telling the audience his rendition he alleviates his own conscience and guarantees that the story will continue to be passed on in true oral tradition.

Amar, the second narrator, quickly resumes drawing attention to his own version of the story by discrediting Salem's, which he states, is "pure perversion." The new storyteller explains to his audience that he bought the true manuscript of Ahmed/Zahra from the attendants at the morgue who disposed of the original storyteller's body. Amar believes Ahmed's death to be much more spiritual than the previous versions of her story have suggested. As in the preceding account, Ahmed does flee from his male persona, but in Amar's story the protagonist's death is depicted as mythical, almost transcendent, wherein the heroine dies in her tower "surrounded by old Arabic and Persian manuscripts on love, drowned by the call of the desire that he imagined" (123).

The most peculiar rendition of the story of Ahmed is that of Fatuma's. She is the only woman who frequents the café and the numerous storytelling gatherings. The old woman states that her freedom in the outside world—the world of men—may be explained by her advanced age and the fact that she has led a solitary life, without husband or children (125-26). Using a carbon copy of Ahmed's story, Fatuma suggests that she too has disguised herself under a male mask, claiming that "it was an extraordinary experience" (130). She confesses to having written her story down in a lost manuscript like Zahra's (133). The possibility that there is more than one protagonist who enjoys transgressing genders seems incredible. Why are these transformations used by women? Fatuma herself admits to not understanding the need to be a male. "Is it out of boredom or lassitude," she ponders, that she hides behind a fake persona? (131).

Ben Jelloun creates through Fatuma a voice for all women. Of all the storytellers, she offers the most insight into the suffering and neglect of women and children in Morocco and elsewhere in the Maghreb: "to be born a boy is the lesser of two evils. To be born a girl is a calamity, a misfortune that is left at the roadside where death passes by at the end of the day" (131). Fatuma, as the author's spokeswoman, acts as a liaison of social conscience between the audience, the various storytellers, and Ben Jelloun. She forces this wider audience to reflect on the question of aggression against the weak, who are the minority.

Fatuma's story, like those of the storytellers before her, fades into another. The Blind Troubadour, who admits he has spent his life weaving tales and "falsifying or altering other people's stories," takes up where the old woman abruptly left off (134). He tells the others gathered in the café of his 1957 encounter with a woman who had a coarse and deep voice. So deep he wonders if it was, in fact, a man (137). In 1961 he meets her again, and this time she brings him an old coin and insists on reading the Qur'an in his office.[19] The obscure woman proceeds to tell him of her plight and her dual identity, but then disappears after their first meeting. Upon her abrupt disappearance, the Troubadour loses his sight. He wonders if there is a connection, and confesses to having "seen" the woman even more clearly in his dreams. His dreams become his sole means of displacement and travel, and he admits that blindness provides the catalyst to self-discovery and to "dream-nightmares" that lead him on nomadic journeys (145).

The blind man continues his hunt for an answer to the riddle of the woman with two identities. In his nightmares he is haunted by her presence. In his dreams the raving diatribes of ghosts, the "woman's voice in a man's body," myth and reality, all become fused and indistinguishable (154). His tale, as well as the identity of the strange woman, for the Troubadour, are lost in a labyrinth of the unknown—what the storyteller defines as being death itself. He states that like death, the voice of the woman is impenetrable and impossible to comprehend, it is made from an unknown dark side of the Self. This very same dark side that Ben Jelloun strives to enter is the other side of the wall of identity—the true Self—that lies beyond social paradigms and prefabricated identities, as well as acceptable norms of literary space.

The Troubadour's speech slips away as vaguely as it began. A man in a blue turban quickly offers the final words on the story of Ahmed. Like the sightless Troubadour, this new storyteller tells his audience that he too has been haunted by that "other" side of the self. He defines it as death. He blames the darkness, this void of nothingness, for having taken away his imagination and his storytelling power. Both story and words, he claims, were stolen from his mouth by the fear hidden away in an otherness that was impenetrable (160). Ahmed/Zahra comes to the storyteller's dreams in a death mask. Subsequently he is visited by Ahmed's father, mother, and wife, Fatima, all of whom beg him to retell the story of Ahmed. It is following this family visit that the storyteller sees clearly and confesses that he is completely engulfed by their story and must continue to deliver it so that it will live on and rest among the living, passed on "through the seven gardens of the soul" (165). His closing words end at the Seventh Door, marking the end of this stage of Ahmed/Zahra's story.

Ben Jelloun's conclusion, "The Gate of the Sands," is the last of the seven doors surrounding the ancient part of the city. It also metaphorically marks the beginning of trajectories toward identity, or lines of flight, toward a becoming-woman that the author follows in his second book, *La nuit sacrée*. These trajectories break away on the other side of the wall of this inner city that has hemmed in the protagonist and the author. In the final paragraphs of *L'enfant de sable*, Ben Jelloun once again alludes to his own "going over to the other side." In crossing over these thresholds he traverses borders onto his own plane of immanence, where he, like the man in the blue turban, seeks true identity: a fusion of French and Arabic, man and woman, and narrator and protagonist.

Affects and Percepts and the Road to a Becoming-Woman and a Becoming-Imperceptible in *La nuit sacrée*

La nuit sacrée continues the story of Ahmed, who now, after having entered a becoming-Zahra, is known definitively as Zahra. As Ben Jelloun explores more profoundly his own becoming-woman (once again the story of Zahra is told in a feminine voice) in this second novel, so does his protagonist take on new appendages of feminine sexuality through modes of affects and percepts. These are the results of events that she encounters during her identity quest.

Zahra, through a series of deterritorializations and reterritorializations (a constant movement from one place to another), accesses new traits for her identity by experiencing events. Colliding with affects means the acquisition of feminine knowledge and sexuality for Zahra. Ben Jelloun opens up an immanent plane to Zahra's self-knowledge in *La nuit sacrée* to draw his own lines of flight also. The metaphors that are evoked in Zahra's discovery of her feminine self are the mirrored images of the author's own decision to wander as a nomad, to let himself go, to leap totally to the other side of the Self in order to discover identity. He plots his own new lines of subjectivity. All reservation and hesitancy on the part of Ben Jelloun in *L'enfant de sable* have all but dissipated in his second novel. The author's committal to transgress fully onto another plane, a true becoming, are evidenced in *La nuit sacrée*. In the opening pages Zahra enters the storyteller's circle, declaring that her principle objective is to put order into her autobiography. She admits that "he" (the storyteller/Ben Jelloun) has given her a face and lines of temperament, but it is now time for her to take charge of her own destiny: "I had arrived in Marrakesh the day before, determined to find the storyteller my story had ruined" (7).

Ben Jelloun's protagonist realizes that in order to discover her true feminine identity she must become a nomad. Only nomads may enter into a becoming. In order to inscribe new traits of identity, Zahra must first venture out. In her case, nomadism aids in building the new multifaceted construct of her feminine self. By wandering she forms a connection of actions and consequences, affects and percepts, that are "nonhuman landscapes of nature" but that allow one to "become with the world" and to contemplate it.[20]

Percepts and affects are blocks of sensations, experiences, and events that constitute a universe—for a woman or a man. They may be consonant or dissonant for an entity but they are necessary in the creation of a Self. One does not experience percepts and affects without becoming a nomad. Affects and percepts are the multiple events Zahra experiences throughout the novel. These events *happen* while Zahra follows her nomadic line, whether in a dream or wakeful state, or in the real or the imaginaire.

In the first part of *La nuit sacrée* Zahra endures several events that begin a chain of affects and percepts. The first takes place after the death of her father (upon which she feels the entire weight of paternal oppression lifted from her shoulders) and marks the beginning of her becoming.

Second are a bizarre series of events that take place once her father's funeral procession arrives at the cemetery. Zahra witnesses an almost supernatural, circuslike scene in which an orator of the Qur'an lies prostrate on a grave, children play in the trees, two lovers embrace hidden behind a tomb, a young student recites *Hamlet*, a young bride dismounts a white horse, and a cavalier walks as if looking for someone. Next, the entourage of mourners is blinded by a bright light; people flee in all directions. The bride comes toward Zahra, offers her a gold-embroidered burnous, and whispers that the cavalier awaits to take her away. Zahra is spirited away to another realm. The passing from an awakened to a dreamlike state is of little importance because Ben Jelloun's objective is to trace lines of identity and subjectivity on his protagonist, no matter her state of consciousness. Therefore he fuses the real and the mythical, creating a new space of dialogue for Zahra, one in which the primary objective is to reconstruct her identity—ultimately ending in a true becoming-woman. In the mythical space of the cavalier, Zahra for the first time experiences certain, almost erotic, bodily emotions and feelings. These emotions begin a birth of femininity, releasing her through what she states is "an inner freedom that warmed my body" (36).

Ben Jelloun further develops Zahra's bodily freedom in chapter 4. His protagonist admits at the gates of the Perfumed Garden, a mythical village inhabited only by children where the cavalier at last deposes her, that her path of becoming lies in her total willingness to negotiate between the imaginary and the real: "I decided to give up trying to distinguish the real from the imaginary or to find out where I was" (39).

Moreover, whether she is in the imaginary or in reality is of little consequence because both spheres afford her space in which to heal and to forget—to begin anew on a smooth plane. Starting from ground zero is her most important goal, as suggested by a little boy who lives in the garden and who tells her she must begin her life by forgetting the past, "the other side of the valley," where she was the victim of oppression and exploitation (39).

The other side of the valley, whether a space of the imaginary or of reality, is the other side of identity—the other side of the former storyteller's Walled-up Gate—where nomadic paths to becoming begin. It is here where liberty of body and of soul set Zahra on the road toward her becoming-woman: "Freedom was giving my body to the wind, the light, the sun, in happy solitude." The affects of nature—water, light and earth—play a significant role even in this mythical world. As Zahra cleanses herself in purifying water, she experiences new sensations of her feminine Self, rejoicing in the fact that "nature was infusing me with new instincts, new reflexes. My body needed water." Water, a symbol for purification (and curiously the usual symbol for women), serves two functions: it washes away her masculine mask and it hydrates her new identity, allowing her to come alive (41).

Purification endows Zahra with strength and resolution and she returns home. After gathering her belongings, she proceeds to her father's freshly dug grave. She digs a hole and buries all traces of her former persona. Undaunted, she takes to the road, declaring, "So long." Or maybe it was, "Farewell, fictive glory, and may we both live, naked and blank, the soul virginal and the body new, however old the words!" (51).

Assembling elements in order to cross thresholds and change perspectives—to inscribe the smooth surface of her new identity—is Zahra's quest, even though her destiny is unknown. Her ceaseless wandering leads her through villages and towns. In each village she is offered water and fruit. She explains that she takes this nourishment with little regard (55). Zahra is nonchalant, almost unaffected by the destitution of her situation. At the end of her first long journey, she is followed out of town by a man. Although she is aware of the danger he represents, she continues on without a care, even when she admits to having "heard talk of rapes in the forest." Fear is not one of the sensations she feels, simply "curious" over the prospect that a "man whose face I did not even know was arousing physical feelings in me with words alone" (55). She considers being followed as simply an event (an affect) that will perhaps provide some clue to love, femininity, and the sexuality she seeks to know.

The man quickens his pace, closing in on her. He then assaults Zahra, throwing her to the ground. Ironically, even as she is being raped, the "normal" reaction of fear never enters her mind. She feels only an ironic satisfaction brought on by the man's forcing body. "I was not thinking," she exclaims, "I was free under the weight of that feverish body. For the first time another body was mingling with mine." So great is her desire to feel "as a woman," neither the idea of rape nor its humiliating consequences enter her mind. She admits, "I was neither unhappy nor disappointed," and unemotionally wonders if this act demonstrates what love really is. Rape, love, sex, and "that union of two bodies" are reduced to one affect—a sensation—which Zahra attempts to quantify (57). Although it blocks her path for a moment, she is not deterred indefinitely by either the violence of the act or its effects on her body, she merely continues her route.

Zahra's process of self-formation begins after her rape and consequent brutal recognition of her feminine sexuality. The consequences of being a woman out alone in a hostile male-dominated environment become apparent. The "outside" nomadic world to which she has fled presents a constant series of compromises, traps, game playing, deciphering of cryptic roles, jealousy, hate, and eventually murder. Identities are obscured and individuality is almost nonexistent, making it difficult for the protagonist to decipher the events that continue to shape her feminine subjectivity. The people she meets are almost nonhuman, just "segments and lines of experimentation" that have functions but no real names.[21] The rapist is an obscure masculine presence. Zahra's encounter in the next village with a strange brother-sister couple is also devoid of all humanism. As we shall see, the Consul, other than his blindness, is never described. His sister, the Seated Woman, is an amorphous creature, possessing hardly any concrete features. They are, for the most part, temporal. What little human capacity they do emit Zahra covets surreptitiously, hoping they will eventually aide in contouring her femininity.

The feminizing of Ben Jelloun's protagonist involves only a single path through a chain of percepts and affects. Because in her world all human substance is absent, Zahra finds that forging her feminine identity depends much on destiny and fate. She does not live events, she is merely marked by them as she maps her encounters, hoping to form a cohesive identity that will efface her past and lead her to a new sphere of subjectivity.

In no other place in *La nuit sacrée* is Zahra's fatalistic attitude so apparent than her first encounter with The Seated Woman, the odious female attendant of the village hammam. The protagonist's body, once more, has become a receptacle for the events that take place around her. Despite forebodings that Zahra confesses having, she reacts indifferently when the Seated Woman offers her employment. Zahra accompanies her new acquaintance home without emotion. She justifies her choice as an act of fate, considering it an integral part of her identity quest. It is an event that crosses her "body without leaving wounds," and is implicated in her choice to teach herself "to forget, to not look back." (74).

Zahra's only duty as housekeeper for the Seated Woman is to take care of her older brother, the blind Consul. His identity also is false and is made up of the make-believe in which "he was only a consul in an imaginary city in a ghost country" (66). She learns that the Seated Woman is responsible for having amplified his position and inventing his title. Despite this false shell, the Consul proves to have significant influence on the creation of Zahra's new self. She admits that because of meeting him the weight of her past has been lifted and the construction of her feminine identity assured, an event she rates as important in her identity quest (86).

Unfortunately, the brief respite Zahra enjoys from her nomadic life once again is abruptly halted. In the world of the Seated

Woman and the Consul all traditional family roles have been replaced with bizarre relationships, bordering the fantastic. The young woman is entangled in this brother-sister ego, in which she felt as if she "had become the plaything of a diabolical couple" (83). Normal designated roles between woman and man are obscured as the Seated Woman admits to Zahra that she raised her younger brother like her own son. As time passes, the heroine remarks on the strange and unnatural love they have for each other. The suggestion of incest becomes even more apparent when the young woman accompanies both sister and brother to the hammam, where they take a communal bath. When she witnesses an intimate moment between them, Zahra is so nauseated she wonders, once again, if she is caught in a space of reality or of the imaginaire: "Was I dreaming or was I still in the baths? I heard languorous cries, followed by groans. Then I saw—at least I think I saw—the Consul curled up in his sister's arms. He was sucking her breast like a baby" (84).

The protagonist becomes more and more aware that the Seated Woman is grossly manipulative. The attendant's conception of "sister" implicates a double role as provider of both maternal and sexual intimacies. She acts as a liaison between sight, sensuality, and sexuality. The sister is a conduit for her brother's happiness and well-being: taking him to the nearby brothel once a month for sex, nursing him in sickness, massaging him in the communal baths, and bathing his feet as an evening ritual. Both brother and sister have signed a pact to which only they are privy (84).

Zahra's own place and space are diminished by the strange name the Consul gives her: the Guest. The name neither connotes individual identity nor status, but simply an uncertain, fleeting presence. Once more Ben Jelloun wields the metaphor of the anomal. Zahra, like the author writing her story, circles a normalized space (although the space of the Consul and the Seated Woman's is perverted and incomprehensible, it still has been normalized by those functioning within it). However, the protagonist is never quite able to enter this twisted sphere.

When she does become the old man's lover, Zahra is caught

again in the middle of the couple and forced to play different roles for each. The young woman represents for the Consul both confidant and lover. Conversely, she is a coveted object of jealousy for the Seated Woman. Zahra knows that she should leave this void of supernatural relationships, but some unknown force compels her to stay. Despite a foreboding, she is resigned to follow fate, acting as a liaison between the couple's dark secrets. They are added to Zahra's repertoire, much like her rape, dreams, and mythical experiences. The couple is a simple "event" along her way, an affect that lies on her plane of self-discovery: "I was firmly convinced that this family—this couple—was my destiny. They lay on my path" (99).

The longer Zahra remains, the more her love for the Consul becomes apparent. For the Consul, Zahra's nomadic persona is appealing. He almost prefers not to know her past. He envies her murky identity and absence of family ties, admitting that her position as one who lives on the fringes of society and human intrigue, uncommitted to anything or anyone, fascinates him (110). While the Consul admonishes Zahra with love, she is hated and despised by her hostess. Jealousy finally pushes the Seated Woman to seek out the answers to her maid's obscure origins. In order to save herself, Zahra must find a way out of the maze of lies caused by her past and the bizarre relationship she endures with the couple. She decides to divulge her story to the Consul even though once again she feels a noose of premonition around her neck.

Ben Jelloun's protagonist's past continues to haunt her: "To forget completely was impossible" (114). The more she is plagued by a past that will not go away, the more she strives for some semblance of normalcy—at least what she perceives as normal. She invests in her relationship with the Consul, believing it to be a means of establishing herself as a woman, free to love and be loved. She defiantly demonstrates this desire by taking him by the arm and walking with him out into the street, remarking, "It was the first time I had walked in the street holding a man's arm. We looked like a normal couple. Nothing at all unusual about us" (115).

Although this scene is ordinary in nature, Zahra is once again haunted by an unnatural feeling; a supernatural presence—an evil eye—lurks "there, behind a door left ajar," watching her in a most unnatural manner (115). Again she feels the ever-present weight of a premonition that affects her body and soul. Is this a metaphorical allusion to Ben Jelloun's own misgivings about rooting himself in a fixed identity—or a nonbecoming—one that does not evolve but becomes stagnant, encumbered by representation and mimeticism, promoting only a false self? Is this evil eye the normalized feminine role in Muslim society into which Zahra is being slowly forced? Is it a role that will halt her nomadism, end her anomal existence, committing her to a life that will never permit a becoming-woman? Zahra's contemplation over the meaning of the evil eye brings about a sudden rupture in the author's narrative. Once again, Ben Jelloun's mediating space of introspection and negotiation resurfaces. Within this space the above questions are reflected upon. This abrupt break in Zahra's process of feminine self-formation, although marking a moment of hesitation, does not diminish her determination to find love. She must accomplish her love affair with the Consul in order to move forward—toward a becoming-woman. She shrugs off the premonition once more, convincing herself that the evil eye, like the rape and the encounter with the Seated Woman, are all part of her larger destiny—one that traces a predetermined path: "Fate led me to the baths. It was the rape in the forest that drove me there. I knew that for a while I would be able to live only with strange people" (127).

Zahra's discovery of love, she acknowledges, is due to the Consul, who she believes has shaped her feminine identity and given her the feminine desire she has so long sought. It is he, she maintains, who has carved her flesh out "of sand and dust, of uncertain identity, crumbling at the slightest gust of wind" (128). Through his love, her body is formed and becomes solid. Yet, she soon discovers that this feminine identity is false and does not truly represent the completeness she seeks. Once again Ben Jelloun fuses the world of the real and the imaginary as his protagonist realizes that hints to her destiny are found through unnatural and supernatural sources. The Seated Woman returns from her absence, accompanied by Zahra's uncle, "the miser my father had told me to be careful of" (132). Her uncle exposes Zahra's masculine past and accuses her of cheating and stealing the family's fortune. Her fragile, burgeoning identity is shattered. Curiously she feels compelled to end the episode with her uncle. Murder seems the only solution to closing her troubled past: "It was my duty to finish it, to put my signature on it with that murder. . . . I was relieved when I saw the greenish-yellow blood flowing from the body as it lay on the ground." As other previous actions, murdering her uncle does not affect the protagonist. The act, she admits, is merely a quantifying part of her destiny. She feels nothing, no "notion of loss" (133). Because of the murder she commits, Zahra—"the Houseless Woman"—"is condemned to spend fifteen years in prison."

Ironically, prison for Zahra represents salvation and liberty because it is in this enclosed and confining space that she at last rids herself of her past life. Her prison is the threshold of another leap onto another plane, the space in which Zahra tears off her many masks: masculine persona, guest, and lover. These masks, she exclaims, were making her lose her "sense of presence in the world" (158). During her stay in prison, she undergoes a process by which she finally enters the last stages of her becoming-woman. However, the process is slow and she is again subjected to a series of arduous events leading up to her final transcendence and total embrace of feminine subjectivity. Darkness, isolation, and physical mutilation are inflicted upon her before she finally ascends to a place of self-knowledge where her whole sense of perception changes.

Zahra's first event in the series of tests thrown her way, is her becoming-blind which she realizes causes her first change in perception. She decides to bandage her eyes in order to "separate from [her] body." In the prison's darkness and isolation her past recedes and she claims, "I ceased to be obsessed with my past as a woman disguised as a man. I forgot all about it. With my uncle's death I had liquidated the past (or so I thought)" (143-44).

Bandaging her eyes is successful for a while in her process of re-birth; however, it does not release her from occasional hauntings and visions. At one point she is visited by her five sisters in what she thinks is a dream. They threaten Zahra with scissors, a scorpion, and a snake. Unable to fight them off, she is sexually mutilated in their search for revenge. Once again she enters another change in perception, one that confuses time—mixing the past, the present, and the future until she is unable to discern where or when the events took place (149). These confusing, dreamlike events are a forewarning, a prelude to another, more horrifying incident that is real: "My legs were held apart, tied on each side. The oldest [sister] stuffed a damp rag into my mouth. She put a hand on my belly and crushed the lips of my vagina with her fingers until what they called 'the little thing' came out. They sprinkled it with something, took a razor blade from the metal box, soaked it in alcohol, and cut off my clitoris. I fainted, screaming inside" (151).[22]

Hurt and now deprived of the very sexuality she has so long sought, Zahra slips into a hallucinatory state in which her fever acts as a catalyst for dreams, visions, and nightmares. Once again she confronts a change in perception, one that takes her into another void of the imaginary. Her space is now fragmented. Both body and soul have been beaten down. Due to her mutilation (which in his view has turned her into a nonfeminine being), the Consul ceases his visits, leaving her once again alone "without anesthetic, facing the final reverses of fortune, disaster, sadness, and violence" (159). Her life becomes her prison, bringing both solitude and refuge (163).

After physically healing, Zahra enters another becoming, which grants her the official title of public scribe for her fellow prison inmates. This becoming marks yet another change in perception. She becomes the voice of others, writing down their stories. Yet, locked into such a becoming does not bring the protagonist peace because it is still not representative of her true being. She feels, once again, as if she is slipping into a void of nothingness. This void is both stagnant and filled with the emotional turmoil of having had to be both man and woman. She is caught in a nonevolving state in which she inhabits "neither a woman's body full and eager, nor a man's serene and strong." She exclaims, "I was now somewhere between the two; in other words, in hell" (168). Ben Jelloun again halts his protagonist's metamorphoses. Caught in a space of nonmovement, she must once find a way out in order to enter the last stage of a becoming-woman. Since she writes and reads, the final way out is found by helping other women inmates who come to her for instruction and guidance. Eventually, Zahra discovers that this last threshold before her becoming-woman is on the edge of a vast plane where sources of understanding lie. It is a plane of knowledge that she must learn to understand and then explain to others. It is equally where the imaginary is, a "mythical place, [a] source of all light" (169). She is released once more on a nomadic quest, the last journey "where the light turns soft and ambiguous, when it drifts away from the sun and joins the sky on the threshold of night" (170). In this desert of light Zahra enters into a *becoming-saint*, a state in which she is visited by countless women. She becomes spokeswoman and healer for all women, forming an alliance with all those who have been mistreated. Through this alliance with women she gains the strength to wipe away the remaining vestiges of her repressive masks and at last to come "out of myself. . . . hurled into the whirlpool of emptiness," or a tabula rasa on which new beginnings will make their marks (173).

When she is at last liberated from prison, Zahra decides to make one final journey to the sea. Water, again, provides purity, cleanliness, and refuge. Once again the imaginary fuses with reality as she passes from feeling wet sand under her feet and the cool breeze of the ocean to another, mythical place, where an "almost unbearable light came down from the sky" (176). The light engulfs her in a final stage of becoming. This is an ultimate transcendence through a becoming-woman to the place of the imperceptible, where there is "a perception of things, thoughts, desires in which desire, thought, and the thing have invaded all perception: [where] the imperceptible finally [is] perceived."[23]

The white light is filled with people Zahra recognizes. Among these ghostlike figures is the Seated Woman, who seems somewhat altered, more human. It is a place where "perceptions as well as actions pass into imperceptibility."[24] Finding the key to the secret of identity provides Zahra with the knowledge that her space is not one continual line of plotted points, but one of a mixture of movement, affects, percepts, and experiences. It is her anomal, yet liberated, position on the outside, where, she claims, "everything was becoming clear. Between life and death, I thought, there was but a thin layer of mist or darkness; the threads of lies were woven between reality and appearance, while time was but an illusion born of our own anguish" (178).

In this divine space Zahra is at last identified for who she is. All barriers to her feminine being have been dismantled. "You're here at last," exclaims a Saint in this paradise of final recognition to which she has been brought (178). The validation of her feminine identity leads Zahra at last to her becoming-woman—pure womanness—marking the end of her quest and the end of her nomadic journey. It is a place where desire directly invests perception, and perception becomes the key to passing to the imperceptible, beyond the hindrances of gender, difference, or marginality.

Ben Jelloun's two novels demonstrate more than just the author's fascination with the feminine side of his Self. They are studies of the affects of an anomalous position, or a critique of the politics of marginalization; the intricacies of being an intellectual, author, and critic in exile. Through his protagonist Ahmed/Zahra, Ben Jelloun traces his own lines of flight toward all sorts of becomings on a smooth plateau of self-discovery. Following these lines, the author deterritorializes to dissimulate all preconceived notions of alterity and otherness to embrace another threshold that forms his own

Third Space, which is both a mediating milieu in the middle of established paradigms of culture, identity, and language, and a transcended beyond that leads to new becomings and perceptions. It is in this outside space where existing ideologies concerning femininity, masculinity, Islam, the East, and the West may be negotiated.

Chapter Three

Assia Djebar's *L'amour, la fantasia* and *Vaste est la prison*

Rewriting History and Feminine Identity

I N HIS DOCUMENTARY novel *La gangrène et l'oubli*, Benjamin Stora, French author and historian, writes that "it is time to put to work a new history, with new books on the Algerian war; from its colonial beginnings to its survival in the memories of the present."[1] Assia Djebar's novel, *L'amour, la fantasia,* echoes Stora's words.[2] Constructing a hybrid narrative of culture, language, and historicity, Djebar reconsiders and renarrates the legacy of French colonialism, which has altered the identity of Algeria. As a social commentary, *L'amour, la fantasia* confronts difference and marginalization and champions the important roles of voice, ethnicity, and diversity in forming a historical narrative. Djebar employs a multivalent perspective to reinscribe the multiple stories of the Other's past and present. She seeks not to wipe the historic slate clean of the former colonial presence in her own country, but to refocus the reader's gaze on overlooked events in France's archives on Algeria. Layers of history are incorporated into her narrative, creating a palimpsest text, a text through which multiple views encompassing both French and Algerian spheres may be read.

Vaste est la prison is a study of exile and duality.[3] It is equally an evaluation of the current political situation and issues affecting women in Algeria. The freedom Djebar finds in exile allows her to critique social, cultural, and historical influences that have formed the idea of womanhood and the role of feminism (or lack thereof) in Algeria. Within her space of exile, the author negotiates new feminist parameters for all women of the Maghreb. However, such parameters are not formed easily. Djebar must first define an intellectual space of agency where she sets herself and her female protagonists beyond established stereotypes concerning Algerian women. The new parameters Djebar forges begin with her autobiography and move to other narrative modalities that encompass colonial/ postcolonial revision and cinematographic journalism. It may be said that the author's works are polyphonic. Such polyphony requires constant metamorphosis; therefore no single site of fixed ideology or subjectivity is favored. The author writes in a transitory space for all her feminine characters. By writing in the transitional, Djebar is setting a new tone for feminine writing and social ethics for the Maghreb.

Defining a New System of Discourse in *L'amour, la fantasia:* The Historiographic Metafiction

The historiographic metafiction is a product of both the postcolonial and the postmodern era. The contemporary Francophone postmodern author, like his or her Western counterpart, seeks to define the link between writing and history. Linda Hutcheon suggests that "[w]hat the postmodern writing of both history and literature has taught us is that both history and fiction are discourses, that both constitute systems of signification by which we make sense of the past." Following this definition of postmodern writing, Hutcheon explains that the historiographic metafiction "refutes the natural or common-sense methods of distinguishing between historical fact and fiction. It refutes the view that only history has a truth claim, both by questioning the ground of that claim in historiography and by asserting that both history and fiction are discourses, human constructs, signifying systems, and both derive their major claim to truth from that identity."[4]

Creating these new human constructs and signifying systems within the parameters of identity requires the destabilizing of established historical empirical concepts of reality. In the case of Djebar's writing, that means destabilizing canonized archival accounts of French colonization in Algeria. The historiographic metafiction destabilizes time by viewing history as having different, but equally valid, constructions of past reality. These new conceptions retextualize existing documents, archives, and eyewitness accounts to favor the unread, the unseen, and the unheard diaspora. In Assia Djebar's text, subversion of French archival accounts of the French colonial mission, actual colonization, and the Franco-Algerian War are all present, but written down (for the first time) not through a Western colonizing French perspective, but rather through the eyes of an Algerian woman and researcher. Djebar uses a reconceptualized schema of Western historical process to problematize what has been written on Algeria by the French. Consequently, *L'amour, la fantasia* is cast in the mode of a historiographic metafiction that reconceptualizes both Western notions of colonial narrative time and thematic structure. Djebar's destabilization of narrative time is most visibly noticed in her re-renditions of French colonial archives. The author's thematic spectrum also promotes one of the key elements of a historiographic metafiction: parody. Through the parodic interpretation of Algeria's colonization, Djebar subverts dominant stereotypes (such as those issuing from French Orientalism) to reinstall the lost presence of her people.

Assia Djebar's rewriting of historic fact is marked by what Paul Ricoeur calls time of narrating and narrated time. The distinction between these two modalities forces us into a problematic that "does not seek in the utterance itself an internal principle of differentiation that would be apparent in the distribution of the tenses, but instead looks for a new key for interpreting time in fiction in the distinction *between* utterance and statement."[5]

Djebar's objective of rewriting historic time within a fictive framework offers an example of a three-stage process that aids in closing the gap between historic and fictitious narratives to favor the creation of a space of enunciation. The first of these stages is an archival document, "time of narration," which is reinscribed in the author's present text in "narrated time," thereupon resulting in a "fictive experience of time."[6]

Djebar's space of enunciation in *L'amour, la fantasia* is founded in the written historical French documents (time of narration) from which she gathers sources for her novel; these include eyewitness accounts and commentary from nineteenth-century French authors, such as Eugène Fromentin, who traveled extensively in Algeria during the latter part of that century. Writing and language are central linking forces by which Djebar penetrates her people's history as well as that of the former French colonizer.

During the colonial period French became a language of force, imperialism, and colonial desire. The colonized-Other was a victim of a "discursive hierarchy" created from the "axes of language and desire."[7] Within this hierarchy, the identity of the conquered Algerian was lost in the paternal representations written down by army reporters and journalists caught up in the glorification of the civilizing mission. Drawing attention to France's banalization and frivolous documentation of the conquering of Algeria, Djebar focuses on the correspondence of French officers whose quasi-poetic discourses written up in newspapers and journals served to narrate the glorious, brutal military campaigns of the 1830s and 1840s in Algeria. Here, the author reappropriates the voice of the young French field marshal, Pierre Bosquet,[8] who writes in 1840, "Our little army is celebrating with feasts. . . . I'll tell you all about it: there's a bit of everything in this *razzia* . . . every possible touch of poetry in the setting which formed the backcloth to the foray'" (*Fantasia*, 54). In exposing Bosquet's commentary, Djebar notes how the officers' stories, letters, and eyewitness accounts generated sentiment in France among the general public for the maintenance of colonialism. These same documents helped found and shape further political goals that sustained France's presence in Algeria for the next 132 years.[9]

Djebar subverts the link between conquest and the French language by achieving two objectives. The first is to use the French language to revive the lost identity of Algerian women and their representation in Algerian colonial history. French allows Djebar not only to see herself through the eyes of the Other, but also "to draw on aspects of the colonizer's model in order to elaborate her own sense of subjectivity."[10] This, in turn, creates a different vision of the world, thereby overturning standardized French depictions of colonial actions. By using French, Djebar transforms it into an-Other language that becomes her own. French is appropriated and thereby reassigned a new mode of expression for the formerly colonized. By appropriating the French language to accent the brutality caused to colonized Algerians, the author ruptures the link between conquest and language. She succeeds in subverting its discourse by exposing the anecdotes of French colonials that have been buried for over a century. By resurrecting these long-forgotten documents, Djebar revives the countless colonized women who lost their lives with little ado during the colonial era. In one brutal scene, the author exposes a short exchange between French soldiers who give details on seven Algerian women who were murdered during a military campaign in 1840:

> Women prisoners crouched on piles of velvet; they wait in outward calm. The oldest one, with uncovered face, stares haughtily at the watching Frenchmen. Bosquet guesses that at the slightest word from them she is prepared to hurl insults. He examines the silent women as he draws near to his commanding officer.
>
> "One is the Aga's daughter, the others are two daughters-in-law and some of his relatives!" explains Daumas, who must have questioned the serving-women who are standing round in the background.
>
> "The girl's a real beauty! She refused to weep for her brother, she's proud of him!" an admiring voice whispers in Bosquet's ear.

Lamorcière curtly asks why some women have nevertheless been slain a little distance away.

"Seven in all were executed by our soldiers," someone explains.

"They greeted us with insults!" (53-54)

Such a small incident becomes the symbolic representation for the widespread senseless suffering and death that characterized the fate of so many Algerian women during the colonizing mission. By acknowledging these seven barely recorded deaths, Djebar brings their lost subjectivity back into a space of agency, therefore rewriting a space of enunciation for them.

The author's second reason for using French is to emphasize how French colonialism deprived women of education and literacy during much of the colonial period.[11] Due to the lack of formal instruction either in French or in Arabic during the colonial period, feminine literary subjectivity was expressed only in oral form.[12] Feminine identity, subjectivity, and history were primarily based on village stories handed down from one woman to the next. Therefore, writing in French for Djebar not only corrects French archival accounts, but reinvests Algerian women with the literary voice they were deprived of.

Once the documents of the enunciation process have been defined and then subverted, Djebar reappropriates and then reinscribes them into the new version of the narrated time of her novel. Narrated time, Ricoeur suggests, is a comparison of archival renditions of history and the author's own vision of his or her novel's time: "But what is the correlate of presentification to which narrated time corresponds? Here we find two answers. On the one hand, what is narrated and is not narrative is not itself given in flesh and blood in the narrative but is simply 'rendered or restored.' . . . On the other hand, what is narrated is essentially the 'temporality of life.' However, life does not narrate itself, it is lived."[13] Djebar's reconstituted time weaves in between historic dates that are among the most significant in Algerian colonial history: 1830 (the French conquest of Algeria), 1954 (the beginning of the war of independence), 1960 (the Battle of Algiers), 1962 (Algerian liberation). Her control over the time line allows her to stop at any moment, to focus on what has been barely noted down by the French. In one instance, the author halts briefly in 1956. She retells the story of a young French soldier, Bernard, as he enters an isolated farm seeking a lovely young girl for his sexual pleasure. Djebar's reevaluation of this obscure incident mixes both a biography and an appropriated autobiography. She is responsible for telling the story of Bernard, who simultaneously tells his own. The author is both inside the Frenchman's text as a soldier combating the enemy during the Franco-Algerian War of 1954–62, and outside it as an Algerian woman narrating the biography of one of her "sexploited" foremothers. She also acknowledges the presence of the other fearful women who are caught in the room when the soldier enters the house:

> He slips in without knocking. It must be half past one in the morning. He hesitates in the darkness, then strikes a match: facing him, a group of women squat in a circle, staring at him; they are nearly all old, or look it. They huddle close to one another; their eyes gleam with terror or surprise. . . .
>
> The Frenchman takes food out of his pockets and hurriedly distributes it. He walks around, he strikes another match; finally his eyes light on "the pretty Fatma" who has smiled at him. He seizes her hand, pulls her to her feet.
>
> The match has gone out. The couple find their way to the back of the vast room, where it is pitch-black. The old women squatting in a circle have not moved; companions and sisters of silence, they crouch, staring with dim pupils which preserve the present moment: could the lake of happiness exist?
>
> . . .
>
> The Frenchman has undressed. "I could have been in my own home," he will admit. He presses the girl close to him; she shudders, she holds him tight, she begins to caress him.

"What if one of the old women were to get up and come and stick a knife in my back?" he thinks.

Suddenly two frail arms are round his neck, a gasping voice begins to whisper: strange, fond, warm words come tumbling out. The unknown hot-blooded girl pours these words in Arabic or Berber into his ear.

"She kissed me full on the mouth, like a young girl. Just imagine! I'd never seen anything like it! . . . She was kissing me! Do you realize?. . . Kissing me! It was the little meaningless action that I shall never be able to forget!"

Bernard returns to the camp about three in the morning. No sooner has he fallen asleep than he wakes with a start: he must leave the village forever. (210-211)

In focusing on this male biography, Djebar exposes the sexual manipulation of Algerian women at the hands of the French during the Franco-Algerian revolution. However, she also bypasses the gravity of this manipulation with the young girl's fervent kiss—an act that is viewed by the young soldier as defiant. Such an act breaks apart the veiled and submissive image of Maghrebian women in the harem so meticulously cultivated by French Orientalist fantasies, to reinstate them as active fighters for their country and freedom. Yet, although in this scene one woman demonstrates a small act of defiance, Djebar is more concerned with the image of the women cowering in the darkened corners of the room—these women are the backbone of her feminine reality. They are the ones the author must reinstate into Algerian history. It is these women for whom she must speak, those who have no power and who have been forced to submit to oppression for centuries. Commenting on this banal scene reinscribes it in the present as a eulogy for all women who have been maimed, beaten, raped, and mutilated by war, colonialism, and present-day conflicts in Algeria. Years after this 1956 event the author warns her feminine readers not to forget their sisters, mothers, and grandmothers who crouched, silenced by fear, in an obscure corner. Djebar's message is clear: women must emerge from their silenced history or risk mute servitude and loss of subjectivity forever.

Djebar's fictive experience of time is a plotting of both historic and autobiographical time within the boundaries of her narrative. These new plotted points have the end result of constituting a fictional narrative of larger scope—or a collective autobiography. Djebar creates a collective fictive experience based on assumptions about the lives of Algerian women in history and by the insertion of her own autobiography within theirs. The author's interplay of different temporalities comprised of her autobiography and that of other women founds a new rewritten time that entirely reshapes the notion of Franco-Algerian history. Djebar's history is an original account written from a woman's point of view.

The feminine autobiography as painful testimony is a product of this reshaped feminine history on which Djebar focuses in *L'amour, la fantasia*. The interweaving of her own story with the autobiographies and stories of many other women demonstrates the power of speech as a linking force that brings together all participants in history, thus rendering more profoundly the fact that, as Roland Barthes notes, "writing is a historic act of solidarity."[14]

Djebar formulates her collective autobiography on two levels. The first is a personal level where childhood and family experiences allow her to explore her feelings of dual identity and the difficulties that arise from living a liminal existence between French and Arab worlds. The second level reflects the author's dedication to cultivate a collective effort among women to learn to write and empower their own discourse, freed of male and colonial domination.

The author uses her experiences as a young girl growing up between two languages, two cultures, and two traditions as metaphors for the lives of many other women. Djebar opens her novel with what is portrayed as a scene from her first day at a French school. Her father, a teacher, walks her to the door of the school, thereby openly defying village taboos by parading his daughter freely in the street. He is doubly condemned for exposing her to a Western education and the language of the colonizer, which in turn provide a link to the "outside," the dissident, the free space of discourse and of open love: "For her the time will come when there will be more danger in love that is committed to paper than love that languishes behind enclosing walls. So wrap the nubile girl in veils. Make her invisible"(3). This seemingly ordinary personal event is transformed into a social commentary as Djebar uses her diary accounts to describe the more global position of women in Algerian society. The noun *outside* (synonymous to school and the streets of her village) becomes a site of dissidence because the young girl defies the normal practice of keeping women illiterate. The young girl ventures out into male space in order to become educated. Here, in turn, she is also presented with the dire consequences of her boldness. Despite the taboos, outside space for the author is equal to empowerment and emancipation.

In another autobiographic scene, Djebar's father sends a postcard written in French to her mother. This scene also informs Djebar's readers about the severe sociocultural ramifications women face in Algeria when they become either an object or an agent of sexual desire. Not only did her father write in French, the language of the colonizer, but he also made public a declaration of love by brazenly writing to her mother for all the surrounding community to see. He addressed this little postcard in "the Western manner as 'Madame So-and-So . . . ', whereas, no local man, poor or rich, ever referred to his wife and children in any other way than by the vague periphrasis: 'the household'" (37). In presenting this open interaction between her mother and father, Djebar alludes to the public pressures on women to remain hidden away as nonsubjects. She further informs her readers that such public demonstrations of love are not looked upon favorably in a society whose Muslim traditions have divided men and women according to strict domestic codes.

However, these codes that define social space are but one reason for the nonrepresentation of women. On another, more global level, Djebar addresses women's loss of subjectivity in modern Algeria as the fault also of Western Orientalist constructions of women's identity that persist in our neocolonial era. The author constructs a collective autobiography to circumvent these paternalistic Orientalist images. Adlai Murdoch accurately states, "Djebar writes woman as object of desire into woman as desiring subject, drawing on the alienation and desire for recognition which are the legacies of a colonialist discourse," thereby recoding Algerian femininity by destabilizing historic colonial representation.[15] In writing a collective feminine biography, Djebar seeks to illustrate women's struggle to find and establish presence through the strength of their links with each other.

The author's collective narrative alludes to larger issues concerning feminine writing. The need to establish presence and subjectivity is a necessity shared by all women. Throughout history, women have incarnated the identity of man's desire as "the objects that succumb to his overall picture of what they ought to be."[16] Under masculine domination, women are socialized to write about themselves through male eyes, thus denying their own identity. The only male encounter with femininity has been femininity as an object of desire, or as the mirror image of maleness. In these terms, women orbit around the masculine world, deprived of any independent subjectivity.[17]

To counter the male mirror image, Djebar frees the women of Algeria both in a historic and feminist context by writing her collective autobiography. Through her own discourse, the author attempts to resist not only the male mold, but the colonized-Oriental one as well. One such example of the destabilizing of accepted stereotypes is Djebar's manipulation of "gazing power." The act of gazing, or viewing, the Other has always been a traditional privileged act of the colonizer, as Edward Said notes in his critique of Flaubert: "The Orient is *watched*, since its almost (but never quite) offensive behavior issues out of a reservoir of infinite peculiarity; the European, whose sensibility tours the Orient, is a watcher, never involved, always detached, always ready for new examples of what [Flaubert calls in] *Description de l'Egypte* . . . 'bizarre jouissance.'"[18]

Pointing out the ways in which European historical accounts

have reduced Algerians "to objects of a dominant gaze,"[19] Djebar seeks to restate what has never before been stated through her narrative, thus giving voice and presence to the colonized Other. In one such scene, the author allows her historic character, the wife of Hussein, to gaze back at her conqueror. Instead of having the reader witness the conquering of Algeria solely through the eyes of the French, Djebar imagines a dialogue among the female residents of Algiers as they witness the encroaching French invasion: "I can imagine Hussein's wife neglecting her dawn prayer to climb up on to the terrace. How many other women, who normally only retreated to their terraces at the end of the day, must also have gathered there to catch a glimpse of the dazzling French fleet" (8). In this scene the power to watch is destabilized, thus breaking traditional Western conceptions of the Other's lack of power. These few women, empowered by the act of gazing back, are no longer the veiled, obscure objects of desire, but rather active players in the denouement of historic events. Djebar strives to unmask the West's view of the Arab as a generalized Oriental stereotype, subtracted from the rest of the world. This stereotype, as Said notes, has been responsible for depicting the Arab as part of an isolated "living tableau of queerness."[20] Unmasking means for Djebar reintegration into history and the redocumenting of women's roles. By rewriting their presence in history, Djebar provides a sphere of active agency through a fictive experience that gives back a collective voice to all Algerian women who were deprived of speech throughout colonial history: "Here are these shrouded women, right in the heart of the parade, their silent presence tolerated, the ones who enjoy the sad privilege of remaining veiled in the very heart of the harem! At last I understand both why they are condemned and why they are fortunate: these women who 'shout' in their daily lives, the ones whom the matrons thrust aside contemptuously, probably typify their need to be seen, to have an audience!" (204-5).

In her historiographic metafiction, Djebar not only rewrites but calls into question "the monologic discourses of power and authority" that have overshadowed the Other's texts. The formerly marginalized must, therefore, step outside, become "ex-centric" to the established centered norm (in Djebar's case, the French text), in order to operate paradoxically and therefore install and then subvert canonized Western representations of themselves.[21]

The paradox is indeed an integral part of the historiographic metafictional novel, and a dimension that Djebar exploits in *L'amour, la fantasia*. Paradoxically, writing of the French colonizing process necessarily brings about confrontation, or a collision between the political and historical processes that have, in Djebar's case, colonized Algeria. Paradoxically, destabilizing Orientalism and the legacy of its stereotype is one of Djebar's principal objectives in *L'amour, la fantasia*. To achieve her parodic reworking of history, Djebar uses the colonial archive. Her text exemplifies the predisposition of the historiographic metafiction to paradox, because, in Hutcheon's terms, "there is no direct access to what may be real, . . . while reality may exist 'out there,' it is unavoidably ordered by the concepts and categories of our human understanding."[22]

In the author's narrative what is real or pure hypothesis is of secondary importance. Djebar's more important agenda is to establish a plan of reconstruction—to rewrite the subjectivity of lost feminine histories. The paradoxical doubling, or the two-sided text of a historiographic metafiction (such as that of the Other and of the colonizer), sets all documents and histories on equal ground. Such equalization allows these histories to be retold and reinterpreted. In this manner, paradox becomes a catalyst by which all subjects gain access to reinscription as new equalized bodies sharing a part in historic events. By using parodies, the normalized colonizing (male) gaze is destabilized, allowing for a new image of feminine representation.

As mentioned above, Djebar notes that either misrepresentation, or worse still, no representation at all, has characterized the West's depiction of the colonized Other in the archives of Western history.[23] These misrepresentations have rooted themselves in Western culture, promoting Oriental stereotypes that remain prevalent even in our post-colonial era. According to Said, these modern-day universals are based on mythical ideals stemming from nineteenth-century European colonial images of sexual pleasure, native exploitation, and rich revenues: "The Orient was Orientalized not only because it was discovered to be 'Oriental' in all those ways considered commonplace by an average nineteenth-century European, but also because it *could be*—that is, submitted to being—*made* Oriental. . . . Orientalism [however] is nothing more than a structure of lies or myths which, were the truth about them to be told, would simply blow away."[24]

Orientalizing stereotypes have been doubly detrimental to women of formerly colonized countries. Just as Europeans fostered convenient stereotypes of Maghrebian lands in general, so too did they create narrow, self-serving visions of Maghrebian women. Colonization conveniently fabricated an identity for the Maghreb, and on a larger scale all of North Africa. Women were easily depicted as erotic divas or dancing girls in nineteenth-century paintings by artists such as Delacroix and Ingres. These Western stereotypes stifled Maghrebian feminine voice, presence, and individuality. In *The Colonial Harem*, Malek Alloula elaborates on the Orientalizing and artistic endeavors of Western painters and photographers. He explains that these artists and authors embarked on a quest to represent the Maghreb, particularly Algeria, as they wanted it to be, "arrayed in the brilliant colors of exoticism and exuding a full-blown yet uncertain sensuality . . . where unfathomable mysteries dwell and cruel and barbaric scenes are staged. . . . [this] has fascinated and disturbed Europe for a long time." Alloula further remarks that "orientalism leads to riches and respectability";[25] therefore, to change the image of North Africa would deflate an entire economy built around this personification. The colonized, mysterious, veiled woman is one such element of Orientalizing construction that ensured the maintenance of feminine stereotypes.

Because she was veiled, unseen, unobtainable, and sequestered away from public space—a representative of "scopic desire"—*La Mauresque* (the Maghrebian woman) became the incarnate of the Western, particularly the French, Oriental dialectic.[26] Unable to possess her, the colonizer's sense of rejection manifested as condemnation of Muslim culture, one that he viewed as directly responsible for her sequestration. The veiled woman became synonymous with a site of sexual desire, anonymous and obscure. Feminine individuality was erased as *La Mauresque* melted into an erotic-exotic feminine collective that was unattainable for the Western man.

Perhaps no other Orientalist author represents to such an erotic degree the feminine-Arab stereotype as Eugène Fromentin in his nineteenth-century travelogues. The author-painter's *Un été dans le Sahara* and *Une année dans le Sahel* (first published in serial form in 1856 and 1857, respectively) chronicle his perceptions of Algeria through a vivid array of colors, odors, sights, and sounds. Fromentin uses these elements to construct rich written accounts much in the same painterly manner he rendered his paintings. The author admits in his preface to *Un été dans le Sahara* that his reports (in the form of letters written to an anonymous friend) were the products of simple amusement: "It was a charming job, which did not cost me effort and gave me great pleasure. It is clear that the letter writing style I adopted for these two stories was a simple artifice that permitted more freedom, authorizing me to discover myself a little more, and saving me from all method."[27]

Most of the scenes he evokes in his novels construed from "refracted images" and "the spirit of things" are the products of "a little imagination" and characterize the colonizer's embrace of the Civilizing Mission begun a few years before Fromentin set foot on Algerian soil.[28] The images of Algerians Fromentin describes in his travelogues echo the colonizer's vision of the colonized as a mimetic idealization of himself. This mimetic ideal, which Albert Memmi explains almost a hundred years later, is dependent on a master-slave dialectic and on the importance of recognition as a means of self-validation for the colonizer.[29] It also assures that the colonized will remain as an Other, "as a subject of difference that is almost the same, but not quite." Ambivalence is the fruit of mimicry and thus constructs a discourse for the colonial subject, fixing him or her "as a partial presence." This "fixity" locks the Other into an *"object* of regulatory power, as the subject of racial, cultural and national representation."[30]

During the time he spent in Algeria, Fromentin's Arab women, like his colors, odors, sights, and sounds, became locked in an Orientalist fantasy that consequently assured their presence in the French reading public's psyche only as ornaments to adorn narratives and paintings. The author-painter's women were essentialized as one of the many "constructions of the colonized subject" of the Arab world that would adorn texts and paintings up to the present.[31]

These "Mauresques" were like mysterious objects placed in sublime settings as part of the Algerian landscape; like sunsets, flowers, birds, or trees, Fromentin admired them from a distance. However, unlike the colonized landscape, Algerian women were unapproachable and could be observed only from afar. On the rare occasion when "the veiled Mauresques" ventured from behind their cloistered milieus, Fromentin was there, lurking in the wings or on the fringes. He writes enthusiastically, "I often witness this scene from afar, hidden in a shadowed place of observation which I have specially chosen. I see everything."[32] In *Une année dans le Sahel* the author hides behind a tree to observe a group of women visiting tombs in a cemetery. He is elated to see them at last discard their veils and relax in the field of Sidi Abd el Kader in the Algerian countryside:

> They do more than converse there; they eat, sit on the tombs; they spread out their haiks as tablecloths; the headstones serve both as a seat and as a table, and in small groups they enjoy cakes and sugared and saffron eggs. The large veils, which are

used when any indiscreet person shows himself in the neighborhood, blow suspended over cacti; they let their brilliant
makeup underneath show—some of which is splendid—because it is an occasion to empty their coffers, to show the splen-
dor of their finery, to cover themselves in jewels. . . . Who can
say, my friend, what goes on during these hours of independence between these women who have escaped from the sever-
ity of sequestration?[33]

The painter, throughout his travelogues, reifies these tranquil images of Arab women and pastoral scenes,[34] pleasing the colonial
milieu and Orientalist Parisian salons during the second half of the
nineteenth century.[35] These images would fuel Orientalist conceptions in Europe for the remainder of the nineteenth century and the
first half of the twentieth,[36] thereby assuring people of the colonized lands a "homogeneous empty time," as construed by Western
discourse. This discourse succeeded in normalizing "its own history of colonial expansion and exploitation by inscribing the history of the other in a fixed hierarchy of civil progress," thus
installing forevermore a basic rhythm of "historylessness" for the
culture, traditions, language, and customs of the colonized.[37]

To counter this "historylessness," Djebar studies Fromentin's
texts for flaws and byways through which to subvert and subsequently reinstall the lost identity of the eroticized-colonized Algerian woman. Her most striking parodic intertext in *L'amour, la
fantasia* again involves her study of Fromentin's *Un été dans le
Sahara*, in which the nineteenth-century painter describes his encounter with a severed hand he finds near the corpses of two dead
Algerian women:

I dismounted in order to examine more closely these mum-
mified corpses, consumed to the bone, but still clothed in their
gray cotton haiks. The earth did not leave anything to gnaw on
these dried up carcasses, and once exhumed, the dogs didn't
even try to disrobe them. A hand was detached from one of the
cadavers and hung from an arm only by a torn, dried thread,

hard and black like *la peau de chagrin*. It was half closed, rigid, from the last struggle with death. I picked it up and tied it to my saddle; it was a funeral relic to bring back to the sad ossuary of El-Aghouat. . . . The hand was suspended next to mine; this small hand lying straight with white nails, which perhaps had not been without grace, which perhaps had been young; there was something still alive in the frightening gesture of these contracted fingers; I began to be afraid, and I set it down when passing [an] Arab cemetery.[38]

Djebar's remanipulation of this scene in *L'amour, la fantasia* is interesting and demonstrates her total control of the recontextualization process used to write her fictive experience. In her effort to re-render history through paradox, she takes certain liberties with the goal of contesting all determined paradigms. Djebar's scene exemplifies Linda Hutcheon's theory of the historic metafiction because it is a "contradictory cultural enterprise . . . one that is heavily implicated in that which it seeks to contest."[39] What Djebar's historiographic metafictional text contests is both any naive realist concept of representation and any equally naive assertions concerning colonized identity. Her narrative becomes a tool that does not attempt to destroy the past but rather excises it to question its meaning.

In her pursuit to revive Fromentin's Algerian woman at any cost as well as to question his motives for being in Algeria, Djebar re-renders the nineteenth-century painter's scene in a new light—a metafictional manner—that enables a contradictory doubleness or, as Hutcheon explains, a paradox that causes "the intertexts of history and fiction [to] take on parallel status in the parodic reworking of the textual past."[40] When Djebar picks up this hand revered by Fromentin in his original text, she disregards any respect he might have demonstrated for the unknown woman's death. Her rendition does not elaborate on how the painter placed the hand later in a sacred cemetery. Instead, this gesture goes unnoticed as Djebar opts to pick up (almost angrily) this single hand in order to fetishize it in martyrdom. For Djebar, the hand becomes not just that of one lost woman, mutilated through the colonizing process, but the symbol for all feminine suffering—an icon for lost feminine subjectivity. It becomes the site of a reinvested collective feminine identity, fomenting the creation of a new active discourse for women:

> And then I intervene, with nomad memory and intermittent voice. Undaunted, I have traveled to the four corners of my native land between the captured City and the ruins of Caesaria, it stretches from Mount Chenoua, in the shadow of the Muzaïa Peak, a languid plain whose wounds have not yet healed. I intervene to greet the painter who has accompanied me throughout my wanderings like a second father figure. Eugène Fromentin offers me an unexpected hand the hand of an unknown woman he was never able to draw.
>
> In June 1853, when he leaves the Sahel to travel down to the edge of the desert, he visits Laghouat, which has been occupied after a terrible siege. He describes one sinister detail: as he is leaving the oasis which six months after the massacre is still filled with its stench, Fromentin picks up out of the dust the severed hand of an anonymous Algerian woman. He throws it down again in his path.
>
> Later, I seize on this living hand, hand of mutilation and of memory, and I attempt to bring it the *qalam*. (226)

By rewriting Fromentin's ending to this one small incident in colonial history, Djebar has once again subverted the dominant French discourse of the colonial era. Her use of the word *qalam* (Arabic for pen) symbolizes physical and metaphorical reinscription for women in historic text while disinvesting the importance of the French language in her creation of an image. This image becomes a universal, evoking once again her quest to bridge the gap, through the written word, between the silenced history of the feminine past and the uncharted feminine present. In the last scene of her novel, Djebar alludes to a larger, postmodern, historic metafictional agenda that problematizes all French historical knowledge. The author's narration of the past questions all facts—whether archival or literary. In condemning Fromentin for having discarded the severed hand (even though in his account he seems to have had some reverence for it), Djebar does not allow any sympathy for the colonizing mission in Algeria. Her historiographic metafiction plays upon the truth and the lies of historical archives and therefore is created to place emphasis purely on an enunciative situation that brings into question previous relationships between text, producer, receiver, historical, and social contexts. Djebar's recontextualization of one lost woman's history founds a new collective voice for all unidentified women, lost not only in textual accounts, but also in the physical, brutal colonization of Algeria. By using Fromentin's "hand," she overshadows what the nineteenth-century author actually wrote, or any sympathy he might have felt for Algerian women.

Djebar's parodic strategy leaves no margin for sympathy for the colonizer nor for any form of feminine oppression. Her principal objective is to subvert the Western (French) normalized images of Algerian women. The disruption of images like Fromentin's peaceful, pastoral depictions causes their passive consumption to erode, forcing us to rethink not only history and its male conception of feminine identity, but also the colonial stereotypes that have been the staples for Western conceptions of the Oriental-Other. *L'amour, la fantasia* is a historic discourse, one that problematizes our reading of history and the domination of Western documentation of the Maghreb. It is a novel, which in Djebar's own words means "to lift the veil and at the same time keep secret that which must remain secret, until the lightning flash of revelation" (62).

Assia Djebar's *Vaste est la prison:* Platform for a New Space of Agency and Feminine Enunciation in Algeria

Vaste est la prison shares many of the historio-linguistic aspects of her earlier novels. In much the same manner as *L'amour, la fan-*

tasia, Vaste est la prison promotes a narrative strategy of extreme diversity, blending historic accounts, legends, and traditional folktales. Added to these, Djebar's narrative agenda incorporates many aspects of her own life.

Besides literary content, Djebar uses visual recreations of her work as well. For instance, she weaves in an element of the cinematographic, reusing scenes and phrases from her films. This cinematic overlay not only adds her experiences as a filmmaker to those she has had as an author, but also includes those stories of other women she has met. Through the literary, visual, and oral, she lays bare for her readers a different interpretation of the accepted masculine renditions of the feminine body, while problematizing women's expected place or role in the phallocratic constructions of Algeria. Through the venues of historic revisionism, autobiographical details, and cinematographic representation a new space of agency is forged, solidified, and destined to be maintained by Djebar, who struggles for human rights as an author and as an intellectual. It is Djebar's exploration of outside agency and the development of a three-pronged narrative strategy promoting modalities of autobiography, postcolonial and colonial historic revision, and her cinematographic accounts that grounds a new intellectual milieu of enunciation for the author and for the exiled of Algeria.

Vaste est la prison is a multiply organized text that crosses positionalities of history, autobiography, and cinematic journalism, thus denoting the constant transitory manner of Djebar's new kind of speech, one that promotes the goal of feminine empowerment. Through the ever-shifting boundaries of these textual modalities, Djebar once again empowers women, as she breaks apart stagnant, traditionally fixed parameters of feminine identity to explore the unknown of Algerian women's unwritten history. Brought out through these varied textual modalities of history, autobiography, and cinematographic accounts, are themes of movement and exploration. Djebar's feminine characters of different socioeconomic strata, like herself, search for identity and feminine place outside stereotypes, masculine domination, and the dogmatic oppression of religion. These constraints, the author attests, have hindered Algerian women's access to self-representation in history as well as to the sociopolitical arena of contemporary Algeria.

Vaste est la prison is not a novel in a traditional sense. Each chapter centers around a different female figure who speaks in either the first or third person. From the countess Adélaïde, exiled to Naples after the fall of Napoléon in 1815, to an Algerian mother who in 1960 takes off her veil to travel to France to visit her son (a political prisoner being detained in Metz, France), Djebar's women grapple with instability and the consequences of experiences outside their designated sociocultural roles. As nomads and fugitives, Djebar's heroines in *Vaste est la prison* tell their stories of war, oppression, and abjection. Often these women are forced to find new spaces of feminine identity in diverse areas.

In her novel, language, love, dance, film, history, and travel all become roads to self-expression and liberty. It may be said that *Vaste est la prison* provides a stepping stone for the reestablishment of Algeria's memory of its history as well as the rewriting of feminine identity in the Maghreb. Establishing enunciative agency is necessary not only for feminine freedom, but also for future intellectual democratic processes in Algeria. Therefore, whether Djebar is listening to the oral stories of the mountain women she studies, reinscribing the historic archives she uncovers, or directing her films about the lives of women,[41] the author empowers a new venue for feminism and intellectual voice in her homeland.

The first few pages of *Vaste est la prison* depict Djebar's struggle not to lose the power of voice. She maintains that construction of such an enunciative milieu implicates a transition from the oral to the written text. The author realizes that although painful, writing is a necessary act; one that stabilizes and counters the passage of time and memory and solidifies the oral stories of Algerian women.

In *Vaste est la prison* Assia Djebar not only rewrites history and critiques the present day violence against Algerian women, she also condemns the oppression of an entire intellectual milieu that is viewed as threatening by the current fundamentalist movement, the Front Islamique du Salut (FIS).[42] Therefore, her objective as an Algerian feminist historian-author-filmmaker-intellectual is to note down not only a history for Algeria as seen from a woman's point of view, but also to fight for intellectual freedom in favor of all those who have been oppressed. The successful outcome of both of these objectives has proved to be dangerous and almost impossible since the end of the Franco-Algerian revolution of 1954–62.

Not only does Djebar seek to write in/on her new space of feminine intellectual discourse, she also hopes to create a platform for a new institution of cultural, intellectual, and artistic thought— something which has had little guarantee in postrevolutionary Algeria. Since 1962, little has been done to offer intellectuals the freedom required to install any tradition of political or cultural debate in Algerian society.[43] Any intellectual practice has had to be set up on the fringes of Algerian society or in exile. For the author, this ex-centric space, which expands outward to France, the United States, and other parts of the Maghreb, recreates a peripheral intellectual milieu. The maintenance of this space has become necessary for some semblance of free intellectual process among Algerian academics, journalists, authors, and philosophers. As Djebar states in her later novel *Le blanc de l'Algerie,* "getting away" and reviewing Algeria's sociopolitical situation from the outside is the only means by which an author or intellectual will gain the courage "to go back there, to the middle of blood that flows, [to] young killers' faces that loom at us."[44]

Djebar implies in her novels that a safehaven must first be created in exile to cultivate intellectualism and to promote its eventual institutionalization in Algeria. Creating an institution that will hold together new systems of discourse is a paramount theme in *Vaste est la prison.* This new institution Djebar defines encompasses not only historic discourse, but also the discourses of feminism, language, culture, and French and Algerian identities. In a sense, within her ex-centric space, Djebar is forming a plane of consistency, or a site of multifaceted thought, on which terms of her identity as a woman, researcher, intellectual, historian, and Algerian author writing in French may be mediated.

The author has been forced to create her space of enunciation outside of Algeria because of a number of factors, the principal one of which is the hostile political climate created by the fundamentalist movement in recent years. As stated previously, this movement has gained momentum, menacing intellectuals, academics, authors, and philosophers since 1990.[45] Second, Djebar's popularity in the West is countered by lack of support in Algeria, both publicly and politically, due to a more deeply rooted social anti-intellectualism begun in 1962 and slowly woven into the fabric of Algerian society. This anti-intellectualism unfortunately is a legacy of colonialism and a product of the postrevolutionary military governments, which, though espousing progressive socialist rhetorics, in reality have chosen to rule Algeria with an iron fist since the revolution. Réda Bensmaïa affirms this, stating that one of the reasons Algerian intellectuals, journalists, authors, artists, and philosophers have been the brunt of so many vehement and violent attacks by Islamic fanatics is that they have never achieved any status, recognition, or support from the public in postrevolutionary Algeria. Therefore, they are little known or recognized for the benefits they would offer society as a whole:

> If we refer to what is happening at this moment in Algeria, what is striking is the contrast which exists between the insignificance of intellectuals as a "group" and the violence which is harming them. If there is a paradox, it is to see the distance which separates the little regard for intellectuals during almost three decades of independence and the fury inflicted upon them now which throws them in prison, forces them into exile, kills them or assures that they loose all taste for being teachers, advocates for political liberty, defenders of personal rights or even architects of a transparent society where the individual and the citizen would coincide.[46]

In the same context, and in light of the current political instability and public hostility toward intellectuals, Djebar's novel *Vaste est la prison* may be considered as targeting two essential items of importance for the fostering of a new intellectual movement in Algeria. First is the need for the written enunciation of women's stories from history (a theme begun in *L'amour, la fantasia*). As the author indicates, it is important not only for women, but for all those who have been oppressed to write *their own* history and stories, and therefore to establish *their own* place in Algeria. This she accomplishes through her writing. The collective "they"—the effaced—become empowered through the author's pen on both a personal and a social level. It is this "they," family and friends who are revived, forced by Djebar to recapture a collective lost voice. Through her pen, "the voice leaves me each night while I call up the sweetish asphyxia of aunts, of cousins, interviewed by me, a young girl who understood nothing, who contemplated them, eyes wide, in order to later imagine them again and to come away with understanding" (337).

Second, it is imperative to create and subsequently maintain a space of intellectualism, where freedom of speech is guaranteed and where feminist, philosophical, and theoretical discourses may be cultivated. The integrity of such a space of enunciation will also guarantee the reinstatement of the lost memory of Algeria that is the result of an unstable postrevolutionary beginning and the subsequent installation of military regimes that have offered little freedom of speech to the Algerian people. Until the power of enunciation is handed over to Algeria's intellectuals, journalists, authors, and philosophers, there will be no intellectual tier within Algerian society.

In order for the philosopher's or the author's language to exist, or for his or her "language to be granted the importance it claims," Pierre Bourdieu notes that "there has to be a convergence of the social conditions which enable it to secure from others a recognition of the importance which it attributes to itself."[47] Creating such social conditions from which to cultivate Algerian intellectual thought, and therefore to promote other aspects of her writing such as feminism and historic revision, Djebar has had to assume an anomalous position, or shift to the outside, on the borders, as an "exceptional individual" with "many possible positions."[48]

As stated many times in my analyses of contemporary Francophone texts of the Maghreb, it is out on the borders where the power of enunciation, and thus the key to subjectivity, is cultivated. Tzvetan Todorov concurs in *Du bilinguisme* that it is this space of enunciation that is the principle component of being. "If I lose my place of enunciation," he writes, "I cannot speak, thus I do not exist."[49] The first few pages of *Vaste est la prison* depict Djebar's struggle not to lose the power of voice, which Todorov proclaims as primordial for an author who is writing from two discursive milieus. Djebar's struggle suggests how her space of agency acts as a safe haven from which she is able to critique all aspects of Algerian society, culture, and history in both collective and autobiographical terms. Within *Vaste est la prison,* all facets of historical revision have equal ground, all places have equal influence, all "prisons are opened," and all women have a voice: "I do not write down, alas, the words of the *noubas*[50] too knowledgeable for me. I recall them: no matter where I go, a persistent voice, whether of a tender baritone or a blind soprano sings them in my head, while I rove the streets of some European city, or *d'ailleurs* when a few steps in the main street of Algiers make me immediately perceive each prison open to the sky or closed" (172).

Reviewing the past and the present, both historically and autobiographically, although painful, is a necessary process in rewriting a feminine history for Algeria. Her polyphonic discourse, incorporating both sides of her own heritage, affords Djebar the means to review her politico-cultural situation as a feminine author writing from abroad about her country's history. Because she is forced to review Algerian history and present-day conflicts from the outside in France, the United States, and elsewhere Djebar is able to redefine the meaning of *biculturality* and *duality*. Her disdain of

France's colonization of Algeria cannot be denied. However, at the same time, because France has provided the author with a platform from which to write, it evokes a certain tolerance for what Djebar calls "l'autre en moi." This Other is explored as an appendage to her Self—as something exterior: "France, thus, was for me simply the outside" (260). Although it is problematic for many contemporary authors to write in French, the language of their former colonizers, Djebar has subverted its stigma in order to find a means to liberty, the freedom to venture out and to explore. French evokes for the author a feeling of detachment, it is thus a method of access both professionally (because it enables her to research Algerian history as depicted in French colonial archives)—and personally—through memories she has of Algerian and French worlds).

As in *L'amour, la fantasia*, Djebar uses her autobiography often to allude to larger social situations concerning Algerian women. The author's introspection is realized through the narrative of her own painful experiences, living as a woman who comes up constantly against seemingly permanent male barriers. Although autobiographical, her pain reflects that of many women who find themselves caught—victims of Muslim tradition, male domination, and limited freedom—within the confines of home and family. Djebar's experience and the subsequent choices she is forced to make because of family, tradition, and culture are offered as examples of the constricting universe most Algerian women face. This universe is split between the freedom of independence (which often carries the price of exile) and the reality of oppression (the product of feminine submission and conjugal imprisonment). Finally, in her own case, resolution to throw off her conjugal confinement "imposed its words." She ruptures all ties between herself and her husband: ". . . from here on out put up a door! Forever." (108).

The author's final choice to rid herself of her domestic bonds seems almost foreign because it is so rare in her traditional Muslim milieu. Even more curious is the fact that the idea to flee from her husband comes to the author in French words rather than her native Arabic.

Blending autobiography and history, Djebar forges a link with Princess Zoraidé, an ancient historic feminine figure whose story the author-researcher uncovers. Like the author, when the young princess ventures out to find her freedom, she too must negotiate between two histories, two cultures, and two languages. Although daunting, fleeing sequestration to journey to an unknown land, where she is forced to negotiate in the in-between, means certain freedom for Zoraidé. The princess, like Djebar, discovers that freedom of movement becomes a catalyst by which to find the words to rewrite her own history. In the same manner as Djebar, Princess Zoraidé also is a "fugitive who doesn't know it," who dares to open a dialogue "with the Other" even though it means risking her life. In the following passage, Zoraidé's and Djebar's voices become intermingled, almost indistinguishable from one another, as "their" story is told:

> I write in the shadow of my mother, who has come back from her wartime journeys—me, chasing my family in this gloomy peace made from muffled interior war, from internal discord, and from the confusion and swell of my native land.
>
> I write to open up my secret path, and in the language of the French privateers who, in the story of the Captive, strip Zoraidé of her diamond-studded gown. Yes, it is in this so-called foreign language that I become more and more renegade. Such is [the story of] Zoraidé, the despoiled princess. Like her, I have lost my wealth from the beginning (in my case, it was my maternal inheritance), and have gained nothing except the simple mobility of a stripped body, except freedom.
>
> Fugitive, thus, and one who doesn't know it. Because, if I know it too much, I will fall silent and the ink of my writing will dry too quickly. (172)

A fugitive who doesn't know it, Zoraidé, a sequestered princess, seeks the freedom to write and to explore on the outside of her paternal prison. This "first Algerian woman who writes" so desires freedom that she enters a pact with an imprisoned Christian soldier who becomes her lover: "she seizes upon a crazy role: she plays liberator for the one who will venture with her into the ultimate transgression." In freeing this foreigner from her father's prison, she frees herself, realizing that the life of a nomad in an obscure country with a lover is better than a life confined within the four walls of her father's domain. As Djebar states, "in freeing the slave-hero from the dungeons of Algiers," Zoraidé "liberates herself from the father who gave her everything except liberty. . . . She trades an encircled space (the richest house in Algiers, where she was queen) for an unlimited but uncertain elsewhere" (168).

By writing down this story, Djebar obliges her readers to reflect on the parallels between the stories of Algerian women in the past and the present. She also exposes the steps they are forced to take to secure freedom. Again the author asks, Is this price worth isolation and destitution in a foreign country? Djebar herself is unable to answer. She concludes that the story of Zoraidé, retold to Don Quixote between 1575 and 1579, is a historic emblem for all Algerian women who find themselves caught between liberty and oppression: "This entire fluid story places itself immediately under the sign of Arabic feminine writing—writing that, through repetition, dulls a gift of gold. The woman scribe is the one who pays, but she's also the thief, the traitor in the eyes of her father and family, the one who, in *le jardin de campagne du Sahel d'Alger*, invents intrigue and sets it in motion, then in the heart of the night faints in the arms of the foreigner, then perseveres in her will to flee. Her journey begins in a diamond-studded robe and ends in the rags of poverty" (169). Djebar is an ally to Zoraidé and to other women forgotten in history. She too remarks on the feelings of "la dépouille," the feeling of being stripped bare—brought on by exile and isolation. Whether from the past or the present, playing large or small roles as queens or peasants, Djebar's heroines prove their strength to persevere and to pull themselves from the depths of seclusion and oppression in order to reach a free space of agency. That free space, as

Gayatri Spivak notes, allows women to "have a self and a world" therefore assuring "a certain kind of being in the world, which [could] be called [a feminine] politics."[51] Political voice is the reward women will enjoy from the reinstallation of their stories in history. Rewriting history, Djebar reestablishes feminine communicative agency. As outlined in chapter 1, such agency benefits women because it grants a space of commonality for feminine subjectivity, politics, and socioeconomic freedom. Therefore, the author's global message favoring feminine intellectual thought also may be viewed as promoting feminine community. Whether from the mountains of Algeria or the streets of Paris, Djebar's women form a circle of political solidarity. This kind of solidarity does not objectify all women under "one guise of sameness," but instead incorporates all the "cultural, personal, and political transformations of women."[52] By rewriting feminine history, Djebar fuses historic and contemporary voices into a space of resistance, reestablishing political solidarity and desire in order to cross-fertilize a new discourse for feminine intellectual thought.

Such cross-fertilization is achieved for Djebar, as well as for her heroines, in part by journeying as a nomad. Being a "fugitive," paying no allegiance to either French or Algerian spheres, linguistic tradition, or cultural paradigms, cultivates a certain schizophrenic discourse. Her schizophrenia compels Djebar to move beyond French and Algerian languages to construct her autobiographical space of agency through a new form of discourse one that does not just reflect bilingualism, but rather a multiple linking of all the aspects that make up her multivalent voice. This multiple linking, or dialogism, is constituted not just from languages but also from history and culture. It is pure movement between the multitiered aspects of the nomad-author's multicultural world. Djebar's world of the multivalent reflects what Bakhtin defines as a multilanguage space favoring a suspension of totalized theories of difference. In the dialogic space, multiple enunciative processes collide, yet none ever takes precedence over another: "A dialogue of languages is a dialogue of social forces perceived not only in other static co-existence, but also as a dialogue of different times, epochs and days, a dialogue that is forever dying, living, being born: co-existence and becoming are here fused into an indissoluble concrete unity that is contradictory, multi-speeched and heterogeneous."[53]

Writing in this world of diglossia leads the dialogic author on a "pathway of frontiers, such as those of migration or exile." Djebar traverses these frontiers to engage in what Todorov explains represents "an invitation to authors to throw themselves out into an enormous polyphony for which all language is foreign, for which *one* language does not exist."[54] Djebar's language in *Vaste est la prison* is shaped between her autobiographic voice and her process of historic revision, thus reifying in her own manner the world of women, silence and love: "The silence of the writing—wind of the desert which turns its unyielding grindstone—while my hand runs, while the language of the father (language from somewhere else transforms into the paternal language) undoes little by little, surely, the languages of dead love. And the feeble murmur of the faraway grandmothers, the hooting moan of the veiled shadows floating at the horizon, so many voices spattering themselves in the slow vertigo of mourning while my hand runs" (11).

The act of writing forges the link of her own autobiography in the present to these historic "veiled shadows," and therefore leads Djebar to resurrect the unsolved mysteries of the pre- and post-colonial specters of her homeland.

Issues from Algerian history, both during and after colonialism, are integrated in the thematic agenda of *Vaste est la prison*. Clarifying women's roles in such issues is the pivotal force of the second and third portions of her novel. One previously orally transmitted story about women in colonial Algeria that Djebar reifies in written form is that of "la fille du mokkadem du saint Ahmed ou Aabdallah." The author renarrates the young woman's story, explaining how she married two husbands "from the mountains," only to leave them in order to migrate back to her native village in order to raise her daughter on her own. This clear act of defiance breaks apart the traditionally subservient role most readers expect of Muslim women. The young girl's defiance is resurrected as an important story for Djebar because it is both an oral tale and a personal experience passed down from generation to generation. Having been only temporal because of its orality, it is finally written down, preserved forever by the author in pen and ink: "And now after three-quarters of a century, I do not know—me, Isma (the narrator, me, the descendant—by the last of the girls) If Lla Fatima (Mama) loved her two husbands one after the other, or one instead of the other, or one more than the other. I am certainly the only one to ask myself this about the dead!" (228).

In writing down the oral story, Djebar gives concrete presence to both the narrative and its protagonist. For the first time, the transitory story has been fixed in time and space. Writing down their histories transforms her female characters into empowered women who are rendered into subjects rather than objects. In such a space, the author's voice becomes a collective one, spreading "the blood of writing" through the veins of her subjects (345). Power and presence are brought at last to those women who were erased during the passage of time: "Write; the dead of today desire to write" (346).

On a more global level, Djebar's rewritten feminine history-as-novel extends outward to what Françoise Lionnet defines as new "border zones" of culture, historicity, intellectual thought, and feminism. These border zones, become the sites of a "creative resistance to the dominant conceptual paradigms" of the West.[55] This resistance thus redefines the processes of the West's appropriation of the language and the culture of the Other's space. Djebar remarks that it is important to maintain these zones in order to reinstall the lost "memory" of Algeria into the modern day. It is out on the borders where new processes of rememorization are embraced. These processes are necessary in the founding of a platform for intellectual discourse in Algeria. As Abdelwahab Meddeb has noted, we cannot conveniently efface memory with regard to the present situation in Algeria. The act of forgetting is one of the causes, he stresses, of the current sociopolitical ills of that country.[56] Although Tunisian, Meddeb voices the opinion of many Algerian authors who have been forced to reside outside Algeria. The "absence of memory" of both the colonial epoch and the tumultuous years during and immediately following the Franco-Algerian War have caused the loss of a collective conscience among the Algerian people. Today, added to these historic legacies, is the fragmentation of an entire social system due to religious fanaticism. The control of this fanaticism has made remembrance of history virtually impossible (due primarily to a religious dogma that annihilates any reference to the West, to the revolutionary-nationalist movement of the 1960s, or to modern intellectualism and rereadings of history). Benjamin Stora reiterates this loss of memory:

> In the actual conflict in Algeria, formulae follow according to the course of fancies, passions, and emotions. In the shuffle of words ("violence," "barbarism," "fundamentalism") a new beginning proves difficult. The demands of urgent solidarity with a society in peril discourage historic references; the extraordinarily rapid disintegration of the situation weakens the work of a "placing in perspective." The incessant looking forward (Where is Algeria going?) without any precise point we should be oriented toward lends to emotion overshadowing reason. The opaqueness of the future seems impenetrable.[57]

Stora and many sociopolitical theorists insist that historical revision of the Franco-Algerian War, as well as of the French colonial period, is absent in Algeria. This is due mainly to the postrevolutionary efforts of the FLN (Front de Libération Nationale) to wipe out the country's past and in its place found a purely Marxist-nationalist regime promoting social-collective unity. Under no circumstances were martyrs, individuals, or certainly the original leaders of the rebellion of 1954, who started the war, to be revered. The "collectivizing" of the war effort, the disregard of certain facts (some of which clearly demonstrated that the majority of Algerians in the earlier years of the revolution did not favor independence), coercion by the FLN of Algerian citizens, tortures, and assassinations—all these influenced the FLN-led government to stifle any memory process other than what it had fashioned for its citizens. Stora and other historians of the Franco-Algerian conflict ask if this falsifying of historic documents and this memory "numbing" are not directly linked to the rise of Islamic fundamentalism in Algeria at the present time. In the last few years a dogmatic "war on the people" has been systematically waged, engulfing a generation of Algerians.[58]

In light of the current urgent situation in Algeria, it is now, more than ever, necessary to reinstate an Algerian memory with a complete feminine presence and to create a platform from which to instigate the commencement of a new process of documentation for postrevolutionary history. These two objectives, at the forefront of Assia Djebar's work, install a cohesive intellectual platform not only for feminism but for humanity in Algeria. Reestablishing Algeria's stability is important for all its citizens and for the Maghreb as a whole. Sociopolitical stability in Algeria will allow free dialogue among intellectuals, feminists, scholars, authors, and filmmakers, therefore subverting the historic "memory loss" that has effaced the subjectivity of many, particularly women. Filling in the gaps of history creates a productive platform for feminine agency and representation. As Fatima Mernissi suggests in her book, *The Forgotten Queens of Islam*, the historic memory loss of Algeria and all of the Maghreb has drastically reduced feminine representation in Islamic countries to a bare minimum. "Muslim women in general, Arab women in particular, cannot count on anyone, educated or not, 'implicated' or 'neutral,' to read their story. This reading is their entire responsibility and their task. Our claim to full and total pleasure and our universal human rights, here and now, necessarily traverse a re-appropriation of memory, a re-reading–reconstruction of a large and open Muslim past. Certain tasks can reveal not austere and constraining obligations, but delicious journeys towards borders of pleasure."[59] Therefore it is necessary for women of the Maghreb to make a transition toward reinscription of their own stories in order to fully reappropriate feminine memory.

In part 2 of her novel Djebar does "read" the history of her feminine ancestors, reflecting once again her historic research and commitment to reinstalling the little-regarded roles of women in Algerian history. In this section, titled "Erasing the Stone" (L'effacement sur la pierre), Djebar's objective is to reinstate her heroines' presence so that it will not be forgotten through the march of time. Delving into the historic, the author chronicles the exceptional occasions when women have broken the bonds of passive interior space to explore these "delicious journeys towards the borders of pleasure." Djebar explores what this new life entails—a life out from behind the veils of Islamic fundamentalism and feminine sequestration—by cultivating the role of the feminine as an active player in a space of productive agency. This is primordial for her heroines, all of whom risk their lives to seek other means of subjectivity than the passive interior ones of harem, court, marriage, and family. Djebar understands that movement into the realm of the public is essential if women are to achieve any influence on public decisions, or participate in the distribution of public recog-nition.

Entering a public space allows women to develop a cognitive consciousness. It also forces the remembrance of loss and destruction. As Djebar suggests, "knowing," "seeing," and "hearing" the empowerment of a liberated consciousness for her heroines and herself exposes all women to pain and destruction:

> Oh, I see (or I hear, I don't know), I see the oldest dead, including my youngest brother, who I never really remembered, except by the trembling voice of the father relating the sorrow of the orphaned mother I see them, the dead from very far, not because I lay claim to the legacy of the magician Lla Rkia . . . . simply because, these past two or three seasons, in my country, all the dead, indistinctly, come back.
>
> Their desire haunts us, us women. . . .

The dead come back to us and what do they desire, in this unexpected desert? (335)

In this passage the author notes that throughout Algerian history there have been women living on the margins who risked "facing the dead," by venturing out into public space, to face death, destruction, or captivity. To Djebar they are heroines. But their heroic acts have been given little regard by male Algerian historians. To counter this lack of recognition, Djebar gives her own version of the precolonial story of Abalessa, "the princess who pushes all the way to the heart of the desert of deserts!" (161). In so doing, the author issues a series of questions concerning the need to flee. Why does this young protagonist choose to flee "from the north of the Berber country," where she is princess, and why did she leave, fleeing friends and family? Was it for discovery or for escape? "For what political or private reason, despite her youth and the fact that she was going to perhaps rule, would she decide to abandon everything, to plunge on beyond the oasis of the Sahara? Was it for her threatened liberty—hers or that of her family, or her group?" (161-62). Abalessa, like so many forgotten women in history offers no answers to Djebar's questions. The author notes that she simply ventured out, and then was lost, apparently without ceremony or historic documentation.

Djebar also constructs her space of agency in *Vaste est la prison* in aesthetic terms, paying considerable attention to the cultivation of the visual, sensual, and musical in her text. In this third section of her novel, the author now also becomes a narrative filmmaker as she casts her characters in filmic roles that mirror her actual work as a cinematographer. In a blend of cinematographic allusions in the text, Djebar compels the readers to follow a textual camera. This section, titled "A Quiet Desire," becomes a narrative film, complete with musical score. Djebar writes seven small movements (each with a separate title) to be used in the montage of her text. These movements tell her autobiographical experiences as a film director, recount the tales she has heard passed down to her, and describe her lifelong efforts to chronicle the lives of other women on film. This filmic section consists of cultural and historical events glimpsed through the lens of her narrative camera as she shoots the diverse aspects of the feminine: body, voice, and imagery.

Within the cinematographic space, "A Quiet Desire" continues the novel's themes of feminine exile and nomadism. This section of the novel moves quickly, developing strength and resonance. Interspersed are short, staccato scenes, each titled "Femme arable" (molded or transformed woman), in which Djebar narrates the difficulty and the pleasure she experiences in directing her films. "Femme arable I" begins with Djebar's personal reflections on making her earlier films in postrevolutionary Algeria. She pays particular attention to her 1978 film *La nouba des femmes du Mont Chenoua*. This film, made in Arabic, also weaves historic feminine stories with contemporary feminine issues. *La nouba* is particularly interesting because its feminine theme forces the audience to take stock of women's position in Algerian society some fifteen years after the revolution. The fact that Djebar, a woman filmmaker, ventures out to discover and expose the real participation of women in the revolutionary process, reminds the audience of the feminine contribution that has been overshadowed because of traditions that only favored the male elite once the revolution was won.

In order to link the themes from her film *La nouba* (now twenty years old) to her 1996 novel *Vaste est la prison*, Djebar brings out the common thread of reviewing feminine history and the significance of a (particularly Muslim) woman's renunciation of interior space to establish subjectivity and to affirm her agency. The particular issue of breaking the traditional boundaries of women is explored in the 1978 film (as well as the 1996 novel) in identical scenes. In the film "her" husband (presumed to be the author's) is a shadowy presence, confined to a wheelchair after a fall from a horse. Her liberty from domestic servitude, poignantly indicated in the film, leaves the young researcher free to travel and to gather information on her own.

As in *La nouba des femmes du Mont Chenoua*, Djebar begins her narration in "Femme arable I" of *Vaste est la prison* with the identical image of a handicapped man, depicted in shadow, confined, and kept from entering the space of women by his own incapacitated body:

> The 18th of December of that year I filmed the first scene of my life: a paralyzed man sitting in a chair watches, stops at the entrance to a room, where his wife sleeps. He cannot enter: two steps hinder his wheelchair. A bedroom like any other, hot, so close, yet at the same time so far: the bed is large, low, encircled by many white sheepskins softening the roughness of the high walls of the peasant house. In the old way, the sleeping woman has pulled back her hair in a red scarf. The immobilized husband watches from afar. He moves his upper body; his hand touches the door frame, a second before the shot is finished. (173)

By rendering this one man physically handicapped, and therefore unable to take part in any story, Djebar is free to form a feminine allegiance with the sleeping woman in the film and with the women of the ancient harems. These women were confined in a space created, formed, and maintained by men. This destabilizing or castrating of the male gaze and dominance ("the immobilized husband watches from afar") turns the tables on masculine power and feminine objectification.

Djebar's male figure is unable to dominate the feminine body with his gaze; he is rendered incapacitated and unable to penetrate the room of the sleeping woman. Disordering the ordered, normalized male role of "gazer" and appropriator of the feminine redefines what Laura Mulvey describes as "a world ordered by sexual imbalance [where] pleasure in looking has been split between active/male and passive/female; [it is here where] the determining male gaze projects its phantasy on the female figure which is styled accordingly."[60]

Djebar's film-text in *Vaste est la prison* gives to Algerian women of all echelons the active world they have rarely enjoyed. Her destabilization of this traditional passive feminine space (in this case an inviting harem room set up for optimal male pleasure) grants women freedom from masculine penetration in both metaphorical and physical terms. The cloistered passive women of Algeria's past succeed in compelling Djebar to act as an agent for their visual and narrative reinscription into history.[61] By evoking her film work in the novel, Djebar calls our attention to the fact that the cinematographic space, like the writing space, allows the author-director to create, and subsequently organize, a feminine third (mixed) space of agency, reconfiguring visual and textual normalized images in favor of feminine control. Djebar's images promote new parameters for Algerian feminine subjectivity. She remarks in her novel on the stimulation she feels as a woman in total control of her subjective space and as the promoter of feminine agency: "The first shots of my work: a sort of defeat of man. . . . I said, 'Action.' Emotion seizes me. As if, along with me, all the women of all the harems had whispered, 'action.' A complicity that excites me. Henceforth, their gaze only matters to me. [It is] set down in these images that I organize and that these invisible presences behind my shoulder help to ferment" (173-74).

The author's cinematographic space built on this "defeat of man" also becomes a negotiating space for feminine freedom. The driving force—the action—behind each scene reinstates "these invisible presences" from the historic past. It is the "ancestors" at her feet who spur Djebar on to refilm what was lost and "to seek out the oral memory of the women of the mountains" (322). All the women Djebar chooses as examples, whether wives, mothers, or sisters, share a common experience: they have been forced to venture out into a hostile world. Women such as "the mother," who leaves for France, where she suffers extreme humiliation when trying to visit her imprisoned son, or Djebar's own daughter, whom she rescues after her participation in the Algerian protests of 1988,[62] allude to the great risks women face when they step outside the boundaries of their designated roles to challenge structures of authority.

Djebar terminates her novel at the end of a journey across years of her own life and across the lives of many other women in history. Not only has she woven in her colonial French past with her postrevolutionary present, she has also linked the diversity of the lives of many women who come from Algeria and France, who are rich, poor, princesses, or historic figures. By connecting these women, Djebar creates a form of resistance that is empowered not through politics but rather through feminine social communication. Such a feminine *socius*, promoting solidarity, extends beyond essentialist glorifications, whether racial, sexual, geographic, or cultural. A world of solidarity is dissident and political, as well as ex-centric and peripheral. Yet, it is this very peripheral space of freedom that promotes the sociopolitical platform from which Djebar is able to write.

The author's closing words in *Vaste est la prison* exemplify her efforts to link Algeria's past and present in a field of multicultural, multivalent discourse. She explains that although Algeria has had a fragmented and violent past, and continues to be split apart by a factionalized political system, the cross-culturalism that is inherent in herself and all her fellow countrymen and women will never be effaced: "the rest, the living and the dead, the masculine (that is, the irredentist pride) and the feminine (the lucidity that hardens or causes insanity) of that which I think of as the soul of this earth, the rest, thus, is wrapped in veils of dust, in the French words masking the shapeless voice gurgling disavowed Berber and barbarous sounds, Arabized and modulated melodies and complaints, the polyform voice of my genealogy. Oh, how badly I extricate myself from it!" (331-32).

Djebar concludes the novel as she began it, from an activist point of view. She devotes the last few pages to a young woman, Yasmina (who the author describes in life and death through what she calls "the blood of writing"). The scene revolves around this "young professor . . . [and] proofreader for an independent newspaper" who died so insignificantly in Algeria (343). This woman provides an example; she is but one martyr among many who dies each day in Algeria. After stating that she could never leave her country, Yasmina, demonstrating strength and courage, like so many women before her, is gunned down in 1994.

In order to keep alive the memory of Yasmina and so many others who have died, Djebar continues to write and to make films in order to hone a new space for intellectual thought and historic revision. She attests that her existence depends on her writing and that she must always write as if tomorrow were her last day: "When I write, I always write as if I am going to die tomorrow. Each time I finish I ask myself if this is really what was expected of me, because the murders continue. I wonder what good it did. If not, I clench my teeth to keep from crying."[63]

For Djebar writing is the sole means of protesting a prison that is so vast, its borders and its exits are almost indeterminable. It is only from her polyphonic place of exile that Djebar finds the means to break free of the violence that characterizes Algeria today. The author must live outside, as a dissident, on the liminal edges of a factionalized Algeria in order to continue to contest the injustice that is imposed there. She insists that a dissident voice is the only means through which an author, placed in an unstable and unjust world, will succeed in developing his or her own strategy of dialogue to effectuate a platform of agency. Defining and constructing an enunciative milieu is the sole manner dissidents "maintain the integrity of the thought process and denounce the contradictions of the world in which they live."[64] From Djebar's dissident, exiled status she can speak out, to question and draw the attention of others to the current violence in Algeria. She and her nation have suffered the perpetuation of a culture of war "which will end up by engendering a questionable automatism in the young generations of Algeria."[65] It is up to Djebar, as well as other authors and intellectuals like her, to reconstruct history as they think it should have been told, with the final objective of forging a new space for future Algerian intellectual discourse, a space that will displace the violence of a country in turmoil for over two centuries and that will foster the remembrance and subsequent rewriting of a forgotten history. Writing in exile as a fugitive who doesn't know it, Djebar nurtures the voice within her Self as well as that of all the Selves of Algeria that cannot speak, or have not yet spoken.

Chapter Four

Seeking the Becoming-Woman in the Third Space of Culture

Leïla Sebbar's Shérazade

A S OFTEN MENTIONED in this book, contemporary Francophone authors, whether writing from the Maghreb or from France, seek to transcend Western stereotypes designed for the Other by the West. This transcendence facilitates the construction of a new identity. The formerly colonized-Other becomes a socially embodied subject, with its own space of active agency. This space is indicative of our postmodern era, which gravitates around an a-centered, or ex-centric, exploration of the subject.[1] This exploration provides a perfect background for new concepts concerning the identity of the literature of authors from the formerly colonized diaspora. These authors, as we have seen, exist on the anomalous fringes—on the outside of the established norm. It is this outside, however, which is the promoter of all becoming, the centering force of a new identity for all those who have been marginalized. This outside is "one general all-consuming flux in which everything is dissolved together in one world."[2] This world of involution means that one identity flows into another, sweeping "one *and* the other away, a stream without beginning or end that undermines its banks and picks up speed in the middle."[3] It is here, in the between things, where things happen.

The in-between is where Leïla Sebbar places her principal character, Shérazade. Sebbar's trilogy, beginning with *Shérazade: Dix-sept ans, brune, frisée, les yeux verts*, continuing with *Les carnets de Shérazade*, and finally ending with *Le fou de Shérazade*, is a study of surviving in the peripheral spaces of France—of living in the in-between—which is a Third Space of culture.[4] Homi K. Bhabha explains that this third, intersubjective space of culture is where "[t]he pact of interpretation is never simply an act of communication between the I and the You designated in the statement. The production of meaning requires that these two places be mobilized in the passage through a Third Space, which represents both the general conditions of language and the specific implication of the utterance in a performative and institutional strategy of which it cannot 'in itself' be conscious."[5]

In the Third Space the Other has the possibility of free exchange. Like Deleuze and Guattari's plane of consistency, the Third Space does not create a hierarchy or foster oppression and inequality—it is an undifferentiated milieu, an abstract machine, "which in turn formalizes contents and expressions according to strata and reterritorializations."[6] The plane is free of all inequalities. What is important is what happens on this plane. It is where an entity forms connections and follows paths to other realms.

Many modes of empowerment take place when one enters the Third Space of culture, but perhaps the two most important capacities one gains are the freedoms to establish modes of dialogue and to confront stereotypes. Within this interstitial space, the Maghrebian Francophone author is free (because there is no hierarchy, no oppression) to open a dialogue with what I call the First Space—that is, the old colonial world of Western stereotypes. Such a non-hierarchical space allows the author to then mediate a second space. This Second Space represents a modernized vision of the "Westernized Other," which has always been the product of a prefabricated stereotype dating back to the colonial era. This stereotype persists today as a neocolonial perception haunting those of formerly colonized countries. It is also a space in which Western post-colonial rhetoric takes shape, allowing the West to mark the Other as different. Those under the different label are packaged in a separate identity, and allowed little freedom to incorporate their own diversity into the impenetrable Western world.[7]

Sebbar's heroine, Shérazade, finds that her Third Space of culture is a place in which to retrace her Algerian heritage. This space provides a springboard off which the young Beur woman deterritorializes (or uproots herself) from France (which she considers as her country of exile) and then effortlessly reterritorializes (reintegrates herself) in other places along her path of self-knowledge. This travel ultimately leads to her becoming-woman and true identity. Shérazade's battle is not just with the West and Western perceptions of North Africa that persist in France today. Wherever she goes, regardless of the country—Israel, Algeria, Lebanon, or France—the heroine must fight a stereotype or a prefabricated identity fashioned for her by those who seek to seal her in a convenient package. Her task is to combat resemblance and mimetic ideals surrounding Maghrebian women. The only way to do this is "to get outside the dualisms. . . . to be-between, to pass between."[8] Her place to become is on the outside of fixed ideals, away from affiliations and stereotypes. She must stay on the outside in an anomal place of existence in order to enter her own becoming.

Sebbar understands the nature of the Third Space. She realizes that it is only in the "in-between" that her characters will find the identities they seek—true identities made from the richness of the inherent diversity of their cultures. This in-between for Sebbar signifies a meeting point of cultures, notions of difference, exile, history, and identity: "[My books] are the sign, the signs of my crossed history, of a racially mixed [woman], obsessed by her route and crooked paths, obsessed by the surrealist encounter with the Other and of the Same, by the intersection of nature and the lyric of the earth and of the city, of the science of the skin, of tradition and of modernity, of the East and the West."[9]

In her *Shérazade* trilogy, as in most of her novels, Sebbar's characters are without a country. They follow maps and paths across cultures, along highways, through towns, cities, and over oceans, rhizomatically constructing their identities. Shérazade's identity is the product of a series of diverse journeys and experiences. Sebbar's first volume of the trilogy, *Shérazade: Dix-sept ans, brune, frisée les yeux verts,* begins at the beginning of a journey that takes her heroine across Paris. The second volume, *Les carnets de Shérazade,* follows the young woman across France on a seven-day journey in the cab of a truck with Gilles, a French truck driver who himself incarnates a perfect French stereotype. In the last novel, *Le fou de Shérazade,* Shérazade sets out for Algeria, but ends up in Lebanon and Israel, where she risks her life in her pursuit of self-knowledge and her Arab heritage. Although she is constantly confronted with unstable environments where she negotiates her identity and often her life, Shérazade never loses her focus on her true quest—to *become* in the margins of a stereotype, to embrace her own individuality. At no time does she leave her Third Space, even though her identity and place in the world (regardless of the country in which she travels) constantly are questioned. The young Beur heroine always finds her freedom on the peripheries of the established norm, as an anomal. She lives under her own conditions and on her own terms; entering her true becoming is something she finally achieves in the last novel, *Le fou de Shérazade.*

The First Space: Reconciling with Orientalism and the Colonial Legacy

Shérazade, like all sons and daughters of Maghrebian immigrants in France (or the Beur generation, as these children call themselves), inherit what Azouz Begag and Abdellatif Chaouite call "a cultural myth." This myth is fabricated from "several morsels or reminiscences of their origins; some are stereotyped images and some are creolized" from the world of their parents and the past.[10] It is a world of ambiguity for these adolescents, who consider their parents' world as both a site of cultural identity and an unbearable weight of difference that makes it impossible to assimilate and to be accepted as French citizens among their French peers. Therefore, the Beur finds him or herself caught in the middle of a battle of identity: hold on to former traditions that evoke some semblance of cultural identity but that will only hinder acceptance by your French milieu, or deny any ties with your parents' world and thereby cut yourself off from your former history, people, and country. It is the indecision caused by these two conflicting realities that marginalizes this young generation. These children feel French, yet it is French society that has relegated them to the spatial peripheries of the everyday Beur reality of HLM ghettos, second-rate schools, and juvenile detention centers.

In the first volume of Sebbar's trilogy, her heroine is caught in this marginal identity. She is pulled between memories of her grandfather and Algeria, and the reality of everyday life as a child of immigrant parents. Such memories of her parentage come to mind in her day-to-day routine and through the people who she sometimes meets in the neighborhood. One such person is an Arab vagabond with "his blanket folded over his shoulder like a carpet seller and his bottle of Evian water in his hand." This dejected man washes his feet before prayers (a Muslim ritual), "just like her grandfather did," only the vagabond uses the "Evian water, under the bridge, near a Metro station" (145–46). These memory associations, as I term them, demonstrate a link to her parentage and heritage, yet at the same time the resulting otherness brought out through them also constantly alludes to the isolation of France's marginalized Arab population. By juxtaposing the old, solitary Arab man who, although destitute, continues to maintain his homeland's rituals alongside the constant Frenchness of the world in which he must live (the Paris streets, the Metro, Evian water), Sebbar calls attention to the situation of immigrants and their children, who find themselves caught between Western and Arab traditions. The instability of the Beur's life, however, is not only caused by the fragmented past evoked by their immigrant parents, it is also brought about by colonial stereotypes that still persist in France and throughout the West. Mysticism, the veiled woman, paintings by Delacroix and Fromentin, and Orientalist texts by Gautier and Loti offer a panoply of Oriental stereotypes that constantly pop up to hinder Shérazade's efforts to create her own identity.

The author's heroine is both intrigued and repulsed by these Oriental stereotypes, but realizes also that they play an important role in her life. Her own name, Shérazade, is an Oriental label. It is a diminutive of the longer name Shéhérazade, given to the famous princess of *A Thousand and One Nights,* who bargained for her life by telling an endless tale to her captor. Therefore, the name of Sebbar's heroine becomes a constant site of intrigue. On the one hand she must defend it when confronted by Arabs who ridicule its Frenchified pronunciation; on the other hand, she must shirk off the exotic and mystic connotations it evokes for the French. On the first page of the first volume, Sebbar describes a scene in which her heroine must defend not only her Beur identity but also the "realness" of her name when questioned by Julien Desrosiers, a Frenchman, who is immediately enamored by the exoticism that the young girl's image evokes. For Julien, Shérazade serves to vivify his Orientalist fantasy, fondly recalling his *pied-noir*[11] youth spent in Oran before the revolution:

> "Your name's really Sherazade?"
> "Yes."
> "Really? It's . . . it's so . . . How can I put it? "You know who Scheherazade was?"
> "Yes."
> "And that doesn't mean anything to you?"
> "No."
> "You think you can be called Sherazade, just like that? . . ."
> "No idea."

He looked at her, standing at the other side of the high, round counter at the fast-food [restaurant], unable to believe his eyes.

"And why not Aziyadé?"

"Who's that?"

"A beautiful Turkish woman from Istanbul who Pierre Loti was in love with, a hundred years ago."

"Pierre Loti I've heard of. Not Aziyadé."

"He dressed as a Turk and learned the Turkish language for her sake. He even went to live in the poor district of Istanbul to see her in secret. Aziyadé belonged to the harem of an old Turk. She was a young Circassian slave, converted to Islam."

"Why are you telling me about this woman? She's got nothing to do with me."

"She had green eyes, like you." (1-2)

As exemplified here, Shérazade's name throughout the course of the three novels is a constant site of contention for the young woman. It becomes both a name of pride when she is among French people (because it marks her ethnic Algerianness and thus, difference), and shame when among Arabs who remind her its beauty was lost by its Frenchification. Such Frenchification, she explains, was an oversight. But, as she realizes in the following scene from *Le fou de Shérazade,* this small manipulation of her name further isolates her from what she most wants to discover: the Algerian world of her parents. France has conquered her difference. Using the simple notion of a name, Sebbar alludes to the power the former colonizer continues to exercise over its immigrant population, those who were most victimized by the colonial legacy:

"Scheherazade?"

"Yes," said Sherazade.

"But why do you pronounce it the French way? You lose the most elegant syllable, the one the most Oriental. . . . "

Sherazade looks at the old woman, stupefied.

> No one had ever talked to her like that about her name, about the lost syllable. . . .
>
> "The French clerk simplified it on the papers. My father didn't say anything; he's a foreigner, and my mother too."
> (164)

For Julien Desrosiers (who eventually becomes Shérazade's lover), his Orientalist fantasies become a reality, reincarnated through the young Beur woman's name and body. He is fascinated by her green eyes and dark skin. She fits the perfect ideal of the Maghrebian woman he views as perfection: voluptuous, dark, mysterious, much like the women depicted in the Orientalist paintings of Delacroix, Matisse, and Ingres. Each gesture Shérazade makes, each breath she inhales, reminds Julien of this mythic, Orientalist past he sadly regards as decomposing in the dust of colonial history (*Missing*, 8-9).

Like Shérazade, Julien is also a victim of the past and of the colonial stereotypes that persist in France. He is engulfed by his own *pied-noir* tradition and the images of the colonial era he views as unfortunately fading in the wake of modernity and capricious French culture. Like Shérazade, Julien seeks to mediate the duality of his own identity. He constantly tries to reconcile his Algerian past with the modern world of Paris in which he feels isolated. Julien sees in Shérazade his link with colonial history. She is a means by which to visualize his nostalgic fantasies and mold his modern ideal of the *odalisque arabe*. Instead of a paint brush, reminiscent of Fromentin's subtlety, Julien uses his camera, taking image after image of Shérazade posed in Orientalized scenes.

Shérazade plays Julien's game for only a short time. She quickly realizes that his Oriental reincarnations of her are just another form of entrapment. Like the hermetically sealed French stereotypes and Julien's attempts to project her into a prefabricated exotic mold, the photographs hinder her identity quest. The photos neither represent who she really is nor the ideal she seeks for her own identity.

The young woman realizes that she must break this eroticized image in order to free herself from Julien's space and find one of her own making. As she frantically tears the photos off the walls of his apartment, she exclaims, "I'm sick to death of seeing my mug everywhere, you understand. . . . you don't need me in the flesh after all." The photos are meticulously shredded and thrown into "the waste-paper basket which she went to empty in the rubbish chute and started again. The photographic paper was best quality, thick and hard to cut. Sherazade continued till the very last pictures were disposed of " (169-70).

Although this prefabricated identity is both physically and metaphorically "thick and hard" Shérazade must destroy it if she hopes to continue on her quest of self-knowledge. Julien is an eternal reminder of the identity she could have if she were to let him take control of her destiny—an identity like those of the former harem odalisques of the nineteenth century who were mute, passive, seductive, and colonized. Leïla Sebbar creates Julien Desrosiers in order to evoke and condemn the Oriental myth that the Western world has upheld for so long. As Edward Said remarks, this myth has been contained in the postcolonial Western rhetoric of our era. This neocolonial discourse maintains and continues to perpetuate the old tendency of exploiting the Oriental world. The Orient essentially becomes a "standardization," a "cultural stereotyping," therefore intensifying "the hold of the nineteenth-century academic and imaginative demonology of 'the mysterious Orient.'"[12] The popular perception, maintained in the nineteenth century, that the Orient was a world weaker and inferior (in all aspects, including economic and social) to that of the West, persists today. These perceptions have paved the way for the Juliens of the West to uphold political doctrines that are still riddled with colonial pretexts assuring the continuation of neocolonial attitudes and the continued exploitation of Oriental exoticism and mysticism. These perceptions have been molded into idioms in the West, forging a "layer of doctrine about the Orient . . . [that] was fashioned out of the experiences of many Europeans, all of them converging upon such essential aspects of the Orient as the Oriental character, Oriental despotism, Oriental sensuality, and the like."[13]

Shérazade and many of her friends realize that to break the Orientalist stereotyped mold means eroding a Western tradition more than 200 years old. However, condemning France's love affair with the Oriental stereotype is often presented as a game for Sebbar's heroines: "[Shérazade's friend] France, who came from Martinique, was always acting the Hollywood heroine from bush, jungle and tropics, revised and improved on to suit her whims as a half-caste trying to charm Paris, while spitting with disgust, Rasta fashion, on Babylon, the corrupting, moribund West of the Whites" (128). It is also interesting to note Sebbar's choice of names for her protagonists. Choosing France as a name for the intrepid young woman from Martinique further subverts a codified colonial image of the erotic black diva of the jungle. Although named after the former imperialist country, France amuses herself by playing up and, subsequently, throwing her eroticism back in the faces of the French. Choosing, at times, to play this eroticized persona, not once does she allow the image to dictate her place in Parisian society.

Breaking the Oriental tradition for Sebbar's young characters often becomes dangerous. Struggling against the Oriental identity presented at each *soirée française* they attend often entails more than denial of a stereotype. The exotic image that these young women evoke for their white French peers is deeply ingrained in the Parisian demimonde of haute couture and therefore familiar. As African or mulatto models for high-fashion magazines, these young women always provide amusement and are attractive additions to any party. Unfortunately, it is only this Oriental appeal that gives Shérazade and her friends access to the white French world. Even more disturbing is the fact that access for these young women is assured only by paying a price—and that price often is life threatening. In many scenes throughout her novels, Sebbar exposes the violence inherent in the Beur culture. Her heroines constantly are caught up in a world of exploitation, drugs, pornography, theft, and racism, as Sebbar acutely portrays in the chapter titled "Jungle" in the first volume in the Shérazade series.[14] Between playing the game and physical violence there is only a very thin line, on which Shérazade and her friends consistently walk. When Zouzou, Shérazade's mulatto friend, signs the young women up with a photographer for some daring photo shoots, violence and exploitation become dangerous realities:

> "Right, let's go!" said the photographer patting her on the behind. "To work." Zouzou put on a leopard outfit consisting of split shorts and a top that barely covered her breasts. She had on red stockings that the photographer asked her to take off, "I prefer legs." Her belt allowed her, like France and Sherazade, to hide her pistol. . . . "You're fantastic. Jungle and virgin forest scenes are very popular at the moment. . . . We ought to have a panther as well. . . . " Wait, I've got an idea, each of you take a sub-machine-gun, like guerrillas. . . . It's going to be fabulous. Well, this is what you do, first you kiss on the lips, you can pretend, as soon as I say "Now" you change partners as if you were dancing in a nightclub, there really are discos just for women—and then you lie down one on top of the other in turn, it's quite simple. But see that your tits and bums are visible, you mustn't be prudish. . . . I've paid you. . . . Well, shit, can we start?" They were standing in front of him, holding their pistols. (166-67).

This passage provides an extreme, but accurate, picture of what young Beur women must endure to be accepted into French culture. Each woman in Sebbar's novels is, in her way, a *lutteuse*—a fighter—who must find a way to destroy the prefabricated Oriental identity fashioned in the Parisian demimonde. In place of this overdetermined identity, young Beur women seek to establish their own individuality. This is attempted by weaving together the threads of the past and present, as well as French and Maghrebian cultures, in order to build a future somewhere in the middle of these oppositional worlds. In the case of young Algerians, they arrived early in infancy and have been, therefore, scholastically formed in the French system. They speak French without an accent and most do not have a grasp of their native Arabic or Berber. Yet, they still insist on saying, "I am Algerian." [15]

To counter Shérazade's experiences of being exploited as an Orientalized object in the French fashion world, Sebbar offers several female characters as role models who have resisted the temptation of playing on the Oriental ideal in order to gain access to white French social circles. From Esther, an African journalist exiled in Paris, to Aurore, a successful computer technician who befriends Shérazade in the second novel, Sebbar makes it known that immigrant women can beat the odds and provide examples of what a young Beur woman should aspire to. Sebbar's women have forged their own identities, regardless of the seemingly impossible fixity of Western stereotypes inflicted on them. Esther and Aurore incarnate the becoming-woman of all young Beur women like Shérazade. Her meeting with Esther in the first volume of Sebbar's trilogy aids the heroine in making her final decision to undertake a journey of exploration—to find other possibilities of identity. Shérazade immediately embarks on a quest away from all Orientalist ideals, committing herself to learn more of her family's history and Algerian heritage. She realizes that she must find a way to bind together her Algerian past with her Parisian cosmopolitanism. Therefore, she leaves her parents' apartment in the immigrant HLM ghetto to explore her heritage and her history.

Unfortunately, as Shérazade discovers in the subsequent novels of the trilogy, locating lost Arab identity in Algeria and in other Arab countries is almost impossible. She quickly learns that it is out of the question to wander alone, unveiled, and freely in societies whose Islamic traditions dictate that women should be sequestered and hidden away. Ironically, it is the Western half of her identity that places her in danger. In the third volume of Sebbar's trilogy,

Shérazade begins her journey in Beirut, where she finds that she is marginalized, isolated, and condemned as a Western woman by Lebanese soldiers for her loose morals and high ideals of equality.

> They sneer:
> "You expect us to think you're Arab?"
> As the men carry her away to their camp, Shérazade says she
> is Arab, like them, that she was born in Algeria.
> "You can say what you like, we won't believe you." (*Fou*, 18)

Defending her Arab heritage in hope of being accepted as a sister to her Arab brothers is once again hindered by her French nationality. Her journey to the Middle East dashes her hopes of ever being integrated into her parents' culture. In Palestine, where she is taken hostage, she finally understands that to be totally Arab she must give up everything French in her life. That would mean that books, education, and her fascination with Oriental history would have to be forgotten. The heroine realizes that even study of her own Arab history has been accomplished in the French language. Her cherished books by famous Arab authors and poets are translated French versions of the original Arabic texts. Moreover, she finds herself often defending her French education and knowledge of Arab culture in front of the very people she wishes would include her. The impossibility of acceptance is most acutely felt by the heroine when she is taken as a hostage by Palestinian terrorists (in the last volume of the trilogy) and forced to burn the books she has in her knapsack. The poet Adonis and Ibn Khaldun, an Arab philosopher of the Middle Ages, are unknown to and ridiculed by her captors. "Let me have my books," Shérazade pleads with her captors. But her cries fall on deaf ears as the leader of the terrorists lights a fire and throws her books on the pyre (33-35).

As Shérazade spends more and more time as a captive of her Arab brothers, her need to be accepted diminishes. When she is set free she gravitates toward someone like herself, who is also seeking to build a bridge between Arab and French worlds. Jaffar also has come to Lebanon from France to seek out his brothers. He tells her, "I came to Lebanon for my Palestinian brothers. Tomorrow I'm going to go to a refugee camp on the border" (169). However, like Shérazade, he is rejected both for his name, which seems too exotic, and for his Frenchified accent and strange manner of speaking Arabic:

> "Jaffar! He's named Jaffar! He was born in France . . . " The militiamen laugh, slap each other on the back, and look at Jaffar. Jaffar answers their questions in Arabic; they sneer:
> "A vizier who doesn't know how to speak the language of his caliph. What language are you speaking, Jaffar? What bastard, son of a whore language? The Arabic of Africa . . . bastardized into French Arabic. . . . Here, you learn our language, the only language. . . . "
> [In Jaffar's pocket they find a book.] [The militiaman] takes it out and scrutinizes it. He reads the title, written in Arabic, out loud: *Nedjmette,* he doesn't read the title written in roman letters: *Nedjma.* . . . The militiaman skims the book, examines it as if he's going to find a coded message; he asks Jaffar in Arabic:
> "Is this a French book?"
> "It's a book written in French."
> "And this title is in Arabic? Was it written in Arabic first?"
> [A second militiaman asks:] "What's the name of the author, is it a Frenchman?"
> "It's Kateb Yacine, he's an Algerian," said Jaffar, "an Algerian."
> "He doesn't write in Arabic?" asks the other militiaman, turning the book over and over.
> "No." Says Jaffar, "He wrote *Nedjma* in French."
> "He's a turncoat, . . . that's it. Give it a rest."
> Jaffar seizes the book from the militiaman, and says in French: "Kateb Yacine says go to hell, *Nedjma* also, and I'll tell you to go to hell too." He puts *Nedjma* back in the left inside

pocket of his coat and places his hand on his heart to calm himself. He refuses to speak anymore. (170-72).

Shérazade and Jaffar both find that their cross-fertilized Parisian cosmopolitanism has produced a Beur identity that no longer may be represented by a unique and singular heritage. Beur culture sets them apart from other nationalities because of this "plurality, [and] fruitful hybridization . . . [that results] from a painful duality, a problematic allegiance, a fragmentation of the self, a tearing apart." Beurs are pulled both by a need to "withdraw into themselves while at the same time revealing the self to the outside world as a means of establishing their own points of reference."[16] These reference points, as Shérazade and Jaffar realize, may only be created through a multiplicity of connections and not by favoring one language, culture, or tradition over another.

By placing Shérazade face to face with her Arab heritage, Sebbar forces all young Beur women and men to take a long, hard look at their past—a past that has been too romanticized and too mythical to hold any real value for them in the present. Shérazade learns, as she makes her way across Lebanon and into Israel, that her true identity is a synthesis of both French and Arab worlds. In any world other than her hybridized one she will always be considered a foreigner. In fact it is her original point of departure, the Paris streets, where Shérazade finds her true identity and where Beur culture in general has recognized its roots.

Shérazade learns that negotiating her heritage and shrugging off Orientalist stereotypes are only the first steps she must take to deterritorialize and enter her true becoming-woman. Her journey is "neither tourism or emigration" but a constant journey. It is also not the beginning of "an exile, but rather a political act, a gesture of solidarity, and an historical event."[17] Shérazade's actions reflect a larger feminine communitarian project. They are done as acts of solidarity with all young Beur women who are trying to mix their past, present, and future in a cultural space of active agency in which they may make their own way.

Dialogue with the Second Space

The Second Space promotes Western cultural theories that have become popular in our postcolonial era. These theories, although recognizing difference as a positive trait of multiculturalism, nevertheless continue to marginalize the Other by only allowing him or her to enjoy subjectivity in terms of difference. If difference is perceived only in these terms it becomes nothing more than "an object of representation always in relation to a conceived identity, a judged analogy, an imagined opposition or a perceived similitude."[18] Therefore, the Other remains stagnant, caught in the fixity of difference, still viewed as being in opposition to the West and its cultural values, history, and traditions. Although some respect is shown for ethnic difference in Western society, cultural theorists argue that this respect often does more harm than good by trapping those of nonwhite European origins in an-Other space, a space of containment where, according to Bhabha, "the Other is cited, quoted, framed, illuminated, encased in the shot/reverse-shot strategy of a serial enlightenment." Therefore, the Other's narratives, as well as the cultural politics that surround them, become the only defining factor of his or her identity. Difference "becomes the closed circle of interpretation" in which the Other loses his or her power to signify, "to negate, to initiate . . . historic desire, to establish [his or her] own institutional . . . discourse."[19]

The status of different applied to ethnic communities in France has made the isolation of the immigrant population and of their Beur children a familiar reality. France's HLMS and ZUPS,[20] which during the 1960s were supposed to furnish affordable lodgings for all (both for immigrants and the French working class), have in recent years become the ghettos of the primarily North African (most significantly, Algerian), unemployed population of urban communities: "opinion affirms it, statistics confirm it: *immigrant* means first of all Algerian."[21] It is the Algerian who incarnates more than any immigrant group the idea of "immigrant" in France. The Algerian-French population is held to be at the root of problems such as juvenile delinquency, unemployment, and excessive high school dropout rates, and is condemned for the general degradation of the French social fabric. The French also regard with disdain Algerian immigrants and their descendants because they are constant reminders of the Algerian war of independence and France's humiliating defeat. This historic resentment, in turn, manifests in full-blown contemporary xenophobia.[22]

For Sebbar's heroine, Shérazade, the marginalized status of delinquency and truancy is further solidified by French males who continuously insist on casting her in roles that further ingrain this delinquent stereotype into accepted normalcy. It is the idea of difference, and therefore opposition, that assures the continuation of the stereotype. When she is offered her first role as Zina (Arabic for "pretty") in a film by a director friend of Julien's, Shérazade almost falls into a trap. The director wants her to live up to the delinquent role designed by French society, wherein she will meet his expectations of an immigrant "gang leader, rebel, poet, unruly, adept with a knife, expert at karate (like his first prostitute heroine), fearless, a fugitive from ZUPs, hanging around housing estates, basements, underground carparks, wandering the streets, as illusive and frightening as a war-leader" (236).

Sebbar's scene draws attention to a crucial element in Beur and immigrant communities: the West continues to write and maintain history according to its parameters therefore granting the Other within its borders little voice with which to state his or her own versions of identity, history, and culture. By ghettoizing the Other, the West succeeds in maintaining stereotypes of alterity associated with Maghrebian cultures. Ghettoization is convenient for French culture because it easily continues the perceived orderliness of the colonial world (which means the maintenance of strict racial barriers), rather than confronting the uncertainty surrounding equality and acceptance of difference as a positive feature of multicultural cosmopolitanism. Sealing the Other in his or her difference on the outside of French culture renders him or her mute and weak. Jean

Bernabé, Patrick Chamoiseau, and Raphael Confiant express to those of the marginalized populations of Western society the necessity of shrugging off the state of dependence generated by this stereotype of containment. The authors call on the formerly colonized diaspora to disinherit this "burden" and to fashion new parameters for their situation in the postcolonial Western world:

> We have seen the world through a filter of Western values, and our foundation was "exoticized" by the French vision we had to adopt. A terrible condition is that to perceive one's interior architecture, one's world, the instances of his days, his own values, through the gaze of the Other. Over determined throughout; in history, in thought, in every day life, in ideas .... In a trap of cultural dependence, of political dependence, of economic dependence, we have been deported from ourselves at each step in our scriptural history. This has determined our writing for the Other a borrowed writing, anchored in French values . . . and which, despite certain positive aspects, has done nothing in our spirits except to maintain the domination of an outside [force].[23]

Shérazade succeeds in tearing down the Western walls and the legacy of dependence that have hemmed her in. She does this by first fleeing from the filmmaker's set and Julien Desrosiers. Freed of their stereotypes of containment, she embarks on a journey across France, a journey she meticulously chronicles in a week-long journey in the second volume of Sebbar's trilogy. *Les carnets de Shéraɀade* is thus a rewriting, or reinscription, of Shérazade's own accounts as a young Beur on the road in France, and the people she meets, mixed with a critique of French Orientalized conceptions of Maghrebian women (she visits numerous museums across France filled with Orientalist paintings to research her opinions). Her journey leads her down a path of self-knowledge and understanding that she faithfully records in her notebooks.

Shérazade's nomadic adventure in *Les carnets* is (not by her own choice) something haphazard. She never leaves the borders of France, but simply criss-crosses the country in the company of the truck driver Gilles, who, enamored by her intriguing personality and her "difference," takes her with him from Marseilles to Paris, stopping many times along the way. What seems like a whimsical journey is in fact meticulously planned by the heroine. Her route is the exact itinerary of the famous 1983 Marche des Beurs that began in Marseilles and continued through Lyon, Strasbourg, Lille, and finally ended in Paris. The Beurs' pilgrimage was one of their first organized movements and definitively solidified their identity, creating what is now known as the Beur Nation. In her notebook Shérazade has scrupulously marked the names of these important places on a map. She keeps track of them constantly, learning by heart the "names along the line that she draws all the way to Paris, with a detour toward the east to Mulhouse, Strasbourg, Metz, Charleville-Mézières, and toward the north, Lille, Roubaix, Tourcoing. Between these towns, hamlets, and villages, are the small towns she notes just because she likes the names" (27).

By retracing these young people's steps she is writing down her history as well as theirs for the first time. Her planned itinerary changes the entire perception of her identity. She is not a *fugeuse*— a runaway—as the French media so enjoy depicting young Maghrebian women whom "sociologists seek to study by transforming them into statistics."[24] Rather, Shérazade is a young woman in full control of her journey, her selfhood, and her identity. By writing her own story and planning her own destiny she is breaking the Western stereotype of delinquency and truancy that has plagued the Beur children. Shérazade is not wandering aimlessly, seeking to run away from an overbearing father who threatens to send her back to Algeria to be married (as French journalists tend to sensationalize), but someone who follows her free will.[25] She is also setting down a new discourse for young women who have had no role as speaking subjects either in history or in the French media. It is now Shérazade who does all the talking and instructing. Providing an ironic twist to her *Thousand and One Nights* namesake, Shérazade takes control, freely telling her stories as a way to keep Gilles and her readers captive in exchange for free passage while on her Beur journey.

Traveling with Gilles, telling her stories, writing in her diary, all help the young protagonist to trace a map to a new identity. She deterritorializes to new encounters and experiences. The importance of tracing this map of identity lies in the fact that it not only is a personal quest, but also one that can be "adapted to any kind of mounting, reworked by an individual, group, or social formation. It can be drawn on a wall, conceived of as a work of art, constructed as a political action or as a meditation." It is a "rhizome . . . that . . . always has multiple entryways."[26]

The young Beur woman's map permits stops and entryways to self-discovery. Each stop she makes on her journey allows her to either encounter someone new or find someone she has met before. All of Leïla Sebbar's novels are interconnected and the *Shérazade* trilogy is no exception. Her heroines and heroes make appearances in multiple places in all of her books, affording readers the opportunity to trace their own maps through adolescent French and Beur cultures. For example Basile, introduced in *Shérazade: Dix-sept ans, brune, frisée, les yeux verts* (volume one of the trilogy), is Shérazade's intrepid friend from Guadeloupe. He is a member of a militant terrorist group and one of her comrades in the Parisian *squat* (dilapidated apartment) they share in the first volume. Basile resurfaces in *Les carnets de Shérazade* and *Le fou de Shérazade* (volumes two and three, respectively) and, like Shérazade, transforms, changing his identity at will. In *Les carnets*, Shérazade meets him in Nantes, where he "no longer champions the rights of the poor, immigrants and the oppressed of all colors . . . who still want to be slaves . . . Now, he says . . . 'I'm a tropical-dandy' and he talked about music and style" (96). In the last volume of the trilogy, *Le fou*, Sebbar's heroine encounters Basile in Jerusalem, where he is conducting research for a book on the Falashas, a black Jewish tribe from Africa.

Like Shérazade, Basile demonstrates his versatile personality, the ease with which he transforms his identity, and his ability to migrate between cultures and nationalities. Such transformations and movements allow Basile, Shérazade, and their friends to map new roads to a positive Beur identity. In other words, no one trait or stereotype holds Sebbar's characters; they are free to transform until they find the true individuality they seek. Shérazade never wavers from her map and the unwritten plan she seems so bent on following to the letter, even when it means risking her life. Her perseverance, daring, and constant good fortune provide endless intrigue for Gilles, her friendly chauffeur and "compagnon de route" in *Les carnets:*

> "You see," says Gilles, "one thinks that you're down and out on the docks of Nantes, that horrible things are going to come your way, and all of a sudden you meet Basile, a friend from Paris who hasn't a damn thing to do in Nantes. You see. . . ."
>
> "But it's true," screams Sherazade. . . . "It's true. I can't tell you anything. You never believe me."
>
> "Yeah, I believe you. But I also realize . . ."
>
> "What? I can run into Basile in Nantes, can't I?"
>
> "The first person [you meet] in a deserted port town is a friend from Paris?"
>
> "You'd rather it had been a savage, tattooed dockworker . . . who kidnapped me . . . ?"
>
> "Kidnapped? Not exactly."
>
> "You always want all the guys to . . . "
>
> "Not all," says Gilles, "but some, yes. A girl like you, alone, on the road, in places where we don't see women, . . . surely."
>
> "That's happened to me," cuts in Sherazade, "but not this time . . . Are you happy? That was Basile. It's true."
>
> "I think you're blessed with good luck. That's possible, isn't it? . . . that girls are blessed with good luck?" (94–95)

Shérazade's risk taking and good fortune overturn the contained stereotype French culture has provided her. The new path she forges for herself, and for all those of the Beur culture of contemporary France, in time will break the vicious neocolonial circle Sebbar describes in her novels. Her heroine realizes that part of breaking this circle means manipulating French contemporary culture to recognize the plight of the Beurs. The young girl is aware of the French media's habitual stereotyping of those of nonwhite French communities. Therefore, it is the media and its various forms—written, audio, and visual—that she decides to use throughout the three novels to create her own Beur image. Beur language and identity are very audiovisual, creating a bicultural world that reflects both French and Arab cultures.[27] The diversity of her protagonist's biculturality is evidenced throughout Sebbar's trilogy.[28] One example of this biculturality is the heroine's ease with language. Shérazade speaks French so well that when Gilles first meets her he isn't really sure if she's "Spanish, naturalized Indian," or "perhaps Lebanese." He finally comes to the conclusion that "over there [in North Africa] Christian and Muslims were mistaken for each other, they all resemble each other, like Jews and Arabs in Tunisia and Morocco; that's what they often told him. He didn't know anything about her. That bizarre name, he didn't know any girls called that. . . . The girl spoke French as well as he, maybe she's French after all, there are French people who don't exactly have a French look" (47).

Conversely, although seemingly "so French," Sebbar's heroine also demonstrates a facility for Arabic on numerous occasions. The Arabic language provides a bridge between herself and those of her parents' community—the representations of a past she seeks to know more about. Unlike many Beurs who do not demonstrate any facility with Arabic, Shérazade has cultivated her knowledge and her native accent to perfection (or at least she thinks this is the case; however, she soon finds that once in an Arabic-speaking country she is treated as an outsider for her substandard pronunciation of the language). Her knowledge of Arabic helps others of the immigrant community to face pain, loss, and the isolation they feel in their country of exile. An example of bridging the gap between

Beur adolescents and their immigrant parents is presented when Shérazade elects to seek out the mother of her friend Farid, recently killed in a Parisian prison. Giving an account of the boy's death in Arabic to his mother, Shérazade forges a link between the mother and her son, mediated across the foreign French space (151-52). The young woman discovers that language may also provide a means by which to mediate her own identity. Communication, whether in French or in Arabic, allows her to move freely across France and to other countries and places. Messages in a bicultural coded language are an integral part of the very verbal aspect of Beur identity. Sebbar's heroine receives messages from Julien (ironically under the code name Mille et une nuits) through the French journal, *Libération*. While on the move Shérazade sends messages via Radio Beur to her sister and family.

The radio and the media play a particularly important role in the mediation of the Beurs' biculturality; one might say they form a rhizome of cultural connections. In *Les carnets* the radio is a constant topic of discussion for Shérazade and Gilles. For the Frenchman it is a link to his Frenchness and a means with which to battle the loneliness of his life on the road: "He spends most of the time flipping from one radio channel to another, certainly in the afternoons, up to the hour of *Grosses têtes* . . . which makes him laugh" (49). For Shérazade, musical communication and her love of music provide a rich source of diversity, from Jessye Norman, the American black opera star, who she knows personally, to Pierre Bachelet, "who she heard constantly in the brasserie where she worked in Marseilles" (53). Moreover, music and the radio become a topic through which Gilles and his companion negotiate their cultural differences. The radio, in particular, represents a site of mediation between French and Beur identity; however, it is also a constant source of argument for the two protagonists. The radio at once presents typical French programs, which Gilles finds amusing, and popular songs, which Shérazade enjoys. Gilles's programs are those popular with stereotypical French males: variety shows and those featuring shows like *Grosses têtes* and media personalities like Jane

Birkin. These programs offer him diversions from the monotony of his daily driving. Shérazade, on the other hand, is drawn to pop rock and the multiculturality of Radio Beur as her source of music. Despite constant conflicts centered around the radio as they make their way across France, both the truck driver and the young woman begin to notice how many similarities they share. After all, Gilles confesses, he too was born "somewhere else"—on the Isle de Ré. They begin to acknowledge their similarities through long conversations:

> "Do you have any bread?" asks Sherazade. "I like bread with nothing on it."
>
> "I do too," replies Gilles. "My grandfather on my mom's side was a baker. . . . If the bakery hadn't been sold I would have been a baker, a famous baker like those in Paris you know them?"
>
> "No." Says Sherazade. "In Paris I eat McDonald's hamburger buns . . . they're not that great."
>
> Gilles talks with his mouth full. He eats a second Roquefort sandwich and drinks from a bottle of island wine.
>
> . . .
>
> "Grandfather spoke of the war. . . . He always said, . . . 'It's thanks to God and bread that I came back whole and alive.' At his place, before cutting bread, we crossed it. . . . "
>
> Sherazade replies, "We don't throw bread away at my house either. It's sacred. If we see a crust on the ground, we pick it up, kiss it, and put it somewhere at eye level, for the birds."
> (48-49)

Shérazade uses not only the radio and the newspaper to pass news of herself, but photos as well. The importance of photography, and capturing images is particularly evident in *Le fou de Shérazade*. Photos and film become sites of manipulation for Shérazade's own use as well as for those who seek to place her in a convenient stereotype. In them she is both star and victim. In the third volume of Sebbar's trilogy, Julien's film aspirations take on gigantesque proportions. With his film director friend (whose name is never mentioned), they "recolonize" Shérazade's HLM neighborhood, creating a perfect soundstage for their neo-Orientalist film. Julien's script calls for an authentic Algerian olive tree, which the director and his team have uprooted and flown in from Algeria. The tree is replanted in the middle of the HLM's central square. Sebbar uses the tree as a symbol for the *déracinement,* the uprooting—of all Maghrebian immigrants and their children. It alone represents the past and the present; past colonial invasions and new, neocolonial conceptions. In addition to the appropriated olive tree used as a backdrop for the re-creation of real-life scenes of Algeria, Julien's film includes incredible publicity in the form of posters and photos. He hopes these images will pave the way for Shérazade's debut as an Arab film star. Each poster reifies an Orientalized image of the self-contained stereotypes mentioned earlier that France has fabricated for its Arab-Other, both through historical and modern-day depictions:

> Julien unfolds gigantic posters that are hung from the balconies of the first floor, the courtyard becomes a dreamlike patio: scenes of war in the Orient, mounted combat between Arab warriors, Turkish baths, odalisques. . . . There are also monumental black-and-white photos, bombed-out Beirut, American helicopters in Vietnam, Algerian *maquis,* women in the baths, and women dressing in French paintings. . . . The filmmaker looks stunned at the posters displayed around the felled-olive tree.
>
> . . .
>
> The filmmaker takes off his sunglasses, he surveys the roll that Julien takes over to the olive tree, this is the last one, an immense portrait of Sherazade:
>
> That's the girl I need . . . I've been waiting for so long, I'll pay her like a star . . . That's her, and nobody else. (30)

However, once again the heroine escapes Julien's Orientalist fantasy. She has set out on yet another quest of self-discovery and therefore is impossible to find to play the role of the heroine. In her absence, it is the young girl's family and community that fight on her behalf against the film's publicity and its "Orientalization" of their neighborhood. In a massive act of solidarity, the women of Shérazade's HLM cover the sexually revealing depictions of Shérazade and the other Maghrebian women in the film. Ironically, the coverings used are the veils from Algerian haiks which, in Algeria, are used to cover women's faces from prying eyes:

> During the night the women of the apartment building and other neighbors had resigned themselves to act against the indecency of the photographs that were displayed to all, children, men, and women. They talked with each other during the mint tea hour and made the decision to hide them in the simplest manner. Each woman went and got the veil she unfolds only on arriving in her native country, the one she keeps with the house linen, for her and her oldest daughters. The veils, large as bed sheets, covered the posters perfectly, and it took most of the night to hide the naked bodies of the women on them. (52)

Shérazade continues to elude the filmmaker and Julien. Julien leaves in order to find the girl and hopefully convince her to return to play the role he has fashioned for her. The filmmaker urges, "Go and find her, your Shérazade . . . so that maybe we can start." Julien replies, "I'm going. Right now. I know where she is" (53). Far away, on the other side of the Mediterranean, in Beirut, Shérazade's photo is serving a different purpose. As a hostage of Palestinian terrorists she is filmed on video so that, as the *chef de bande* suggests, "all over the world, from Beirut to Peking, from Tokyo to New York, from Paris to Johannesburg, from Moscow to Rabat, Algiers, and Tunis, you'll be seen on TV, star in a day" (103). Her photo is circulated in every major newspaper as her captors gleefully remark, "We'll see what France does for a French Arab . . . for a runaway girl, without papers, who thinks she's Parisian . . . We'll see"

(102). Curiously it is not political pressure from France that frees Shérazade, but her own captors, who find a better hostage and tell Shérazade, "we need your cell" (126). Neither French foreign authorities nor the French government come to Shérazade's aid. Once again Sebbar alludes to the lack of interest France demonstrates for the sons and daughters of its North African immigrants.

Once freed, Shérazade continues her exploration of Lebanon. She walks the streets of Beirut, again placing herself in danger. Ducking behind a car, she bumps into her old friend Michel. Working as a photographer, he too seeks to use her hostage image for fame and fortune back home. He tells her, "You'll see, your photos, there, in this street in the forbidden zone, a bandanna covering your eyes, your duffel bag in your hand . . . I have big plans, I'm sure no one else took those photos. . . . I'm going to send them off and make a fortune . . . I'm not asking you to agree to them, I don't give a damn" (129-30).

For Michel, it is the violence and the terror in which he sees Shérazade caught that are intriguing. The outside elements that cause the heroine's constant danger make his photos so unique because, he says, "you couldn't fabricate them, it's total surprise, reality more real than fiction" (131). Strangely, Shérazade is indifferent. The blurring of the lines between reality and fiction are, in fact, representative of her own identity. Michel's photos are just one other representation of this mélange. The role of terrorist victim and hostage in Beirut, whether real or unreal, is not, however, a true depiction of who she really is. Thus, Shérazade leaves Michel and continues on her way.

In the last few pages of Sebbar's trilogy, Shérazade finds the path away from the constant battle between reality and fiction that for so long has taken over her own identity. When she leaves Michel in the Palace de Beyrouth (an old reconverted colonial palace converted into a hotel overlooking the sea), her quest takes a new turn toward the truth. In order to protect and nurture her real self, Shérazade realizes she must face what she left behind: the world of the Beur, a world encompassing a series of identifications that reflect a positive, multicultural identity.[29]

Confronting and, subsequently, surmounting the obstacles in this Second Space of difference, Shérazade definitively assures her own identity in French society. She successfully overthrows the Oriental idealized stereotype and the "normalized" codes of Western discourse concerning difference, representation, and alterity. She detaches herself from these codes to become a subject—that is, to become the product of the knowledge she has gained abroad. Sebbar's heroine is able to reach another notion of difference, one that is a "grouping of a plurality of signs that constitute the individual part of identity."[30]

Shérazade's Becoming-Woman

Resisting Westernized stereotypes is only part of Leïla Sebbar's message to her Beur audience. Shérazade must also forge her identity as an independent woman. This, however, is something that all women must do—resist the identity that men have created for them in literature as well as in society. It is up to women to learn to consider their roles in society and culture as freed of all constraints constructed by the masculine world. As Shoshana Felman insists, they must "resist [their] woman's duty" and subsequently resist male recognition by "refusing to ground secularity as meaning, to serve as a narcissistic mirror for man and thereby to reflect back simply and unproblematically man's value."[31] As mentioned above, Leïla Sebbar's heroine resists the masculine, erotic-exotic persona Julien and other French males have constructed for her. Shérazade has equally thwarted the French stereotypes of truancy and delinquency associated with her Beur culture. However, the heroine's struggle has left her to fight a lonely battle, exiled in a space, that is thrilling yet daunting; it is a space of becoming.

The space of becoming allows one to "arrive at a correspondence of relations" that in the end always necessitates a series of

transformations. One transforms until one arrives at one's own becoming. However, such transformation does not impose a hierarchy of changes, but rather an "evolution." One forms a block of
one's own becoming, a block that runs its "own line between the
terms in play and beneath assignable relations."[32] In Sebbar's Third
Space, all terms have a possible and assignable relation to her principal character, Shérazade. It is, however, for the heroine to decide
which assignable relations will be acceptable for her becoming-
woman. Shérazade's Third Space of Culture affords her the liberty
to transform her identity many times before finally arriving at her
becoming-woman, or her true identity. As Sebbar's principal heroine travels in her multicultural space she changes her *carte d'identité*
at will, mystifying Julien and her friends:

> "You look stunning! Lovelier than Marilyn, a thousand
> times lovelier. Why don't you always dress like that?"
> "Wonderful! And what about the cops?"
> "What about the cops?"
> "Because I haven't got my forged identity card yet. I'm still
> waiting for it. Pierrot's buddies are seeing to it. My name'll be
> Rosa. Rosa Mire and I'll be eighteen, I'll be of legal age you
> understand. I'll have been born in Paris and be studying [psy-
> chology]. So now you know."
> "And your nationality?"
> "I'm Algerian."
> "But on your forged card, what'll you be?"
> "It'll be false. I'll be French." (*Missing*, 192)

For Shérazade changing identities at will enables her to negotiate
the isolation in which all Beurs feel caught when living between two
different nationalities and cultures. Out of this space of exile she
creates a new multiple persona, or a block of identities that form
her subjectivity. The women after whom she chooses to model her
new unstereotyped Self are always beautiful, strong, and intrepid.
Such famous characters as Rosa Luxemburg and Flora Tristan are

representative of strength and perseverance while also being beautiful and revolutionary.[33] Like Shérazade, these heroines lived for a cause and sought to change social and cultural perceptions of women in France and in Europe. Curiously, however, these historic women's nationalities do not prevent Sebbar's young heroine from idolizing them. The protagonist prefers their ideals and the similarity of their lives to her own, rather than their nationalities or ethnic backgrounds. For the heroine, extending herself beyond stifling burdens of culture and nationality and embracing an ideal are what is important. Shérazade admires the fact that, like herself, Rosa Luxemburg and Flora Tristan were exiled in their own countries, condemned for their own ideals, and marginalized for having fought for a cause. The name she chooses to adopt, Mire, also evokes numerous connotations that, when studied, add to the complex metaphoric character Sebbar has created in Shérazade. In French *mire* has several pertinent definitions that enhance Shérazade's personality and identity: (1) the verb *mirer* means "to target or take aim at something" *(prendre sa mire, viser)*; (2) *point de mire* means "aim" or "the targeted point"; (3) the figurative meaning of *point de mire* is "the center of attention"; (4) the technical meaning is "conduit for directing; determining a course of action, direction, or plan."

Although mentioned most often, Rosa and Flora are just two of the many famous figures after which the young heroine models her identity. Authors, politicians, military heroes, and revolutionaries representing all races, nationalities, and ethnicities: Joan of Arc, the Saracens, 'Abd al-Qādir, V. S. Naipaul, and Arthur Rimbaud and are among just some of the people Shérazade adds to her Third Space of culture, an interactive place from which she forges her new identity.[34] It is the exceptional qualities of all these people and their histories that she incorporates into her new carte d'identité.

The constant reformulation and transformation of her own identity also reflect the need to come to some sort of closure through memory and history. This need is primordial, because, for the Beur generation, "identity is necessarily linked to History and to memory; a memory destroyed and rebuilt."[35] This world of *croisements* (intersections—of histories as well as of identities) is, as Shérazade discovers, an integral part of her true becoming. In this world of croisements identity is something easily substituted, interchanged, and rearranged. Because Shérazade chooses aspects from a range of cultures, nationalities, and ethnicities, no one central point is favored over another. As Michel Laronde remarks, this point of intersection is more appropriately thought of as a site of *métissage* (cross-breeding) that marks her identity as being at the same time "*self* and being different from the other and *self* and being similar to the other."[36] In such a site, difference is not polarized. It has no opposite because it is an amalgam in which entities are transforms into an affirmation rather than a negation of identity.[37]

Instead of fighting against being different, Shérazade amplifies her difference, making it more acute than it really is. Her identity becomes a series of palimpsests—disguises on top of disguises. Not only does she adopt the name of Rosa Luxemburg, Flora Tristan, or Camille, along with their enigmatic personalities, she further transforms these names into something new, original becomings of her identity. Shérazade drops the surnames, preferring to use simply Camille or Rosa. This subverts the historic European connotations the surnames evoke and replaces them with qualities of the heroine's own identity. By adopting the first names only, Shérazade refuses to entirely appropriate a prefabricated identity, or again, to be something she is not, such as a Spartakist revolutionary or a French feminist. Like the odalisque persona of women of the Maghreb, the historic personalities she explores are only *outside* personifications, devoid of any substance other than serving her utilitarian purpose. They are simply a means to an end. Shérazade explains to Julien that a name such as Camille suggests positive identity in France while also furnishing the means to be mobile, a way to go unnoticed, or "to be imperceptible," as one passes in-between cultures. It is also both a male and female name, thus granting Shérazade even further freedom by allowing her to play not only an identity game, but a gender one as well:

> "In France my parents don't travel. For the holidays I used to go to the country with my sister, we didn't see the sea."
> "We'll go straightaway, if you like."
> "When I get my papers, the forged ones. When I'm called Rosa."
> "I prefer Shérazade."
> "I'm also called Camille. You didn't know?" (*Missing*, 193)

The French-sounding names disassociate Shérazade from her Algerianness, allowing her to slip into an identity that facilitates achieving her goals. A false identity is a means of movement to other places that Shérazade would not enjoy if she succumbed to the marginalized community of the stagnant HLM ghetto. Movement between cultures as Shérazade/Camille or Shérazade/Rosa mark points of transfer from one culture to the other: West and East, French and Algerian, Muslim and Christian.[38] However, because she oscillates between both Western and Maghrebian identities so easily, a balance is achieved without either ethnicity totally engulfing her. Shérazade aligns her identities in a series of movements a process of circulation that displace recognizable markers of difference. The act of circulating constructs a new method of discourse for those who find themselves on the margins of Western culture. As one circulates between cultural spaces "an apparatus that turns on the recognition and disavowal of racial/cultural/historical differences" is construed. This in turn marks the "creation of a space for a 'subject of peoples.'"[39]

But how does this displacement of cultural/racial/historical differences and constant transformation from one persona to another constitute a becoming-woman? What is the ultimate end in Shérazade's quest? As explained in chapter 1, becoming is a product of the communication of beings and of connections. Becoming also is always entered from a minoritarian position. To understand a true becoming one must first be Other—that is, destabilized from the established and accepted norm. Becoming-woman is a becoming par excellence because it signifies deterritorializing from a minoritarian position to a new, independent, feminine space of enunciation. This space of enunciation encompasses cultural and social levels, placing them both into one communicating world, a world in which "one has suppressed in oneself everything that prevents us from slipping between things and growing in the midst of things."[40]

Shérazade does combine everything to fit into her world. She grows from the midst of things, discovering that history, memory, her Algerian heritage, her French present, odalisque images, and her intrepidity all make up her special Beur world. It is a world that she finally realizes is possible. Sebbar demonstrates in the last few pages of the last volume of her trilogy how real the concept of the Beur Nation is and how essential it is for it to be accepted as an integral part of French culture. Unfortunately, as the author underscores in her narratives, the world of the Beurs must still be constantly negotiated. France has not yet totally accepted their role in contributing to a multicultural society. In the closing scene of *Le Fou de Shérazade* the director of Shérazade's film proclaims that he "doesn't agree with Julien on how the last scene should be shot" (201). Going against the wishes of Julien, who up to this last scene is still attempting to maintain his Orientalist vision of the world, the director states that he is "against folklore." As if to end symbolically all Orientalist representation, the director, who seems to have been won over by the Beur children of the HLM community, opts to blow up the scene—a bedroom harem in which Shérazade and the other feminine heroines of the film are languidly lying, posing as odalisques in a bombed-out Beirut mansion. In the staged scene, as if to sum up Shérazade's Oriental-French dialectical world, the patrician who owns the house tells the women, "you are as lovely as the harem odalisques, but not quite the same" (202). In other words, the actresses are similar but "not quite" good enough for a true Western Orientalist odalisque image; they fall short of fitting into their mold and, thus the "accepted" persona.

The director orchestrates a war scene. The bombs fall in realistic fanfare, killing all in make-believe carnage. Frantically looking for her, Shérazade's mother believes it to be real, "My daughter, Sherazade, you've killed her. My girl is dead. . . . Talk to me . . . .They killed you." She is haltingly convinced by Shérazade's sister that the scene is only make-believe. "Shérazade isn't dead. It's a movie . . . Your daughter is alive . . . Imma, don't cry, your daughter is alive . . . Look at her, she's not dead, Imma, Shérazade is alive, alive . . . alive!" (203). Symbolically, this scene is crucial for Sebbar's heroine and all Beur women, all of whom have suffered the neo-Orientalizing images modern France has concocted for them. Demolishing the odalisque image, Sebbar enables her heroine to realize who she really is: a young Beur woman named Shérazade living in a multicultural world.

The dialogue made possible in the Third Space of Culture is a product of all cultures and beings who are in circulation, living in exile in a world on the margins of established norms. This space is one of production—where the desire to explore cultural dimensions is achieved. It is a beyond that, as Bhabha notes, "marks progress, promises the future . . . [allowing] us to live beyond the border of our times." This space is made for a "present [that] can no longer be simply envisaged as a break or a bonding with the past and the future . . .[but] comes to be revealed for its discontinuities, it inequalities, its minorities. . . . [it is] the blasting of a monadic moment from the homogenous course of history, establishing a conception of the present as the 'time of the now.'"[41]

The Beur culture of France constructs its identity through the blasting away of the historical paradigms that have encased and sought to suppress it. Beur identity is a confrontation with a past that cannot be romanticized but must, as Sebbar attests, be painfully deciphered, picked apart, and disassembled. Writing on the borders and in the margins of this space of croisement places the author at the crossroads of a multicultural becoming, one that exists beyond all Western codified images of the Other:

> For me, fiction is the suture that is taped over the wound, the gap between two banks. I am there, at the crossroads, at last serene in my place, partly because I am a "croisée" who looks for a relation and who writes in a line, always the same, linking history to memory, to identity, to tradition, and to transmission, I want to say to the research from an ascendant and from a descendant, from a place in the history of one family, from a community, a people, in the eyes of history and the universe. It's in this fiction that I feel like a subject free (from father, mother, clan and dogma) and fortified by the charge of exile.[42]

Sebbar's characters reflect her own personal experiences of living at the crossroads of identity, ethnicity, alterity, history, memory, and culture. Shérazade enters into her true becoming-woman because she joins together all these notions that make up her identity in one environment, at one central point—a point of croisement. She forms links and connections in a Third Space that is multicultural, acentered, and racially nondetermined. These links and connections are empowering and revolutionary, placing the heroine in a role that is actively engaged in the politics and culture of two conflicting yet historically connected worlds: Algerian and French. As Deleuze and Guattari point out in *Anti-Oedipus,* there can be no revolutionary actions, "where the relations between people and groups are relations of exclusion and segregation."[43] The young women and men of the Beur Nation have realized the importance of destabilizing prefabricated stereotypes. Like Shérazade, these adolescents realize that "groups must multiply and connect in ever new ways, freeing up territorialities for the construction of new social arrangements."[44]

Epilogue

Current Themes in Francophone Feminine Texts of the Maghreb

Deterritorializing New Roles for Women
in Hajer Djilani's *Et pourtant le ciel était
bleu . . .* and Malika Mokeddem's *L'interdite*

I T HAS BEEN the goal of this book to call attention to contemporary themes of Francophone literature of the Maghreb. From 1962 to the present, authors from this region, in general, and more particularly Algeria, have distanced themselves from the revolutionary schematics of earlier works during the years 1950–1962. The contemporary body of work considered here spans the years 1980 to the present and reflects, in particular, the role of feminine authors in redefining new sociocultural and literary debates as well as legal issues in all three Maghrebian countries: Tunisia, Algeria, and Morocco. Today, when we consider the works of nonnative French authors writing in French and their place in French literary studies, it becomes obvious that this corpus not only takes to task linguistic issues, but also represents an effort to define "a space which implicates analysis and historic, economic and social reflection."[1]

The contemporary themes of particular importance to women of the Maghreb encompass feminine emancipation, both in legal and social spheres in their respective countries. These themes promote current feminine research that touches upon religious values, law, society, and culture.[2] Women's emancipation requires first and foremost the breaking away from (and of) traditional phallocratic/centric roles that have hemmed women within the confines of a traditionally male-dominated Maghreb. Such emancipation unfortunately has progressed unevenly throughout the region. In contemporary Francophone literature, the theme of deterritorializing, means venturing out of traditional boundaries to explore identity as a woman in a space of agency. Exploration is important because it promotes a new feminine social project where the historic, the sociologic, and the economic all come into play. Such a space of agency, as Gayatri Spivak suggests, deconstructs "the opposition between the private and the public" and allows women to exert "the desire to have a self and a world."[3] It is in this empowered space of exterior free agency that women change the world, instead of simply interpreting and explaining it. Contemporary Francophone women's writing seeks to not only foster reflection on fundamental theories on the condition of women in the Maghreb, but also to foment a new activism that will lead Maghrebian women to solidarity, changing their social and political condition for the better. From feminine authors, researchers, and academics of immense notoriety, such as Assia Djebar and Fatima Mernissi, to those recently entering the arena of the contemporary Maghrebian literary field, women of Tunisia, Algeria, and Morocco are striving to gain an active presence in order to shape their roles in feminine politics, literature, and history. Maghrebian women authors and intellectuals continue to stress that their identity is a complex intertextual relation, forged as women writing in French who, also, address a plurality of themes important in today's world. The ultimate objective of the contemporary feminine author of the Maghreb is to reach a site of multiculturalism accessible and relatable to all readers.

In this book we have studied works by men and women that exemplify current trends in Francophone writing of the Maghreb. In this epilogue, I would like to conclude with two recent novels that move women of the Maghreb to a supreme space of active agency.

Malika Mokeddem (Algeria, currently residing in France) and Hajer Djilani (Tunisia) explore the theme of deterritorialization and its consequences for not only their heroines, but all women of the Maghreb. Both Djilani and Mokeddem demonstrate the importance of breaking out of/from traditional boundaries to embrace a new deterritorialized space of active agency in their novels. Both novels redefine women's roles. Much like Djebar and Sebbar, Djilani and Mokeddem cultivate a deterritorialized space that does two things: first, it allows Maghrebian women to break the traditional feminized interior area of Muslim space (represented by home, veil, etc.); second, it fosters the building of a new platform of agency in public exterior space (that of politics, law, and cultural activism, thus recontextualizing previous representations of women in a number of areas).

The breaking of traditional boundaries in order to embrace what Fatima Mernissi has defined as a reappropriation of memory for women that will allow them to embrace a pure feminine essence[4] is precisely the objective of Hajer Djilani's *Et pourtant le ciel était bleu* . . . and Malika Mokeddem's *L'interdite*.[5] In both works a strong young woman doctor (Djilani's Chems, and Mokeddem's Sultana) is the central figure who must bear up against aggressive cultural mores, traditional stereotypes, loneliness, isolation, and the desperate, hostile political climates in which they are caught. The daunting events each heroine faces, not only as a doctor but also as a woman trying to survive in a very masculine theocratic environment, are compounded by her individual quest for identity, desire, freedom, and love. Even when she is often the victim of political circumstances, her quest—the uprooting of her Self from what is traditionally expected—is never abandoned. In both novels, as Sultana and Chems confront their own destinies, their individual pursuits redefine Maghrebian women's roles universally, as each woman calls to task feminine survival in a phallocentric world. Attesting to the difficulty of this survival in the opening pages of *L'interdite*, Sultana (upon returning home to her native Algeria after fifteen years of self-imposed exile), reflects on the inequalities between the sexes and on the abuse that she and all women have had to bear in her native homeland: "I had not forgotten that the boys of my country have a perturbed childhood, one that is gangrenous. I had not forgotten that their clear voices pronounce only obscenities. I had not forgotten that, from the earliest age, the *other* sex is a ghost of their desires, a confusing threat. . . . I had not forgotten that they beat dogs, that they throw stones and injure girls and women who pass by" (18; emphasis mine). Curiously, deterritorialization, and consequently the heroine's propulsion to a new, acentered space of redefinition and public agency in Mokeddem's and Djilani's works, is caused by catalysts of recent events that implicate violence and political confrontation. In Mokeddem's *L'interdite*, the current political civil strife and fundamentalist policies of the Front Islamic du Salut (FIS),[6] unfavorable to women, are the backdrop to Sultana's fight for survival in her small native village, Aïn Nekhla, in southern Algeria. In *Et Pourtant le ciel était bleu . . .*, Djilani sets her heroine, Chems, in the midst of the Gulf War. She questions what really happened on Iraqi soil and draws the attention of the reader to the death and destruction imposed on Iraqi civilians—predominately women and children—during the Gulf conflict. Djilani, through the voice of her heroine, forces her readers to consider the pointless loss of human life in Iraq, view rarely acknowledged, certainly in the West. However, her novel does not support the political and military actions of Iraq, but rather through the voice of Chems, openly condemns the whole world's political policy surrounding the Gulf conflict. It was all of humanity, she suggests, that is to blame: "For the moment, all of humanity is responsible for what I have seen and lived yesterday; some are guilty because of their silence, others by their connivance, some by their indifference, and still others by their selfishness. . . . I so need someone to convince me of the right of others to commit such butchery" (75).

It is only after confronting, and subsequently persevering over, these violent political conflicts that both women, in the final scenes of each novel, are able to reach a place of true self-knowledge, the result of a process of deterritorialization that is enriching, fulfilling, and emancipatory. Yet neither author nor heroine is able to right any of the political wrongs of their respective countries single-handedly. Moreover, the freedom granted to Chems and Sultana does not come without stipulations. Deterritorialization—a life of nomadism—condemns them both to a destiny of wandering and of *étrangeté;* their lives bizarrely skewered by strange events and people. Sultana remarks, "How can I make them understand my terror over the choice, over the rupture? . . . that my survival lies only in displacement, in migration?" (234). It is precisely this need to move, to never stop the quest for the self, that spurs these two young heroines, accomplished independent women, to question the current political situations in the Maghreb, and the Muslim world in general. What is important to Mokeddem and Djilani is how these situations compromise women's lives. Of equal importance in both novels is the *déplacement* of the feminine self as a key factor in determining feminine identity. This self-movement is a painful process because it involves confronting the past in order to look forward. Each heroine reviews, and then relegates, tradition in order to achieve her individualism—regardless of the consequences. And those consequences are a life destined to wandering in feminine flux. Both characters find that it is impossible to take root in one set system. Chems is forced to give up part of her self to Iraq, while Sultana is torn between her Algeria of the past and her France of the present. This incapacity to root one's Self in a "home" place on a more universal scale, as Mokeddem and Djilani allude, will not be attained until the women of the Maghreb, and other regions of the Muslim world, can enjoy full equality with men culturally, traditionally, sociologically, and economically.

Et pourtant le ciel était bleu . . . *:* Qui suis-je?

Hajer Djilani's first novel not only presents a woman in a strong central role but also takes up the larger political conflicts of the Gulf

War. These include dissension among Arab nations, the international politics of East and West, and the internal oppositions among the Iraqi people. The events surrounding the Gulf War are reviewed through the eyes of a woman Tunisian doctor, Chems. Unable to live with the knowledge of the ongoing suffering in Iraq in 1991, the young woman uproots herself from Tunis in order to fly to Baghdad as a member of a team of Tunisian doctors offering humanitarian medical aid. The story is told both through Chems's personal journal entries and through letters to her family. The third person voice of the author also contributes to the weaving of an intricate dialogue that reflects the personal relationships between the characters, as well as political commentary on the actions of Iraq and, more generally, on the state of politics in the Arab world. Underlying these three important textual layers are the author's subtle views on the status of Muslim women, primarily in Iraq. As she implies, it is women who bear the brunt of the horrors of war, famine, death, and poverty. In times of war, they and their children are the most vulnerable.

Chems, like the author who invents her character, does not take sides in the political conflict. Like the government of her native country, Tunisia, she remains neutral throughout the novel.[7] The young woman's sole aim is to offer her medical training as a humanitarian gesture to the people of Iraq, who are the constant targets of indiscriminate bombs and gunfire. Her direct confrontation with the war and its death and destruction force her to question the actions of humanity as a whole. Chems's desire to fathom humanity's incomprehensible actions are aligned with her own quest of self-knowledge. It is her aspiration to answer these questions that activates her decision to remain in Iraq and travel still closer to the front lines of the war, long after her Tunisian colleagues decide to abandon their efforts because of the escalating danger. Her personal quest for self-knowledge is aligned with her efforts to reconcile the absurdity of war with her own place in the world as a woman, doctor, and member of the Muslim world "as a woman and person on this earth who has seen spring from man the spark of his grandeur . . . I hope that one day the world will abolish violence . . . the death of man by man, the death of children, the death of the innocent" (265).

It is the catalyst of war, Chems's headlong flight directly into it, and her efforts to combat its destruction that jettison all the past taboos and restrictions she has been taught. She is left with a tabula rasa on which she is able to embrace a new place, acentered from what is normally acceptable. "She runs toward this place, the taboos are forgotten, the forbidden explodes like bombs" (67). It is a propulsion into an uncharted space that is both a place of horror, pain, and suffering and of self-discovery, movement, and constant flux. Here she explores her own inner self, love, and the power of loving as she is drawn toward a man she has only just met: "She is running toward the room of a man she hardly knows, she, whose parents saw each other for the first time on their wedding day" (67). Salah is an Iraqi doctor who is disdainful of war and, like Chems, seeks only the good for humanity as a whole (101). As she falls more and more in love with him, Chems realizes that she must reach a place of peace in order to love and be loved. This place lies beyond the borders of conflict and does not contain any rules or conventions. However it is a space where she and Salah must mediate their differences. Even thought they speak the same language they are worlds apart. Salah, already widowed once (his pregnant wife, Mériam, was the victim of a bomb), hesitates to again embrace the void of love, which Chems offers him. However, each realizes it is precisely this space of turmoil—of war, bombs, and destitution— that draws them together, allowing them to mediate their differences and their pasts. Chems writes in her journal that existing only for the present makes it easier to require no tradition, no past, and no sense of future in order to survive. Her path is left open for union with Salah. War and the sexual consent of the two lovers have created a new space of equilibrium in which they enjoy no boundaries and no preconditions: "If happiness exists, it tastes like this morning. . . . Mother please forgive me for the stolen taboos. I offered Salah the dearest thing I have, I offered Salah my life. He picked up, in both hands, all the incoherence of my life and with a magic gesture, brought it into balance" (181).

This open space of freedom, where there are no restrictions, is not without complications. Chems becomes pregnant by Salah, thus compromising her situation and her work. Their equilibrium becomes tenuous and fragile. It is eventually shattered when Chems herself falls victim to the war. Hurling herself upon a child in order to shield him from an exploding bomb, the heroine is severely wounded: "The sniper didn't miss. On the dusty, warped asphalt, she was hit, a white corolla, eyes half closed, a smile on her lips, a red stain slowly coloring her shirt, yet, the sky was so blue" (289). Paralyzed by the fear that Chems will die on the operating table, Salah asks his close friend Farès to save her. The bullet is successfully removed and she lives. She becomes a heroine, a saint, for the village people, particularly for the women whom she has struggled to save from death, even at the cost of risking her own life. She and Salah become renowned for their healing abilities. However, although supported wholeheartedly and held in esteem as miracle workers by the villagers they have been sent to save, the doctors are asked to leave the village by the Iraqi military, who find their presence and godlike popularity too disruptive. The villagers, who demand to know Chems's health status, threaten to storm the hospital in order to catch a glimpse of her and thus be reassured of her continuation among them. Nevertheless, she is forced to leave, despite Salah's protests. They hastily marry before she sets out in an ambulance for Baghdad. Once again Chems takes flight, leaving one place of territorialization for another. In her last journal entry, on 5 April 1991, as she leaves for Tunis, she writes to Salah, whom she has been forced to leave behind, "You are my life" (330). Out of the pain, suffering, and loneliness she has endured, caught up as both player and victim of the Gulf War, she uncovers a self she has never known. At the end of her journey Chems has found the key to her question, Qui suis-je? (Who am I?). She uncovers the answer in the very multiplicity of her being as she completes her long journey from Tunis to Iraq and back to Tunis. She finds as she closes this long nomadic circle that her true self is not rooted in a single stagnant persona, but in one that is manifold: woman, doctor, lover, wife, mother, and survivor.

L'interdite: Exile and the Language of Women

Malika Mokeddem sets her heroine, Sultana, between two worlds: one French, a symbol for an adopted refuge, a place where she has developed her professional career as a doctor and lived freely as a woman, and one Algerian, representing a past full of tormented memories, lost love, and death. "No, it's not a tragedy to be foreign, it's a tormented richness." (253) Sultana exclaims as she tries to come to terms with her French present and her Algerian past from which she has been barred as "l'interdite" (the forbidden woman) by the villagers of her childhood home, Aïn Nekhla. Coming back after her long absence allows her to efface the feelings of attachment she once had for her native country: "Returning here at least let me destroy my last illusions of anchorage. How can I persuade them of that when I myself took so many years to admit it?" (253).

Sultana is forced to return and confront her childhood memories because of the death of her former lover, Yacine. A doctor in the village, Yacine dies of an unknown cause immediately after posting a letter to Sultana, who resides in Montpellier, France. She is compelled to come back. "I would never have thought I could come back to this region. Yet I never really left. I just incorporated the desert and the inconsolable into my displaced body. They split me in two" (11). Yacine's death offers a window to the past to at last find a means of closing the gap between the memories of her *ksar* (native village) and her new life in France, which she defines as "a privileged corner of exile" (12). Yet, what does she find upon returning? Not only the childhood hostility she endured because of her foreignness (her father was considered an outsider because of his tribe, the Chaâmba, a mountain people known for their skill in fighting against the French colonizers), but also the new popularity in the village of the FIS fundamentalist movement, which poses a constant threat to her from the first hours of her arrival. These factors are compounded, as her friend Vincent remarks, by age-old Algerian traditions denying women equal access to the outside world: "I wouldn't want to be a woman here. I wouldn't want to bear the permanent weight of their looks, their multiple violence, kindled by frustration. For the first time, I realize that the most banal act of an Algerian woman immediately takes on symbols and heroism because masculine animosity is so huge, pathological" (93). Sultana's free circulation in the streets is seen as a constant threat to the men who watch women and those considered to be foreigners (the doctors at the hospital, for example). The tension is compounded when she decides to stay after Yacine's funeral to take up his position as town doctor. Sultana's objective is to support the *Koulchi*—the women who from abuse, distress, and isolation have become quivering shadows, devoid of voice and presence, "silent and full of fury" (243). Her work becomes a lifeline to her own sanity as well as to that of other women. Work also provides an excuse for becoming involved in the village's current political issues, while avoiding her childhood memories. Even though she is in her native village she refuses for days to go and visit her childhood home: "this house," she states, where "I haven't set foot since I left. As for the rest, what can I find? The ruins of my memory have preceded those of the *ksar*, for such a long time" (122). It is only later that we learn it was here that her mother was murdered by her father in front of Sultana. As a village woman explains to the young woman, it was because of her father's foreignness and her mother's murder that she was condemned to the status of "l'interdite." As the old woman points out, "you came from somewhere else, with mannerisms from somewhere else. Bad luck made you even more foreign. So you left also" (254). Saved and adopted by a European doctor, Challes, she leaves for France, where she studies, learns, and resigns herself to never return to Algeria. However, the protagonist learns little by little that her foreignness extends even further back (as the village women tell her), to before her exile to France or her mother's murder. Curiously, it is her mother's murderer—her father—she describes as "my first heartbreak, my first experience of suffering" (256). It is he who breaks with tradition and sends his daughter to school. As one of the village women explains "the proof was that he put you in school while no other girl in the ksar had yet set foot there. Your father was a foreigner here. An educated foreigner, different" (255). Her father, more foreign than the foreign, as the village women explain to Sultana, also paraded his daughter freely in public, despite protest from the men of the village, who implored him not to be seen with his daughter because it was against custom. Her father protested: "You pack of ignoramuses, take a good look at my daughter, she's worth more than all your boys put together" (255). It is therefore long before "le malheur"—the incident—that Sultana's destiny is marked as different from that of her fellow villagers.

Malika Mokeddem does not simply tell the story of one woman's flight from and back to her past, but rather her tale is one of an interwoven *métissage* of two traditions, countries, and histories: one French and one Algerian. Interwoven into Sultana's autobiography is that of another character, Vincent. He is Sultana's opposite—male, blond, French—but also her ally. Like the young woman, he searches for this "Other" which he feels resides in him because of a kidney implant he received from a young Algerian girl, killed in a car accident.[8] The match is perfect, but it adds to a feeling of multiple identity that he too seeks to delve into, uncover, and come to terms with: "Gascon and Christian-turned-atheist on my father's side, Jewish on my mother's side, Polish and believer in solidarity, Maghrebian by my donated organ, and without borders by my 'interwoven identity.' . . . My identity. . . . It's mixed, adapted" (87). Vincent and Sultana are hurled together purely by the common factor they share: foreignness. She seeks her past in memories, he his in a culture he knows nothing of. Their destiny is further intertwined because of Vincent's resemblance to Yacine, Sultana's former lover.

Overlaying Mokeddem's story is her political commentary on the current upheaval caused by the FIS, which she does not deny has infested the social fabric of Algeria.[9] The author's disdain over the treatment of women and the deterioration of women's social and political status because of the rise of religious fundamentalism render her novel more than a fictional account. It is a critical commentary on the demise of civil liberties for those who have no voice in Algeria. Through the voice of Sultana's coworker and sometime lover, Salah, Mokeddem's views on the current disarray of Algerian politics can be heard: "Whether or not they're Islamic, there are so many nervous and rejected people in this country. . . . Now with the decrepit authority of the State, any imbecile thinks he's been granted divine right and can act out justice according to his principals! Populism and cretinous nationalism, those are the two breasts of Algeria today" (215).

Like Hajer Djilani, Malika Mokeddem sets out to draw the reading public's attention to the ongoing sociocultural and political strife of a country laid waste by inner conflict, factionalism, fundamentalism, and abuse of human rights. As both authors reveal, that strife is often the product of the contemporary Arab world, which is constantly pulled between its history and its present. Other hurdles—such as the need to hold onto traditional values, contrasted with movements toward secularization in some areas—also contribute to heated dialogue and sociopolitical dissatisfaction. In the center of these points of conflict, women find themselves facing insurmountable barriers. The women of the Maghreb, whether authors, intellectuals, journalists, or mothers, are slowly voicing their opinions and questioning the male-dominated, archaic system of their Arabic heritage. As Sultana realizes in the closing pages of *L'interdite*, it is only through the solidarity of women that political, social, and cultural gains favoring change will be made. Standing up in unison to the patriarchal status quo, as one old woman tells Sultana, will be the only solution for women in Algeria: "when one is cornered, one is obliged to counterattack. That's perhaps where our strength comes from. Individually, they can enslave or break us. [But] they will think twice if we are unified" (251).

Sultana's predestined life of nomadism leads to the realization that her multiple identity is really made up of her Algerian history, French schooling, and the present bonds she shares with the village women. These contributors to her identity are the key to her true self. "I am multiple and torn apart," she states in defiance (191). Although Sultana is eventually forced to leave by members of the FIS ruling the village, she takes with her the knowledge that she is no longer alone. She has formed a rhizome of feminine connections that will all contribute to the continuation of feminine solidarity and the struggle against male oppression in favor of human rights: "Tell the women, even from far away, I'll be with them" (264).

Maghrebian Women's Texts: Sites of Exile and New Agendas beyond Postcolonial Discourse and Patriarchal Regimes

It cannot be disputed that today's feminine texts of the Maghreb written in French are the products of exile, self-discovery, and reappropriation of feminine history. The narratives of Hajer Djilani, Malika Mokeddem, Assia Djebar, Leïla Sebbar, Nina Bouraoui, Naïla Imaksen, sociologist Fatima Mernissi, and political activist Khalida Messaoudi, among many others, implicate the daring act of speaking out as women in a masculinized social arena. These narratives also forge links of solidarity among women in order to discover answers to pressing questions voiced by the female population of the Muslim world. In the case of the current situation in Algeria, the voicing of issues in the language of the former colonizer is both a political and a textual act of defiance. By writing in this foreign tongue, Algerian women demonstrate their dissatisfaction with the broken promises made by the revolutionary FLN government in the 1960s. Promises for equality and social advancement for the women of that country have never been achieved. As Khalida Messaoudi exclaims, "We have never had our place in the world of the outside."[10] On the brink of a new century and a new era for Maghrebian women's writing in French, it is hoped that the efforts of these women will not go unnoticed. It remains to be seen if women of the Maghreb who choose to write will be forever destined to seek their paths in the outside, the nomadic deterritorialized space of uncharted subjectivity and acentered margins.

In no other context is the revision of colonial historical Western depictions more important than in the case of feminine identity and representation in the Maghreb. Not only do the women authors studied in this book seek to rewrite the West's despotic rendering of the Maghreb, but they also strive to rectify the political injustices committed against them (particularly in Algeria) since the independence movements of the 1950s and 1960s. The women of the Maghreb have endured a double bind, one made up from the colonial Orientalist legacy as well as from the patriarchal oppression of postindependence governments. In general, women in this region are left today questioning the roles they have been assigned in postrevolutionary history as well as in modern Muslim society.

Unfortunately, nowhere in the Maghreb is the status of women and the threat to their identity more acute than in Algeria. In an interview conducted with Elisabeth Schemla, Messaoudi poignantly points out that the women of Algeria "exist only as 'daughter of' or 'mother of.' They are not wholly individual."[11] Identity as an individual and as a woman have been totally denied the feminine half of the Algerian population. The very existence of feminine subjectivity is at risk because of a democratic process that never bore fruit once the revolution of 1954–62 was won. Although Algerian women, for one brief moment, saw themselves treated as equals fighting alongside their male countrymen to end the burden of colonization, as Messaoudi explains, they were duly betrayed by the FLN long before the decolonization process began: "Never, never would we have imagined that those whose sides we fought beside would conduct our country like that; we do what they make us do

. . . . Our 'sequestration' did not begin in 1962 but before independence. Little by little during the war the FLN eliminated us from the maquis, sending us to the borders or abroad. Our role was defined at that moment. We did not have a place in the world 'outside.'"[12]

Today as we witness the closing of the twentieth century, we sadly note that for Algerian women the exploration of their feminine identity, historic roles, and feminism itself have had to be achieved beyond the phallocentric/cratic structures of their homeland. Algerian women authors, such as Assia Djebar and Malika Mokeddem, have had to formulate new feminist agendas for Algeria and the Maghreb outside, on the fringes, expatriated from their native country. These authors have become anomalous, nomadically plotting lines and points of subjectivity to form new platforms of intellectual thought. Such an existence on the borders, although painful and often life threatening, does lead the author, philosopher, and critic to what Edward Said suggests is an "exile" that forces you "to see things not simply as they are, but as they have come to be that way." Situations that mold cultures and societies, he states, are not inevitable but are a "series of historical choices made by men and women, facts of society made by human beings and not as natural or God-given, therefore unchangeable, permanent, irreversible." Exile means "that you are always going to be marginal," but that you will also embark on nomadic roads that will lead to more knowledge and empowerment.[13]

Women of the Maghreb—those who are exiled and those who must live underground fighting for human rights—are conceptualizing new ways to study their past as well as to plot new plans for their future. They are entering into a becoming-woman, an identity that is beyond all preconceived notions, whether historically, phallocratically, or religiously ordained. Authors of the Maghreb who are formulating a new agenda for feminism in the Maghreb seek to promote the cultural as well as the historical. Their discourse posits a multiply embodied feminine subject that reflects a panoply of connections criss-crossed by many cultures, languages, and nationalities. Instead of embracing an essentialized ideal of femininity, the contemporary Francophone author embraces conceptualizations of identity that transgress the boundaries of gender and ethnic dualisms to empower and promote new political agendas for the Maghrebian woman.

Contemporary Francophone authors of the Maghreb have restructured the idea of feminine subjectivity as one that contributes to both the cultural and the political facets of Maghrebian society. Women authors of the region writing in French uphold a sense of womanhood that is formed from a multiple, complex process of subjectivity promoting the revision of history, politics, and traditions. The agenda of feminine identity for contemporary Francophone authors is to deconstruct all preconstructed paradigms. The idea of woman is truly placed at Deleuze and Guattari's "Dawn of the World," a world that is communicating and interactive. She connects with others in a space where enunciation of both the cultural and the historic fuse, giving her voice and agency. Here she communicates with all Others to embrace a mondialiste conception of feminine subjectivity. The contemporary Francophone author has placed woman into a becoming—the cautious stage that will allow her to move in flux, writing herself into culture and history as an embodied, multifaceted, active player.

Notes

Introduction

1. Linda Hutcheon, *A Poetics of Postmodernism: History, Theory, Fiction* (New York: Routledge, 1988), 4.

2. Abdelwahab Meddeb, "Postcolonialisme: Arguement" (typescript of a paper given in Paris on 8 December 1995), 1.

3. Gilles Deleuze, *Difference and Repetition* (New York: Columbia University Press, 1994), 52.

4. Ibid., xi.

5. Ibid., xix.

6. Gilles Deleuze and Félix Guattari, *Mille Plateaux* (Paris: Editions de Minuit, 1980); translated by Brian Massumi under the title *A Thousand Plateaus* (Minneapolis: University of Minnesota Press, 1987), 282.

7. Abdelkebir Khatibi, *Maghreb Pluriel* (Paris: Denoël, 1983).

8. Ibid., 32.

9. F. F. Centore, *Being and Becoming: A Critique of Post-Modernism* (Westport, Conn.: Greenwood Press, 1991), 21.

10. Rosi Braidotti, *Nomadic Subjects: Embodiment and Sexual Difference in Contemporary Feminist Theory* (New York: Columbia University Press, 1994), 115.

11. Ibid.

12. Donna Haraway, *Simians, Cyborgs, and Women: The Reinvention of Nature* (New York: Routledge, 1991), 176.

13. Réda Bensmaïa, "The Vanished Mediators: The Algerian Intellectuals Facing Power," *Diacritics,* Fall 1997, 1.

14. Jürgen Habermas, *Moral Consciousness and Communicative Action* (Cambridge, Mass.: MIT Press, 1993), 122.

15. Gayatri C. Spivak, *In Other Worlds: Essays in Cultural Politics* (New York: Routledge, 1988), 103. Spivak further explains that other binary oppositions that have oppressed women are: rational/emotional, assertive/passive, and strong/weak. These are oppositions that she and others maintain have privileged men at the expense of women by relegating women to an inferior status in society. In *Postmodern Theory: Critical Interrogations* (New York: Guilford Press, 1991), Steven Best and Douglas Kellner note that it is these ideological discourses that "go back as far as Plato and Aristotle [in order to] justify the domination of women by men, enslaving women in domestic activities, and excluding them from public life and the voice of reason and objectivity" (207).

16. Spivak, *Other Worlds*, 103.

17. Habermas, *Moral Consciousness*, 135; emphasis Habermas's.

18. Jean-François Lyotard, *The Postmodern Condition: A Report on Knowledge*, (Minneapolis: Minnesota University Press, 1993), xxxv.

19. A Beur is a second-generation Maghrebian born in France. See chapters 1 and 4.

Chapter One

1. Interview with a staff writer from *Le monde*, 28 April 1995, 12. My translation.

2. Simone de Beauvoir, *The Second Sex*, translated by H. Parshley (New York: Knopf, 1952), xvi.

3. Shoshana Felman, *What Does a Woman Want? Reading and Sexual Difference* (Baltimore: John Hopkins University Press, 1993), 23; Felman's emphasis.

4. Linda Hutcheon, *The Politics of Postmodernism* (New York: Routledge, 1989), 62.

5. Ibid., 66.

6. Hutcheon, *Poetics*, 122.

7. Habermas, *Moral Consciousness*, 125.

8. See Fatima Mernissi, *Beyond the Veil: Male-Female Dynamics in*

Modern Muslim Society (Bloomington: Indiana University Press, 1987), particularly part 1, "The Traditional Muslim View of Women and Their Place in the Social Order" (29–85), and Azouz Begag and Abdellatif Chaouite *Ecarts d'identité* (Paris: Seuil, 1990), 67–68.

9. Children born in France to Maghrebian immigrants. In a primarily urban slang known as Verlan, *Beur* is the French word *Arabe* said backwards. Using two-syllable words in which the last syllable is placed before the first, young adolescents are able to speak in a code virtually incomprehensible to authorities. Verlan is popular among France's ethnic populations because it is viewed as subversive and is often thought of as a key element in the counterculture movements of France's nonwhite citizens.

10. Beauvoir, *Second Sex*, 249.

11. Habitation à loyer modéré (public housing).

12. Jean Déjeux estimates this date to be 1891 and credits the first novella, "la vengeance du cheikh" written in French by an Algerian author to M'Hamed Ben Rahal. The novella was published in "*Revue algérienne et tunisienne, littéraire et artistique* (Algeirs, no. 13, 26 Sept - 3 Oct, 1891, pp. 428-433.)Jean Déjeux, *Maghreb: Littératures de langue française*, (Paris: Aracantère, 1993), 31.

13. When I refer to contemporary Francophone literature of the Maghreb I include all works written by Tunisian, Algerian, and Moroccan authors after 1962, the end of the French colonial presence in the Maghreb.

14. I prefer the term *emerging literatures* because it is free of the pejorative overtones associated with *postcolonial*, which is generally used to designate the literature written by the formerly colonized (i.e., authors from Maghreb, the Caribbean, Central and West Africa, etc.).

15. Neil Lazarus, *Resistance in Postcolonial African Fiction* (New Haven: Yale University Press, 1990), 18.

16. One example of such a postrevolution group is the Berbers living in the Kabylie region of Algeria. This group has been both marginalized and persecuted by the Arab majority throughout history.

17. Frantz Fanon, "On National Culture," in *Colonial Discourse and Postcolonial Theory*, ed. Patrick Williams and Laura Chrisman (New York: Columbia University Press, 1994), 48.

18. Kristin Ross, *Fast Cars, Clean Bodies: Decolonization and the Reordering of French Culture* (Cambridge, Mass.: MIT Press, 1995), 159.

19. Ibid., 164.

20. Vijay Mishra and Bob Hodge, "What is Post(-)colonialism?" in *Colonial Discourse and Postcolonial Theory*, ed. Patrick Williams and Laura Chrisman (New York: Columbia University Press, 1994), 276.

21. Ibid.

22. Bill Ashcroft, Gareth Griffiths, and Helen Tiffin, *The Empire Writes Back: Theory and Practice in Post-Colonial Literatures* (New York: Routledge, 1989), 2.

23. Ibid.

24. Jean Franco suggests that Western sociopolitical theorists have created three convenient discourses in order to define the Third World: (1) *exclusion*—the Third World is irrelevant to theory, (2) *discrimination*—the Third World is irrational and thus its knowledge is subordinate to the rational knowledge produced by the metropolis; and (3) *recognition*—the Third World is only seen as the place of the institutional. Jean Franco, "Beyond Ethnocentrism: Gender, Power and the Third World Intelligentsia," in *Colonial Discourse and Post-Colonial Theory*, ed. Patrick Williams and Laura Chrisman (New York: Columbia University Press, 1994), 361.

25. McClintock, "The Angle of Progress: Pitfalls of the Term 'Post-Colonialism,'" in *Colonial Discourse and Post-Colonial Theory*, ed. Patrick Williams and Laura Chrisman (New York: Columbia University Press, 1994), 291, 1; emphasis McClintock's.

26. Ibid., 292.

27. Ibid., 293.

28. Homi K. Bhabha, *The Location of Culture* (New York: Routledge, 1994), 40.

29. Ibid., 89; italics Bhabha's.

30. Jacques Derrida, *Margins of Philosophy* (Chicago: University of Chicago Press, 1982), 4.

31. Bhabha, *Location of Culture,* 151.

32. Aschroft et al., *Empire Writes Back,* 185.

33. This very apt term was borrowed from Alice Walker. Authors Toni Morrison and Ama Ata Aidoo have also called upon the ideal of womanism as a basis for a new worldview of feminism.

34. Abdelkebir Khatibi, *Le roman maghrébin: Essai* (Paris: Maspero, 1968), 10.

35. Ibid., 17.

36. Nabile Farès, commenting on the work of Albert Memmi, "La littérature maghrébine de langue française," *Français dans le monde,* 189 (November-December 1984): 68.

37. Assia Djebar, *Oran, langue morte* (Arles: Actes Sud, 1997), 220.

38. Farès, "Littérature maghrébine," 96.

39. Abdeljalil Lahnomri, quoting Khatibi, in "Enseignement de la langue française au Maroc et dialogue des cultures," *Français dans le monde* 189 (November-December 1984): 21.

40. Déjeux, *Maghreb,* 28.

41. Armistice Day. Many Algerians fought for France during World War II. At the end of the war, the Algerian people thought that their efforts would be rewarded by France's agreement to grant them independence. In Sétif, as in villages and towns across Algeria, people went out into the streets to celebrate and brandish the Algerian nationalist flag. The Sétif French police saw these as acts of aggression and fired upon the crowd, killing men, women, and children. In the ensuing months acts of revenge against the French escalated throughout the country. This violence was a prelude to the Franco-Algerian War of 1954–62.

42. Déjeux, *Maghreb littératures,* 36.

43. Charles Bonn, *Le Roman algérien de langue française,* (Paris: L'Harmattan, 1985), 52.

44. Ibid., 57.

45. Ibid., 54.

46. Kateb Yacine, *Nedjma: Roman* (Paris: Seuil, 1956), 175.

47. Ibid., 179.

48. Winifred Woodhull, *Transfigurations of the Maghreb: Feminism, Decolonization, and Literatures* (Minneapolis: University of Minnesota Press, 1993), 57.

49. Déjeux, *Maghreb*, 12.

50. Begag and Chaouite, *Ecarts d'identité*, 85.

51. A proliferation of Beur narratives has occurred in the last fifteen years. Some of the most important include: Azouz Begag, *Le gone du Châaba* (Paris: Seuil, 1986); Farida Belghoul, *Georgette* (Paris: Barrault, 1986); Mehdi Charef, *Le thé au harem d'Archi Ahmed* (Paris: Mercure de France, 1983); Leïla Houari, *Zeïda de nulle part* (Paris: L'Harmattan, 1985); Ahmed K., *L'encre d'un fait divers* (Paris: Arcantère, 1984); Ahmed Kalouaz, *Point kilométrique 190* (Paris: L'Harmattan, 1986); Nacer Kettane, *Le sourire de Brahim* (Paris: Denoël, 1985); Mehdi Lallaoui, *Les Beurs de Seine* (Paris: Arcantère, 1986); Mustapha Raïth, *Palpitations intra-muros* (Paris: L'Harmattan, 1986); Akli Tadjer, *Les A.N.I. du "Tassili"* (Paris: Seuil, 1984); Hocine Touabti, *L'amour quand même* (Paris: Belfond, 1981); Jean-Luc Yacine, *L'escargot* (Paris: L'Harmattan, 1986); and Kamal Zemouri, *Le jardin de l'intrus* (Algiers: Entreprise Nationale du Livre, 1986).

52. Bonn, *Roman algérien*, 81.

53. Ibid., 82.

54. Djebar is perhaps evoking Fanon's text, *A Dying Colonialism*, where he contradicts his former views of women (as seen in *Black Skin, White Masks*, notably with the example of Capecia) by hailing the important roles Algerian women played in the war of liberation. In the following statement he considers these roles as an emancipating and liberating process, creating a new Algerian modern woman: "The Algerian woman who walks stark naked into the European city relearns her body, re-establishes it in a totally revolutionary fashion. This new dialectic of the body and of the world is primary in the case of one revolutionary woman" (Frantz Fanon, *A Dying Colonialism* [New York: Grove Press, 1965], 59).

55. *Les allouettes naïves: Roman* (Paris: Juillard, 1967) and to some extent *Femmes d'Alger dans leurs appartement: Nouvelles* (Paris: Des Femmes, 1980), *Vaste est la prison: Roman* (Paris: Albin Michel, 1995), and *Le blanc de l'Algérie: Récit* (Paris: Albin Michel, 1995) also explore Djebar's uncertainty about the political future of Algeria, both historically and in the present. Indeed, many of the same issues the author raised in her earlier novels resurface in her most recent work, *Oran, langue morte* (Arles: Actes Sud, 1997).

56. Most particularly France's cultural revolution of May 1968, of which women's issues were an essential component in the liberal movement.

57. Anne-Marie Nisbet, *Le Personnage féminin dans le roman maghrébin de langue française des indépendances à 1980: Représentations et fonctions* (Sherbrooke, Québec: Naaman, 1982), 13.

58. Reiterated time and again by politicians such as Guy Mollet, Charles De Gaulle, and François Mitterand (Ross, *Fast Cars, Clean Bodies*, 123).

59. Ibid., 124.

60. Ibid., 125.

61. Ibid., 151.

62. The Algerian population residing in France grew from 211,675 in 1954 to 350,484 in 1962, and reached 473,812 in 1968 (Ross, *Fast Cars, Clean Bodies*, 153). Despite numerous expulsions following the events of May 1968, Algerian presence in France continued to grow. In the early 1970s police surveillance and racist violence against this immigrant population increased. In 1974 newly elected Valéry Giscard d'Estang stopped all work visas for Algerians. Marianne Amar and Pierre Milza, *L'immigration en France au XXème siècle* (Paris: Armand Colin, 1990), 42.

63. Driss Chraïbi, *Les boucs: Roman* (Paris: Denoël, 1955, republished in 1989, Paris: Denoël), 50.

64. Tahar Ben Jelloun, *Hospitalité française: Racisme et immigration maghrebine* (Paris: Seuil, 1984), 104.

65. Ibid.

66. Chraïbi, *Les boucs*, 182.

67. Nabil Farès, *Yahia, pas de chance* (Paris, Seuil, 1970), 25.

68. Jeanyves Guérin, ed., *Albert Memmi: écrivain et sociologue* (Paris: L'Harmattan, 1990), 139.

69. Albert Memmi and Joelle Bahloul, eds., *Ecrivain francophones du Maghreb: Anthologie* (Paris: Seghers, 1985), 166.

70. Perhaps Albert Memmi was influenced by new writing and typeface styles introduced by French authors such as Maurice Roche, who in 1966 published *Compact*. Roche's work is thought of as an exemplary illustration of the Tel Quel group's revolutionary theories about language, which included experimentation in typographies, fragmented narrative, and a reference to new ideas in the the fields of linguistics and psychological analysis. However, *Compact* was written before Tel Quel existed and while the novel did anticipate the developments of Tel Quel it was still an original work. See the forward by Mark Polizzotti to the 1988 English translation of *Compact* (Elmwood Park, Ill.: Dalkey Archive Press, 1988). For additional information on the Tel Quel group see George Alexander's article "The Group Tel Quel" (Darlington, Australia: Working Papers in Sex, Science and Culture, vol. 1, issue 2 [Nov. 1976]: 3–11).

71. Albert Memmi, *Le scorpion, ou, la confession imaginaire* (Paris: Gallimard, 1969), 295: "The reader will have understood that this book should have been printed in characters of different colors. I explain this in *Dialogues sur une écriture colorée*. The technical objections made by the editor, particularly singling out the excessive price of such a work, forced us to content ourselves with typographic variations. We count on the reader for a complementary effort of imagination. That will be his part in this communal work."

72. Ibid., 251.

73. Isaac Yetiv, "Du *Scorpion au désert:* Albert Memmi Revisited," *Studies in Twentieth-Century Literature* 7.1 (Fall 1982): 84.

74. Ibid., 86.

75. Most significantly in *Le chinois vert d'Afrique* (Paris: Stock, 1984) and the Shérazade trilogy: *Shérazade: Dix-sept ans, brune, frisée, les yeux verts* (Paris: Stock, 1982), *Les carnets de Shérazade* (Paris: Stock, 1985) and *Le fou de Shérazade* (Paris: Stock, 1991). See chapter 4.

76. Michel de Certeau, "Idéologie et diversité culturelle," in *Société industrielle, état national* (Paris: L'Harmattan, 1984: 231–32). Cited in Winifred Woodhull, "Exile," 11.

77. Woodhull, "Exile," 17.

78. Leïla Sebbar, *Lettres parisiennes: Autopsie de l'exil* (Paris: Barrault, 1986), 126.

79. Ibid.

80. Khatibi, *Roman maghrébin*, 17.

81. Ibid., 39.

82. Bhabha, *Location of Culture*, 37.

83. Ibid.

84. Khatibi, *Maghreb pluriel*, 11.

85. Donna Haraway, *A Manifesto for Cyborgs: Science, Technology and Socialist Feminism in the 1980s, Socialist Review*, no. 80 (1985): 74.

86. My interpretation of recolonizing, here, means reappropriating the Other text and subsequently interpreting it to fit a Western conception. For example, the film *Out of Africa* has often been criticized as representing a neocolonizing ideal. Even in modern-day depictions of the colonial era, natives are subservient and rarely visible while the narrative centers around a single white European protagonist in this case, a woman battling the harsh elements of Africa.

87. Homi K. Bhabha *(The Location of Culture)* and Gayatri Spivak (see "Subaltern Studies: Deconstructing Historiography" in *Other Worlds*) have warned Third World critics, philosophers, and theorists of the dangers of appropriating Westernized canonized views in order to recontextualize their own countries' postcolonial era, texts, and narratives. Further study of their apprehensions is certainly warranted.

88. Braidotti, *Nomadic Subjects*, 5; italics Braidotti's.

89. Gilles Deleuze and Félix Guattari, *Nomadology: The War Machine* (New York: Semiotext(e), Columbia University Press: 1986), 36.

90. Deleuze and Guattari, *Thousand Plateaus*, 243.

91. Ibid.

92. Khatibi, *Maghreb pluriel*, 18.

93. Leïla Sebbar. *Shérazade: Dix-sept ans, brune, frisée, les yeux verts*

(Paris: Stock, 1982); translated by Dorothy Blair under the title *Sherazade: Missing, Aged Seventeen, Dark Curly Hair, Green Eyes* (London: Quartet Books, 1991). Page numbers in this book refer to the English translation. See chapter 4.

94. Deleuze and Guattari, *Thousand Plateaus*, 8.

95. Deleuze and Guattari, *Nomadology*, 51.

96. Tahar Ben Jelloun, *L'écrivain public: Récit* (Paris: Seuil, 1983), 150.

97. Bhabha, *Location of Culture*, 1.

98. Ibid., 2.

99. Ibid., 4.

100. Gilles Deleuze and Félix Guattari, *Kafka: Toward a Minor Literature* (Minneapolis: University of Minnesota Press, 1986), 17.

101. Seen in such terrorist events as the Oklahoma City bombing in April 1995, immediately after which Middle Eastern or Arab men were branded the culprits; Americans, the media, and the West in general asked, How could it be anyone else?

102. Sebbar, *Shérazade*, 190.

103. Ben Jelloun, *HospitalitÈ française*, 16.

104. The concept of the rhizome is explained in detail in Deleuze and Guattari's introduction to *A Thousand Plateaus*. Basically, a rhizome is a system of roots that have no beginning nor end, but cross and connect in an intricate fashion. There are no dialectical oppositions within the rhizome.

105. See Bhabha's discussion of the intervention of the Third Space of enunciation. Bhabha, *Location of Culture*, 37.

106. Deleuze and Guattari, *Thousand Plateaus*, 251.

107. Bhabha, *Location of Culture*, 37.

108. Ibid., 38.

109. Ben Jelloun, *L'enfant de sable* (Paris: Seuil, 1985), 38.

110. Assia Djebar, *Vaste est la prison: Roman* (Paris: Albin Michel, 1995), 47.

111. Paul Ricoeur, *Oneself as Another* (Chicago: University of Chicago Press, 1993), 2.

112. Abdelkebir Khatibi, *Amour bilingue* (Montpellier: Fata Morgana, 1982), 11, 28; my translation.

113. Ibid., 128.

114. Deleuze and Guattari, *Thousand Plateaus,* 272.

115. Ibid., 273.

116. Ibid., 275.

117. Ibid., 291.

118. Ibid.

119. Ibid., 292.

120. Here Western feminism is defined as that influenced by a generally Marxist-socialist agenda.

121. bell hooks, *Feminist Theory from Margin to Center* (Boston: South End Press, 1984), 1.

122. Ibid., 5.

123. Braidotti, *Nomadic Subjects,* 160.

124. Ibid., 57.

125. Fatima Mernissi, *Sultanes oubliées: Femmes chefs d'Etat en Islam.* Paris: Albin Michel, 1990; translated by Mary Jo Lakeland under the title *The Forgotten Queens of Islam* (Minneapolis: University of Minnesota Press, 1993), 4.

126. Current Algerian feminist activism has centered its agenda around the struggle against the Code de la Famille, reinstalled by the FLN-postrevolutionary government in 1984. Marie Aimée Hélie-Lucas suggests that women in Algeria have thus had to struggle against colonization twice once under the French, and currently under Islamic law. "Bound and Gagged by the Family Code," in *Third World, Second Sex: Women's Struggles and National Liberation* (London: Zed Books, 1983), 3–15.

Chapter Two

1. Tahar Ben Jelloun, *L'enfant de sable* (Paris: Seuil, 1985); translated by Alan Sheridan under the title *The Sand Child* (Orlando, Fla.: Harcourt Brace Jovanovich, 1987); *La nuit sacrée* (Paris: Seuil, 1987);

translated by Alan Sheridan under the title *The Sacred Night* (Orlando: Harcourt Brace Jovanovich, 1989). All page numbers cited in my text are those of the English translations.

2. Deleuze and Guattari, *Thousand Plateaus*, 279.

3. By winning the 1987 Prix Goncourt, Ben Jelloun has upset "traditional" literary French practice. The prize, usually awarded to novels like Dominique Fernandez's *Dans la main de l'ange* (Paris: Grasset, 1982) and Frederick Tristan's *Les égarés* (Paris: Balland, 1983), demonstrates that in the past members of the Goncourt committee have had little regard for authors who stray from traditional frameworks of the novel as it "has evolved in the West during the course of centuries." For insight into Ben Jelloun's work, I am grateful to Mustapha Marrouchi, particularly his article "Breaking Up/ Down/Out of Boundaries: Tahar Ben Jelloun," *Francographies* 21.4 (Winter 1990): 71–83; his evaluation of the Goncourt prize, quoted here, appears on p. 71.

4. Marrouchi, "Breaking Boundaries," 73.

5. Deleuze and Guattari, *Thousand Plateaus*, 4.

6. Tahar Ben Jelloun, "Tahar le fou, Tahar le sage," interview by Philippe Gaillard, *Jeune Afrique* 1404 (2 December 1987): 44.

7. Mustapha Marrouchi states, "*Wijdan* is the affirmation of being (l'être) in regard to self and others. It is both an awakening and a presence that ties the individual to his surroundings" (23; Marrouchi citing Fethi Benslama). However, in a becoming-woman context *wijdan* would only be a beginning stage. Once one has developed ties to "one's" surroundings, one must deterritorialize—transcend—to other heights that are not tied to anything.

8. The title of this section was inspired by Ricoeur, *Oneself as Another*.

9. Mernissi, *Beyond the Veil*, 30.

10. A public bathhouse segregated by gender.

11. The Arabic word *fitna* is used to designate civil strife disorder and chaos in society. The word is further convoluted by its meanings of "beautiful woman" and "femme fatale," two concepts that depict

women as a threat to men's self control (Mernissi, *Beyond the Veil*, 31). Mernissi equally suggests,

> The Muslim woman is endowed with a fatal attraction which erodes the male's will to resist her and reduces him to a passive acquiescent role. He has no choice; he can only give in to her attraction, whence her identification with *fitna*, chaos, and with the anti-divine and anti-social forces of the universe. (41)

12. Begag and Chaouite, *Ecarts d'identité*, 67–68.

13. See Marrouchi, "Breaking Boundaries," for a comprehensive explanation of the blending of Maghrebian and Western narrative strategies in Ben Jelloun's texts.

14. Ibid., 72.

15. Bhabha, *Location of Culture*, 48.

16. Ibid., 66.

17. Pierre Bourdieu, *Language and Symbolic Power* (Cambridge, Mass.: Harvard University Press, 1994), 57.

18. Deleuze and Guattari, *Thousand Plateaus*, 172.

19. Mustapha Marrouchi interprets Ben Jelloun's use of the coin as an explication of the entire theme of Zahra's story. In *The Sand Child*, The Blind Troubadour identifies the two coins as Bâttène and Zahir. These terms date back to the eleventh century in Andalusia, where there existed a remarkable school of advanced Islamic philosophic grammarians whose literary quarrels "anticipated twentieth-century debates between structuralists and generative grammarians, between descriptivists and behaviorists" (80). Among the groups of scholars where Ibn Hazm, Ibn Jinni and Ibn Mada 'al-Qurtobi, all of whom belonged to the Zahrite school, all antagonists of the Bâtin school. Batinists believed that meaning in language is concealed within words, whereas Zahrites derive their name from the clear, the apparent, and the phenomenal aspects of it. Zahrites also argue for only a surface meaning, "one anchored to a particular usage, circumstance, historical and religious situation" (80). It is interesting to

note, as Marrouchi points out, that the Consul in The Sacred Night and the Blind Troubadour in The Sand Child both seem to be products of the Bâtin school, while Zahra (a name derived from *Zahrite* perhaps), like Ben Jelloun himself, judges the world from the outside only and "what is visible on the surface" (80).

I am grateful here to Mustapha Marrouchi's article (see bibliography) and his study of these two schools and the history associated with them. His work has provided enormous insight and allowed me to further understand Ben Jelloun's numerous allusions to Islamic history and religion.

20. Gilles Deleuze and Félix Guattari, *Qu'est-ce que la philosophie?* (Paris: Minuit, 1991); translated by Hugh Tomlinson and Graham Burchell under the title *What is Philosophy?* (New York: Columbia University Press, 1994), 169.

21. Deleuze and Guattari, *Thousand Plateaus*, 61.

22. Ben Jelloun states, "I must make it perfectly clear that there is no female excision in the Maghreb; it simply isn't done there. There is no female excision in Islam; it is expressly forbidden. It is a practice that has been imported from [sub-Saharan] Africa. In the terrible world of my heroine, it belongs to the realm of her nightmares. Even so, this allows me to write that excision can exist in an act of extreme violence . . . but not in a sociological tradition as is the case in certain African nations. When I wrote this scene, I was terrified." André Rollin, "La nuit sacrée au peigne fin," *Lire* 146 (1987): 137–39; cited by Marrouchi "Breaking Boundaries," notes.

23. Deleuze and Guattari, *Thousand Plateaus*, 283.

24. Ibid., 289.

Chapter Three

1. Benjamin Stora, *La Gangrène et l'oubli: La mémoire de la guerre d'Algérie*, (Paris: La Découverte, 1991), 321.

2. Assia Djebar, *L'amour, la fantasia: Roman* (Paris: Albin Michel, 1985); translated by Dorothy S. Blair under the title *Fantasia: An Al-*

gerian Cavalcade (Portsmouth, N.H.: Heinemann; London: Quartet Books, 1993). Page numbers cited in this chapter are those of the English translation.

3. *Vaste est la prison* has not yet been translated, therefore all translations of this novel are my own. This novel is the third in a series that Assia Djebar calls her Algerian Quartet. The quartet's first three volumes are: *L'amour, la fantasia* (Paris: J.-C. Lattès, 1985; reprint, Albin Michel, 1995); *Loin de Médine: Filles d'Ismael* (Paris: Albin Michel, 1991); and *Vaste est la prison* (Paris: Albin Michel, 1995).

4. Hutcheon, *Poetics,* 89, 93.

5. Paul Ricoeur, *Time and Narrative,* vol. 2, (Chicago: University of Chicago Press, 1985), 77; emphasis Ricoeur's.

6. Ibid., 77. "Time of narration," "narrated time," and "fictive experience of time" are concepts developed by Ricoeur.

7. Adlai Murdoch, "Rewriting Writing: Identity, Exile and Renewal in Assia Djebar's *L'amour, la fantasia,*" *Yale French Studies* 83 (1993): 77.

8. *Fantasia,* 54. *Razzia,* from the Arabic *ghazwa,* means "foray" or "raid." French field marshal Pierre Bosquet, born in Mont-de-Marsan in 1810, distinguished himself in military campaigns in Algeria and the Crimean. He died in 1861.

9. The Civilizing Mission in Algeria began immediately after Thomas Bugeaud (1784–1849), Marshal of France and initial military organizer of the colonization of Algeria, entered the country. The Civilizing Mission, or those promoting the colonizing endeavor in Algeria, was made up of colonials, missionaries, and convicts exiled from France.

10. Murdoch, "Rewriting Writing," 74.

11. Although French government officials set up education programs as early as the 1880s, the masses of children needing education grew constantly, particularly in rural areas. Girls were allowed to attend school, but this was a rare phenomenon; it was common only among the wealthier families of the cities. Pierre Nora reported that in 1939, out of 1,250,000 children ages 6 through 14, only 110,000

were in school. In the first year of the Algerian revolution (1954–55) only 15.5% of children in Algeria ages 6 through 14 were schooled. *Les Français d'Algérie* (Paris: Julliard, 1961), 218.

12. Curiously, French schools later became a primary source for French assimilation of the Algerian people. In the twentieth century it was thought that forcing women out into the open, metaphorically unveiling them, would break the patriarchal male rebellions and strike a blow to Islamic traditionalism. According to Fanon, the settlers believed, "If we want to destroy the structure of Algerian society, its capacity for resistance, we must first of all conquer the women; we must go and find them behind the veil where they hide themselves and in the houses where their men keep them out of sight." *Dying Colonialism*, 37–38.

The French also believed that by coaxing young Algerian girls to French school, they could be convinced to "remove themselves from the barbaric and medieval influences of Algerian men" who wanted to sequester them. Peter Knauss, *The Persistence of Patriarchy: Class, Gender, and Ideology in Twentieth-Century Algeria*, (New York: Praeger, 1987), 26.

13. Ricoeur, *Time and Narrative*, 78.

14. Roland Barthes, *Le degré zéro de l'écriture* (Paris: Seuil, 1953), 14.

15. Murdoch, "Rewriting Writing," 75.

16. Felman, *What Does a Woman Want?*, 18.

17. Ibid.

18. Edward Said, *Orientalism* (New York: Vintage, 1979), 103; emphasis Said's.

19. Mary Jean Green, "Dismantling the Colonizing Text," *French Review* 66 (May 1993): 962.

20. Said, *Orientalism*, 103.

21. Hutcheon, *Poetics*, 101.

22. Hutcheon, *Poetics*, 146.

23. Alain Grosrichard proposes that these depictions became necessary to insure the West's maintenance of the constant division be-

tween Us and Them. This division assured the continuation of an *imaginaire occidental,* which would keep the "despot Oriental" at bay, weak, and submissive. Alain Grosrichard, *Structure du sérail: La fiction du despotisme asiatique dans l'Occident classique* (Paris: Seuil, 1979), 101.

24. Said, *Orientalism,* 5–6.

25. Malek Alloula, *The Colonial Harem* (Minneapolis: University of Minnesota Press, 1986), 3.

26. Alloula, *Colonial Harem,* 7.

27. Eugène Fromentin, *Un été dans le Sahara,* (Paris: Plon, 1856), xvi.

28. Fromentin, *Un été dans le Sahara,* xvi.

29. See Albert Memmi's *Portrait du colonisé* (Paris: Payot, 1957). See Françoise Lionnet, *Postcolonial Representations: Women, Literature, Identity* (Ithaca: Cornell University Press, 1995), 15.

30. Bhabha, *Location of Culture,* 86, 90; Bhabha's emphasis.

31. Ibid., 80.

32. Fromentin, *Un été dans le Sahara,* 75.

33. Eugène Fromentin, *Une année dans le Sahel* (Paris: Plon, 1893), 74.

34. See paintings such as *La chasse au héron* (1865) and *Fauconnier arabe* (1863) for examples of vibrant, pastoral scenes painted by Fromentin. His painting *Femmes des ouled-Nayls dans un village du Sahara* (1867) depicts Algerian village women in eroticized, seductive poses. Both types of paintings incarnate the classic Orientalist conception of the Arab Other. James Thompson and Barbara Wright, *La vie et l'oeuvre d'Eugène Fromentin,* Les orientalistes (Paris: ACR Edition International, 1987), 224.

35. In the second half of the nineteenth century, Parisian *Turqueries* became the rage among high society. Harem pants, satin slippers, and turbans were routinely worn by intellectuals, poets, painters, and popular figures of the time. The concept of *keyf* ("fulfillment in sweet nothingness") spread in popularity as Europeans embraced new Oriental perceptions of harmony and quiet euphoria. Smoking

opium and hashish was frequently indulged in by such cognoscenti as Gérard de Nerval, Eugène Fromentin, Théophile Gautier, and Charles Baudelaire, who gathered in the Hôtel Pimpodan, where they formed the Club des Haschischins to partake in secret smoking sessions. Alev Lytle Croutier, *Harem: The World behind the Veil* (New York: Abbeville Press, 1989) 177.

36. The Colonial Exhibitions in Marseilles in 1922 introduced another Orientalist marketing technique in the form of posters and postcards. During the first three decades of the twentieth century the French in Algeria produced postcards of unveiled and scantily clad women. In the early part of the twentieth century this "marketing" of Arab harem women, like the nineteenth-century paintings of Fromentin and Ingres, was successful in maintaining stereotypes of sexual fantasy and desire. Croutier, *Harem*, 196.

37. Bhabha, *Location of Culture*, 96.

38. Fromentin, *Un été dans le Sahara*, 280–81.

39. Hutcheon, *Poetics*, 106.

40. Hutcheon, *Poetics*, 122.

41. Assia Djebar's 1978 film *La nouba des femmes de Mont Chenouba* vividly depicts the mountain life of the Berber women of Algeria and the oral stories they have passed down from one generation to another. This film is studied later in this chapter.

42. Curiously, as Djebar states in an interview with Clarisse Zimra in 1992, the fundamentalist group, the Front Islamique du Sabet, accuse her of "pandering to the expectations of the former masters," rather than targeting her gender as the principal reason for their actions against her. See Clarisse Zimra, "Disorienting the Subject in Djebar's *L'amour, la fantasia*," *Yale French Studies* 87 (1995): 169.

43. Bensmaïa, "Vanished Mediators," 2.

44. Assia Djebar, *Le Blanc de l'Algérie: Récit* (Paris: Albin Michel, 1995), 21.

45. At the writing of this book it is widely believed that, although highly visible as an organized body that inflicts violence on the populace, the FIS is not the sole group to be blamed. Many Algerian ex-

perts believe that the official military (predominately the Front de Liberation Nationale) is also to blame for a number of the murders of intellectuals and journalists.

46. Bensmaïa, "Vanished Mediators," 2.

47. Bourdieu, *Language and Symbolic Power*, 72.

48. Deleuze and Guattari, *Thousand Plateaus*, 243.

49. Tzvetan Todorov, "Bilinguisme, dialogisme et schizophrénie," in *Du bilinguisme*, ed. Jalil Bennani et al. (Paris: Denoël, 1985), 24.

50. A *nouba* is a women's circle where singing, telling stories, and dancing are favorite activities.

51. Spivak, *Other Worlds*, 105–6.

52. Lionnet, *Postcolonial Representations*, 3.

53. Mikhail Bakhtin, *The Dialogic Imagination: Four Essays* (Austin: University of Texas Press, 1981), 365.

54. Todorov, "Bilinguisme," 13; Todorov's emphasis.

55. Lionnet, *Postcolonial Representations*, 6.

56. Abdelwahab Meddeb, "L'interruption généalogique," *Esprit* (January 1995): 81.

57. Benjamin Stora, "Algérie: Absence et surabondance de mémoire," *Esprit* (January 1995): 62.

58. Stora, "Algérie," 63.

59. Mernissi, *Forgotten Queens*, 188.

60. Laura Mulvey, "Visual Pleasure and Narrative Cinema," in *The Sexual Subject: A* Screen *Reader in Sexuality* (New York: Routledge, 1992), 72.

61. The original, nonclassical, nonlinear screenplay of the film also caused a certain destabilization of the usual spectator-film relationship expected by Algerian audiences of the late 1970s. Réda Bensmaïa remarks:

> What struck the Maghrebian audience when the film first
> came out, was the general absence of any centering themes
> which would prevent them from becoming "engaged" or
> taken in by the film. In *La Nouba*, no perspective of classical
> narration is offered to the audience so that they may "close

> the gap" and feel wholeheartedly the sense of the film. [There is no] "story," or rather, no continuous "narrative"; no central dominant character. Is *La Nouba* a film about the martyr, Zouleikha? The quest of Lila? Or a homage to the numerous Algerian women who participated in the Revolution. Certainly, there is no one central guiding line to guide the audience towards a sense of final synthesis. Instead, the film seems to take mischievous pleasure in deceiving all the audience's desire for a "closing" or an end to the film's intention.

Réda Bensmaïa, *"La Nouba des femmes du Mont Chenoua:* Introduction à l'oeuvre fragmentale cinématographique," *World Literature Today* 70.4 (1997): 887.

62. In 1988 it was reported by the Western media that five hundred students lost their lives in protests and demonstrations in Algiers and other cities across Algeria due to the antiprotest action taken by the government at that time. Students and other citizens were protesting the high rates of unemployment and the eroding Algerian standard of living.

63. Interview with Assia Djebar in *Le monde,* vol. 12, 1993, n.p.

64. Todorov, "Bilinguisme," 15.

65. Stora, "Algérie," 67.

Chapter Four

1. The ex-centric is defined by Linda Hutcheon as that literary and cultural realm which encompasses minoritarian discourses that shape and challenge canonized theories and practices of Western discourse. Hutcheon, *Politics,* xi.

2. Centore, *Being and Becoming,* 22.

3. Deleuze and Guattari, *Thousand Plateaus,* 25; Deleuze and Guattari's emphasis.

4. *Shérazade: Dix-sept ans, brune, frisée, les yeux verts* (Paris: Stock, 1982); *Les Carnets de Shérazade* (Paris: Stock, 1985); *Le Fou de Shérazade* (Paris: Stock, 1991). In this chapter I use the translated

version of the first volume in the trilogy: *Sherazade: Missing, Aged Seventeen, Dark Curly Hair, Green Eyes,* translated by Dorothy Blair (London: Quartet Books, 1991). Citations from the other two novels are my own translations from the French.

5. Bhabha, *Location of Culture,* 36.

6. Deleuze and Guattari, *Thousand Plateaus,* 141.

7. Nonracial assimilation in France is blamed on the polarization of ethnic groups in French society. Much of this polarization is due to the 1990 Law of Difference, which declares, "All discrimination founded on ethnicity, a nation, a race, or a religion is forbidden." Instead of harmonizing France's ethnic groups, which is what the law intended, it has drawn barriers of racial strife. As Pierre-André Taguieff declared in a 1992 interview, "the reference to race presupposes the existence of distinct human races, in the sense of old anthropological categories," and therefore nourishes segregation. Taguieff, *Nouvel observateur,* 1 April 1992, 7, my translation. *Le droit à la différence* (the Right to Difference), as it has become known, is in fact a form of auto-exclusion that is just one manifestation of the identity crisis we find in all Western societies that contain many diverse ethnic groups. See my article "Le droit à la différence et l'individualisme moderne: La république française, est-elle menacée en 1993?" *Romance Review* 4 (Spring 1994).

8. Deleuze and Guattari, *Thousand Plateaus,* 277.

9. Sebbar, *Lettres parisiennes,* 126; my translation.

10. Begag and Chaouite, *Ecarts d'identité,* 48.

11. *Pieds noir* is the name given to the white Europeans who settled in Algeria, Morocco, and Tunisia during the colonial period.

12. Said, *Orientalism,* 26.

13. Ibid., 203.

14. In *On tue les petites filles* (Paris: Stock, 1978), Sebbar vividly studies the marginalized world of the poor working classes of France as well as its immigrant populations. As a social caseworker, Sebbar explores the effects of poverty and unemployment as direct causes of the abuse, abduction, pornography, and mortality of disadvantaged children in France. Her essay particularly explores the plight of

young women caught up in cycles of abuse and neglect in urban France.

15. Michel Laronde, *"Leïla Sebbar et le roman croisé: Histoire, mémoire, identité,"* *Celfan Review* 7 (1987-88): 9.

16. Tahar Djaout, "Black Beur Writing," *Research in African Literatures* 23 (1992): 217.

17. Mireille Rosello, "The Beur Nation: Toward a Theory of Departenance," *Research in African Literatures* 24 (1993): 21.

18. Deleuze, *Difference and Repetition,* 138.

19. Bhabha, *The Location of Culture,* 31.

20. A ZUP or *zone à urbaniser en priorité* is a zone designated for priority public housing development—in other words, partly rural and partly urbanized. These zones are marginalized, existing on the outskirts of Paris and other large urban centers. Usually they are poor and house only immigrant families.

21. Amar and Milza, *Immigration en France,* 36.

22. Ibid., 43.

23. Jean Bernabé et al., *Éloge de la créolité* (Paris: Gallimard, 1989), 14.

24. Rosello, "Beur Nation," 21.

25. Camille Lacoste-Dujardin and Mhand Khellil have criticized the French media for the way in which they have reported news centered on the plight of young Beur women in France. They fault the media for "a few cases [that] make headlines and sell newspapers." These few cases rarely offer detailed substantiation and do nothing but whip up sensationalism, which in turn fuels more racism between French and Maghrebian communities. More particularly, this sensationalism does little to help the young women in question. These young women are transformed into instant media "stars, but justice is not done to their situation, and they are never given a 'voice' of their own." Cited in Rosello, "Beur Nation," 16.

26. Deleuze and Guattari, *Thousand Plateaus,* 12.

27. Alec Hargreaves, "Language and Identity in Beur Culture," *French Cultural Studies,* (1990): 47.

28. Hargreaves states that accurate information about the "linguis-

tic condition of the immigrant community is very fragmented." For many of the 2,600,000 people of Arabic-speaking roots living in France, Arabic is a foreign language (this number includes 85,000 harkis [native Algerians who fought the French army against the Rebels] and their descendants, a total of 500,000). "The Beurs learn the language of their parents within the family home. As soon as they begin to move outside the home, however, French rapidly takes over as their principle language." Hargreaves, "Language and Identity," 48.

29. Michel Laronde, *Autour le roman beur: Immigration et identité* (Paris: L'Harmattan, 1993), 15.

30. Ibid., 16.

31. Felman, *What Does a Woman Want?* 4.

32. Deleuze and Guattari, *Thousand Plateaus,* 236, 239.

33. Rosa Luxemburg (1870–1919), German socialist and leader, with Karl Liebknecht, of the German Social-Democratic party, protested against the war of 1914. She was incarcerated from 1915 to 1917 and was assassinated during the Spartakist insurrection, an insurrection of which she herself had conceived in her *Letters to Spartacus.* She developed Marxist concepts concerning imperialism and workers' strikes and wrote *The Accumulation of Capital* (1913). Flora Tristan (1803–1844) was one of the nineteenth century's most celebrated socialists, and was instrumental in introducing the idea of feminism in France.

34. Saracens was the name given to the nomadic Arabs who came from Syria and the Arabian peninsula to threaten the African and eastern frontiers of the Roman Empire during the Middle Ages. They were noted for their strength, courage, and military conquests, particularly, under the banner of Islam, against the Christians of medieval Europe.

'Abd al-Qādir al Hādjdj was an Arab emir born near Mascara (1808–1883). Leader of the Algerian resistance against the French (1832–1847), who finally recognized his rule over the Western part of Algeria in 1837, upon the signing of the Treaty of Tafna. However, in 1844 his armies were virtually defeated and his lands taken. In 1847 he was brought and then detained in France. He was released in 1852 contingent upon his promise not to foment further rebellion in Algeria; and finally retired to Damascus in 1855. His remains were returned to Algeria in 1966. *Petit Larousse* (1984), 1089.

Indian writer Vidiadhar Surajprasad Naipaul was born in 1932 in Trinidad and has lived most of his life in London. His novels evoke the impossibility of the native Indian's assimilation into British culture, identity, and society. He advocates the return to one's origin as a means of finding one's true identity; this, he maintains, is found after a long, nomadic journey of self-discovery. Most of his novels' protagonists seek out their destiny in exile.

Arthur Rimbaud (1854-1891), a French poet whose work promoted a rebellion against all forms of political, religious, and artistic authority, had a profound influence on many poets of the twentieth century. Rimbaud produced most of his work before he was twenty, then wandered the globe, winding up in Abyssinia, where he became involved with French political interests.

35. Laronde, *Roman beur,* 166.

36. Ibid., 199; Laronde's emphasis.

37. Deleuze, *Difference and Repetition,* 55.

38. Laronde, *Roman beur,* 201.

39. Bhabha, *Location of Culture,* 70.

40. Deleuze and Guattari, *Thousand Plateaus,* 282.

41. Bhabha, *Location of Culture,* 4.

42. Sebbar, *Lettres parisiennes,* 138.

43. Gilles Deleuze and Félix Guattari, *Anti-Oedipus: Capitalism and Schizophrenia* (Minneapolis: University of Minnesota Press, 1983), xxii.

44. Ibid.

Epilogue

1. Habib Salha and Hamdi Hemaidi, preface to *Écrire le Maghreb* (Tunis: Cérès Editions, 1997), 5.

2. R. Bourquia, M. Charrad, and N. Gallagher, *"Femmes au*

Maghreb: Perspectives et questions," in *Femmes Culture et Société au Maghreb* (Tunis: Afrique Orient, 1996), 1:10.

3. Spivak. *Other Worlds,* 103.

4. Mernissi, *The Forgotten Queens of Islam,* 188. See chapter 3 for discussion of Mernissi's definition of "delicious voyages towards rivers of pleasure."

5. Hajer Djilani, *Et pourtant le ciel était bleu . . . : Roman* (Tunis: Éditions Techniques Spécialisées, 1994); Malika Mokeddem, *L'interdite: Roman* (Paris: Grasset, 1993). All translations of these two novels are my own.

6. See also chapter 3.

7. Although Tunisia upheld the general resolutions of the League of Arab Nations' convention—held in Cairo 3 August 1990 to condemn the "Iraqi aggression" against Kuwait and the immediate withdrawal of Iraqi troops from the area—the Tunisian government refused to support foreign intervention and declined any military involvement by its own military forces. This policy was supported by President Zine El Abidine Ben Ali's address to the Tunisian people at Carthage, 11 August 1990, wherein he stated: "Tunisia, both as a State and as a people, enjoying excellent relations with both Irak and Kuwait, and in view of her national and historical duty, refuses to ratify *faits accomplis* or side with one party or another." *Tunisia and the Gulf Crisis: A Constant Commitment to International Legality,* collection of speeches and acts on the Gulf War made public by the Tunisian government (Tunis: n.p., 1990), 68–69.

8. One cannot help remark here the metaphor of marriage between France and Algeria. A union that no matter how much both countries have sought to absolve, is forever present. See chapter 1.

9. In the last few years, Mokeddem has been threatened by the FIS, even while residing in France.

10. Khalida Messaoudi, a professor of mathematics, has fought for feminine and human rights since the early 1970s. She has been condemned to death by the religious fundamentalists of the FIS, but continues to live clandestinely in Algeria. She is one of the only radical

feminist leaders left in Algeria, and today continues her struggle to fight against the Code de la Famille (legislated in 1984) and to end all negotiation with the FIS and the despotic rule of incompetent and corrupt FLN governments. She fights for a new political and cultural agenda in Algeria, one that includes a democratic ideal promoting freedom, secularism, and equality for all citizens residing in her country. Khalida Messaoudi, *Une Algérienne debout: Entretiens avec Elisabeth Schemla* (Paris: Flammarion, 1995), 84.

11. Elisabeth Schemla is editor-in-chief of *Le nouvel observateur* and author of *Edith Cresson, la femme piégée*. Messaoudi, *Algérienne debout*, 86.

12. Ibid., 84.

13. Edward Said, *Representations of the Intellectual* (New York: Vintage, 1996), 61.

Bibliography

Ahmed, Leila. *Women and Gender in Islam: Historical Roots of a Modern Debate*. New Haven: Yale University Press, 1992.

Albert Memmi: Prophéte de la décolonisation. Ed. Edmond Jouve. Paris: Académie diplomatique internationale Agence de Coopération culturelle et technique SEPEG International, 1993.

Alloula, Malek. *The Colonial Harem*. Minneapolis: University of Minnesota Press, 1986.

Amar, Marianne, and Pierre Milza. *L'immigration en France au vingtième siècle*. Paris: Armand Colin, 1990.

Arnaud, Jacqueline et al. *Hommage à Mohammed Dib in Kalim*. No. 6. Algiers: Office des Publications Universitaires, 1985.

Ashcroft, Bill, Gareth Griffiths, and Helen Tiffin. *The Empire Writes Back: Theory and Practice in Post-Colonial Literatures*. New York: Routledge, 1989.

Aurbakken, Kristine. *L'étoile d'araignée: Une lecture de Nedjma de Kateb Yacine*. Paris: Publisud, 1986.

Bakhtin, Mikhail. *The Dialogic Imagination: Four Essays*. Austin: University of Texas Press, 1981.

Barthes, Roland. *Le degré zéro de l'écriture*. Paris: Seuil, 1953.

Beauvoir, Simone de. *Le deuxième sexe*. 2 vols. Paris: Gallimard, 1946. Translated by H. Parshley under the title *The Second Sex* (New York: Knopf, 1952).

Beauvoir, Simone de, and Gisèle Halimi. *Djamila Boupacha: The Story of the Torture of a Young Algerian Girl Which Shocked Liberal French Opinion*. New York: Macmillan, 1962.

Begag, Azouz. *Béni, ou, le paradis privé*. Paris: Seuil, 1989.

Begag, Azouz, and Abdellatif Chaouite. *Ecarts d'identité*. Paris: Seuil, 1990.

Benhabib, Seyla, and Drucilla Cornell. *Feminism as Critique: On the*

Politics of Gender. Minneapolis: University of Minnesota Press, 1987.

Ben Jelloun, Tahar. *Harrouda: Roman*. Paris: Denoël, 1973.

―――. *Hospitalité française: Racisme et immigration maghrébine*. Paris: Seuil, 1984.

―――. *La nuit sacrée*. Paris: Seuil, 1987. Translated by Alan Sheridan under the title *The Sacred Night* (Orlando, Fla.: Harcourt Brace Jovanovich, 1989).

―――. *L'écrivain public: Récit*. Paris: Seuil, 1983.

―――. *L'enfant de sable: Roman*. Paris: Seuil, 1985. Translated by Alan Sheridan under the title *The Sand Child* (Orlando, Fla.: Harcourt Brace Jovanovich, 1987).

―――. "Tahar le fou, Tahar le sage." Interview by Philippe Gaillard. *Jeune Afrique* 1404 (2 December 1987): 44–47.

Bensmaïa, Réda. "The Exiles of Nabile Farès: Or, How to Become a Minority." *Yale French Studies* 2.83 (1993): 44–71.

―――. "*La nouba des femmes du Mont Chenoua:* Introduction à l'oeuvre fragmentale cinématographique." *World Literature Today* 70.4 (1997): 877–84.

―――. "The Vanished Mediators: The Algerian Intellectuals Facing Power." *Diacritics*, Fall 1997.

Bergner, Gwen. "The Role of Gender in Fanon's *Black Skin, White Masks.*" *PMLA* 110 (January 1995): 75–88.

Bernabé, Jean, Patrick Chamoiseau, and Raphael Confiant. *Éloge de la créolité*. Paris: Gallimard, 1989.

Best, Steven, and Douglas Kellner. *Postmodern Theory: Critical Interrogations*. New York: Guilford Press, 1991.

Bet, Marie-Thérèse. "La littérature maghrébine francophone." Communication au XLIIIe Congrès de l'Association, 22 July 1991.

Bhabha, Homi K. "The Discourse of Colonialism." In *Literature, Politics and Theory: Papers from the Essex Conference, 1976–84*, ed. Francis Barker et al. London: Methuen, 1986.

―――. *The Location of Culture*. New York: Routledge, 1994.

―――. "The Other Question: Difference, Discrimination and the Discourse of Colonialism." In *Literature, Politics and Theory: Pa-*

pers from the Essex Conference, 1976–84, ed. Francis Barker et al. London: Methuen, 1986.

————. "Representation and the Colonial Text: A Critical Exploration of Some Forms of Mimeticism." In *The Theory of Reading,* ed. Frank Gloversmith. Totowa, N.J.: Barnes and Noble, 1984.

Bonn, Charles. *Bibliographie de la littérature maghrébine, 1980–1990.* Paris: EDICEF, 1992.

————. "L'irrégularité de l'écrivain maghrébin francophone." *Revue de l'Institut de Sociologie* (1990–91): 129–38.

————. *La littérature algérienne de langue française et ses lectures: Imaginaire et discours d'idées.* Sherbrooke, Québec: Naaman, 1974.

————. *Littérature maghrébine, répertoire des chercheurs.* Paris: Centre National de la Recherche Scientifique, 1976.

————. *Nabile Farès: La migration et le marge.* Casablanca: Afrique Orient, 1986.

————. *Le roman algérien de langue française.* Paris: L'Harmattan, 1985.

Boumediene, Amel. "Quand les femmes sont un butin de guerre: Le martyre de Kheira." *Nouvel observateur,* 25 January 1995: 30–31.

Boundas, Constantin, and Dorothea Olkowski. *Gilles Deleuze and the Theater of Philosophy.* New York: Routledge, 1994.

Bourdieu, Pierre. *Language and Symbolic Power.* Cambridge, Mass.: Harvard University Press, 1994.

Braidotti, Rosi. *Nomadic Subjects: Embodiment and Sexual Difference in Contemporary Feminist Theory.* New York: Columbia University Press, 1994.

————. *Patterns of Dissonance: A Study of Women in Contemporary Philosophy.* New York: Routledge, 1991.

————. "Toward a New Nomadism: Feminist Deleuzian Tracks; or, Metaphysics and Metabolism." In *Gilles Deleuze and the Theater of Philosophy,* ed. Constantin Boundas and Dorothea Olkowski, 159–86. New York: Routledge, 1994.

Burke, Edmund, III, and Ira M. Lapidus, eds. *Islam, Politics, and Social Movements.* Berkeley: University of California Press, 1988.

Bibliography

Butler, Judith. "Contingent Foundations: Feminism and the Question of 'Postmodernism.'" In *Feminists Theorize the Political,* ed. Judith Butler and Joan Scott. New York: Routledge, 1992.

Butler, Judith, and Joan Scott, eds. *Feminists Theorize the Political.* New York: Routledge, 1992.

Caute, David. *Frantz Fanon.* New York: Viking, 1970.

Centore, F. F. *Being and Becoming: A Critique of Post-Modernism.* Westport, Conn.: Greenwood Press, 1991.

Chraïbi, Driss. *La Civilisation, ma mère!* Paris: Denoël, 1972.

————. *Les boucs: Roman.* Paris: Denoël, 1955.Croutier, Alev Lytle. *Harem: The World behind the Veil.* New York: Abbeville Press, 1989.

Déjeux, Jean. *Maghreb: Littératures de langue française.* Paris: Arcantère, 1993.

————. *Mohammed Dib: Écrivain algérien.* Sherbrooke, Québec: Naaman, 1977.

————. "Romans algériens et guerre de libération." *Esprit créateur* 26.1 (Spring 1986): 70–82.

De Lauretis, Teresa, ed. *Feminist Studies, Critical Studies.* Bloomington: Indiana University Press, 1986.

Deleuze, Gilles. *Difference and Repetition.* New York: Columbia University Press, 1994.

Deleuze, Gilles, and Félix Guattari. *Anti-Oedipus: Capitalism and Schizophrenia.* Minneapolis: University of Minnesota Press, 1983.

————. *Kafka: Toward a Minor Literature.* Minneapolis: University of Minnesota Press, 1986.

————. *Mille plateaux.* Paris: Minuit, 1980. Translated by Brian Massumi under the title *A Thousand Plateaus: Capitalism and Schizophrenia* (Minneapolis: University of Minnesota Press, 1987).

————. *Nomadology: The War Machine.* New York: Semiotext(e), Columbia University Press, 1986.

————. *Qu'est-ce que la philosophie?* Paris: Minuit, 1991. Translated by Hugh Tomlinson and Graham Burchell under the title *What Is Philosophy?* (New York: Columbia University Press, 1994).

Derrida, Jacques. *L'Écriture et la différence*. Paris: Seuil, 1967.

————. *Margins of Philosophy*. Chicago: Chicago University Press, 1982.

Dine, Philip. *Images of the Algerian War: French Fiction and Film, 1954-1992*. Oxford: Clarendon Press, 1994.

Djaout, Tahar. "Black Beur Writing." *Research in African Literatures* 23 (1992): 217–21.

Djebar, Assia. *Les alouettes naïves*. Paris: Julliard, 1967.

————. *L'amour, la fantasia: Roman*. Paris: Albin Michel, 1985.

————. *Le blanc de l'Algérie: Récit*. Paris: Albin Michel, 1995.

————. "Du français comme butin." *La quinzaine littéraire* 436 (Mar. 16–31, 1985): 25.

————. "Fugitive, et ne le sachant pas." *Esprit créateur* 33.2 (summer 1993): 129–33.

————. *Les enfants du nouveau monde: Roman*. Paris: Julliard, 1962.

————. *Les impatients: Roman*. Paris: Julliard, 1958.

————. *Oran, langue morte*. Arles: Actes Sud, 1997.

————. *La soif: Roman*. Paris: Julliard, 1958.

————. *Vaste est la prison: Roman*. Paris: Albin Michel, 1995.

Djilani, Hajer. *Et pourtant le ciel était bleu . . . : Roman*. Sidi Bou Saïd, Tunisia: Éditions Techniques Spécialisées, 1994.

Donadey, Anne. "Assia Djebar's Poetics of Subversion." *Esprit créateur* 33.2 (summer 1993): 107–17.

Du Plessis, Nancy. "Leïla Sebbar, Voice of Exile." *World Literature Today* 63.3 (summer 1989): 415–17.

Elbaz, Robert. *Le discours maghrébin: Dynamique textuelle chez Albert Memmi*. Longueuil, Québec: Editions du Préambule, 1988.

Fanon, Frantz. *A Dying Colonialism*. New York: Grove Press, 1965.

————. *Black Skin, White Masks*. New York: Grove Press, 1967.

————. *Les damnés de la terre*. Paris: Maspero, 1961.

————. "On National Culture." In *Colonial Discourse and Post-Colonial Theory*, ed. Patrick Williams and Laura Chrisman. New York: Columbia University Press, 1994.

Farès, Nabile. *Le champ des oliviers*. Paris: Seuil, 1972.

Bibliography

————. "La littérature maghrébine de langue française." *Français dans le monde* 189 (November-December 1984): 68–71.

————. *Mémoire de l'absent*. Paris: Seuil, 1974.

————. *Un passager de l'Occident*. Paris: Seuil, 1971.

————. *Yahia, pas de chance*. Paris: Seuil, 1970.

Felman, Shoshana. *What Does a Woman Want? Reading and Sexual Difference*. Baltimore: John Hopkins University Press, 1993.

Flax, Jane. "The End of Innocence." In *Feminists Theorize the Political*, ed. Judith Butler and Joan Scott. New York: Routledge, 1992.

————. *Thinking Fragments: Psychoanalysis, Feminism, and Postmodernism in the Contemporary West*. Berkeley: University of California Press, 1990.

Foucault, Michel. *The Archaeology of Knowledge*. Translated by A. M. Sheridan Smith. New York: Pantheon, 1972.

————. *Discipline and Punish: The Birth of the Prison*. Translated by Alan Sheridan. New York: Vintage, 1979.

Franco, Jean. "Beyond Ethnocentrism: Gender, Power and the Third World Intelligentsia." In *Colonial Discourse and Post-Colonial Theory*, ed. Patrick Williams and Laura Chrisman. New York, Columbia University Press, 1994.

Franklin, Sarah, Celia Lury, and Jackie Stacey, eds. *Off Centre: Feminism and Cultural Studies*. London: HarperCollins Academic, 1991.

Fraser, Nancy. "What's Critical about Critical Theory? The Case of Habermas and Gender." In *Feminism as Critique: On the Politics of Gender*, ed. Seyla Benhabib and Drucilla Cornell. Minneapolis: University of Minnesota Press, 1987.

Fromentin, Eugène. *Une année dans le Sahel*. Paris: Plon, 1893.

————. *Un été dans le Sahara*. Paris: Plon, 1896.

Fuss, Diana. "Interior Colonies: Frantz Fanon and the Politics of Identification." *Diacritics* Summer-Fall 1994: 20–33.

Gontard, Marc. *La violence du texte: ...tudes sur la littérature marocaine de langue française*. Paris: L'Harmattan, 1981.

Gordon, Linda. "What's New in Women's History." In *Feminist*

Studies, Critical Studies, ed. Teresa de Lauretis, 20–30. Bloomington: Indiana University Press, 1986.

Grosrichard, Alain. *Structure du sérail: La fiction du despotisme asiatique dans l'Occident classique.* Paris: Seuil, 1979.

Grosz, Elizabeth. "Sexual Difference and the Problem of Essentialism." In *The Essential Difference,* ed. Naomi Schor and Elizabeth Weed. Bloomington: Indiana University Press, 1994.

———. "A Thousand Tiny Little Sexes: Feminism and Rhizomatics." In *Gilles Deleuze and the Theater of Philosophy,* ed. Constantin Boundas and Dorothea Olkowski, 187–210. New York: Routledge, 1994.

Guérin, Jeanyves, ed. *Albert Memmi: Écrivain et sociologue.* Paris: L'Harmattan, 1990.

Habermas, Jürgen. *Moral Consciousness and Communicative Action.* Translated by Christian Lenhard and Shierry Weber. Cambridge, Mass.: MIT Press, 1993.

Haraway, Donna. "Ecce Homo, Ain't (Ar'n't) I a Woman, and Inappropriate/d Others: The Human in a Post-Humanist Landscape." In *Feminists Theorize the Political.* Ed. Judith Butler and Joan Scott. New York: Routledge, 1992.

———. "A Manifesto for Cyborgs: Science, Technology, and Socialist Feminism in the 1980s." *Socialist Review,* no. 80 (1985): 65–107.

———. *Simians, Cyborgs, and Women: The Reinvention of Nature.* New York: Routledge, 1991.

Hargreaves, Alec. "Beur Fiction: Voices from the Immigrant Community in France." *French Review* 62.4 (March 1989): 661–68.

———. "Figuring Out Their Place: Post-Colonial Writers of Algerian Origin in France." *Forum for Modern Language Studies* 29.4 (1993): 333–45.

———. "In Search of a Third Way: Beur Writers between France and North Africa." *New Comparison,* Autumn 1990: 72–83.

———. "Language and Identity in Beur Culture." *French Cultural Studies* 1.1 (February 1990): 47–58.

Bibliography

————. "Sexualité et ethnicité dans le roman beur." *Celfan Review* 7.1–2 (1987–88): 18–20.

Henderson, Mae. "Speaking in Tongues: Dialogics, Dialectics, and the Black Woman Writer's Literary Tradition." In *Feminists Theorize the Political,* ed. Judith Butler and Joan Scott. New York: Routledge, 1992.

Hooks, Bell. *Feminist Theory from Margin to Center.* Boston: South End Press, 1984.

————. *Yearning: Race, Gender, and Cultural Politics.* Boston: South End Press, 1990.

Hutcheon, Linda. *A Poetics of Postmodernism: History, Theory, Fiction.* New York: Routledge, 1988.

————. *The Politics of Postmodernism.* New York: Routledge, 1989.

Irigaray, Luce. *Ce sexe qui n'en est pas un.* Paris: Minuit, 1977.

Jardine, Alice. *Gynesis: Configurations of Woman and Modernity.* Ithaca: Cornell University Press, 1985.

Khatibi, Abdelkebir. *Amour bilingue.* Montpellier: Fata Morgana, 1983.

————. *Maghreb pluriel.* Paris: Denoël, 1983.

————. *Le roman maghrébin: Essai.* Paris: Maspero, 1968.

Knauss, Peter. *The Persistence of Patriarchy: Class, Gender, and Ideology in Twentieth-Century Algeria.* New York: Praeger, 1987.

Lahnomri, Abdeljalil. "Enseignement de la langue française au Maroc et dialogue des cultures." *Français dans le monde* 189 (November-December 1984): 21.

Laronde, Michel. *Autour du roman beur: Immigration et identité.* Paris: L'Harmattan, 1993.

————. "Leïla Sebbar et le roman croisé: Histoire, mémoire, identité." *Celfan Review* 7.1–2 (1987–88): 6–13.

Lazarus, Neil. *Resistance in Postcolonial African Fiction.* New Haven: Yale University Press, 1990.

Lévi-Strauss, Claude. *Anthropologie structurale.* 2 vols. Paris: Plon, 1973.

Lionnet, Françoise. *Autobiographical Voices: Race, Gender, Self-Portraiture.* Ithaca: Cornell University Press, 1989.

———. *Postcolonial Representations: Women, Literature, Identity.* Ithaca: Cornell University Press, 1995.

Loomba, Ania. "Overworlding the Third World." In *Colonial Discourse and Post-Colonial Theory,* ed. Patrick Williams and Laura Chrisman. New York, Columbia University Press, 1994.

Lyon, David. *Postmodernity.* Minneapolis: University of Minnesota Press, 1994.

Lyotard, Jean-François. *The Postmodern Condition: A Report on Knowledge.* Translated by Geoff Bennington and Brian Massouri. Minneapolis: University of Minnesota Press, 1993.

Madelain, Jacques. *L'errance et l'itenéraire: Lecture du roman maghrébin de langue française.* Paris: Sindbad, 1983.

Marrouchi, Mustapha. "Breaking Up/Down/Out of Boundaries: Tahar Ben Jelloun." *Francographies* 21.4 (Winter 1990): 71–83.

Marx-Scouras, Danielle. "The Poetics of Maghrebine Illegitimacy." *Esprit créateur* 26.1 (Spring 1986): 3–10.

McClintock, Anne. "The Angle of Progress: Pitfalls of the Term 'Post-Colonialism.'" In *Colonial Discourse and Post-Colonial Theory,* ed. Patrick Williams and Laura Chrisman. New York, Columbia University Press, 1994.

McClure, Kirstie. "The Issue of Foundations: Scientized Politics, Politicized Science, and Feminist Critical Practice." In *Feminists Theorize the Political,* ed. Judith Butler and Joan Scott. New York: Routledge, 1992.

Meddeb, Abdelwahab. "L'interruption généalogique." *Esprit,* January 1995: 74–81.

———. "Postcolonialisme: Arguement." Typescript of a paper given in Paris on 8 December 1995 (copy courtesy of Réda Bensmaïa).

Mehrez, Samia. "Azouz Begag: Un di Zafas di Bidoufile (Azouz Begag: Un des enfants du bidonville) or The Beur Writer: A Question of Territory." *Yale French Studies* 2.82 (1993): 25–42.

Memmi, Albert. *Albert Memmi: Un entretien avec Robert Davies.* Outremont, Québec: Editions L'Enticelle, 1975.

———. *Anthologie des écrivains français du Maghreb.* Paris: Présence Africaine, 1969.

———. *Portrait du colonisé, précedé du portrait du colonisateur.* Paris: J.-J. Pauvert, 1966.

———. *Le scorpion, ou, la confession imaginaire.* Paris: Gallimard, 1969.

———, ed. *Ecrivains francophones du Maghreb: Anthologie.* Paris: Seghers, 1985.

Merad, Ghani. *La littérature algérienne d'expression française: Approches socio-culturelles.* Paris: Oswald, 1976.

Mernissi, Fatima. *Beyond the Veil: Male-Female Dynamics in Modern Muslim Society.* Bloomington: Indiana University Press, 1987.

———. *Le harem politique: Le prophéte et les femmes.* Paris: Albin Michel, 1987.

———. *Sultanes oubliées: Femmes chefs d'Etat en Islam.* Paris: Albin Michel, 1990. Translated by Mary Jo Lakeland under the title *The Forgotten Queens of Islam* (Minneapolis: University of Minnesota Press, 1993).

Messaoudi, Khalida. *Une Algérienne debout: Entretiens avec Elisabeth Schemla.* Paris: Flammarion, 1995.

M'Henni, Mansour, ed. *Tahar Ben Jelloun: Stratégies d'écriture.* Paris: L'Harmattan, 1993.

Miller, Christopher. *Theories of Africans: Francophone Literature and Anthropology.* Chicago: University of Chicago Press, 1990.

Mishra, Vijay, and Bob Hodge. "What is Post(-)colonialism?" In *Colonial Discourse and Post-Colonial Theory,* ed. Patrick Williams and Laura Chrisman. New York, Columbia University Press, 1994.

Mokeddem, Malika. *L'interdite: Roman.* Paris: Bernard Grasset, 1993.

Mortimer, Mildred. "The Desert in Algerian Fiction." *Esprit créateur* 26.1 (Spring 1986): 60–69.

———. "Language and Space in the Fiction of Assia Djebar and Leïla Sebbar." *Research in African Literatures* 19.3 (1988): 301–11.

———. "On the Road: Leïla Sebbar's Fugitive Heroines." *Research in African Literatures* 23.2 (1992): 195–201.

M'rabet, Fadéla. "Les Algériennes." In *Middle Eastern Muslim Women Speak,* ed. Elizabeth Fernea and Basima Bezirgan. Austin: University of Texas Press, 1977.

Mulvey, Laura. "Visual Pleasure and Narrative Cinema." In *The Sexual Subject: A* Screen *Reader in Sexuality.* New York: Routledge, 1992.

Murdoch, Adlai H. "Rewriting Writing: Identity, Exile and Renewal in Assia Djebar's *L'amour, la fantasia.*" *Yale French Studies* 83 (1993): 71–92.

Nisbet, Anne-Marie. *Le personnage féminin dans le roman maghrébin de langue française des indépendances à 1980: Représentations et fonctions.* Sherbrooke, Québec: Naaman, 1982.

Nora, Pierre. *Les Français d'Algérie.* Paris: Julliard, 1961.

Ottavj, Marie-France Vanina. "La structure en étoile de scorpion." In *Albert Memmi: écrivain et sociologue,* ed. Jeanyves Guérin, 61–70. Paris: L'Harmattan, 1990.

Ricoeur, Paul. *Oneself as Another.* Translated by Kathleen Blamey. Chicago: University of Chicago Press, 1992.

———. *Temps et récit.* Vol. 2: *La configuration du temps dans le récit de fiction.* Paris: Seuil, 1984. Translated by Kathleen McLaughlin and David Pellauer under the title *Time and Narrative: The Configuration of Time.* (Chicago: University of Chicago Press, 1984.

Rivas, Pierre. "Littérature nationale et littérature sous dépendance." In *Albert Memmi: Écrivain et sociologue,* ed. Jeanyves Guérin. Paris: L'Harmattan, 1990.

Rosello, Mireille. "The Beur Nation: Toward a Theory of Departenance." *Research in African Literatures* 24 (1993): 13–24.

Ross, Kristin. *Fast Cars, Clean Bodies: Decolonization and the Reordering of French Culture.* Cambridge, Mass.: MIT Press, 1995.

Roumani, Judith. "A Literature of One's Own: A Survey of Literary History and Criticism of Maghrebian Francophone Literature." *Esprit créateur* 26.1 (Spring 1986): 11–21.

Said, Edward. *Orientalism.* New York: Vintage, 1979.

———. "Orientalism Reconsidered." In *Literature, Politics and Theory: Papers from the Essex Conference, 1976–84,* ed. Francis Barker et al. London: Methuen, 1986.

———. *Representations of the Intellectual.* New York: Vintage, 1996.

Scharfman, Ronnie. "Starting from Talismano: Abdelwahab Meddeb's Nomadic Writing." *Esprit créateur* 26.1 (Spring 1986): 40–49.

Schneider, Judith Morganroth. "Albert Memmi and Alain Finkielkraut: Two Discourses on French Jewish Identity." *Romanic Review* 81 (1990): 130–36.

Schor, Naomi, and Elizabeth Weed, eds. *The Essential Difference.* Bloomington: Indiana University Press, 1994.

Sebbar, Leïla. *Les carnets de Shérazade.* Paris: Stock, 1985.

———. *Fatima, ou, les Algériennes au square.* Paris: Stock, 1981.

———. *Le fou de Shérazade.* Paris: Stock, 1991.

———. *Lettres parisiennes: Autopsie de l'exil.* Paris: Barrault, 1986.

———. *Shérazade: Dix-sept ans, brune, frisée, les yeux verts.* Paris: Stock, 1982. Translated by Dorothy Blair under the title *Sherazade: Missing, Aged Seventeen, Dark Curly Hair, Green Eyes* (London: Quartet Books, 1991).

Sharpe, Jenny. "The Unspeakable Limits of Rape." In *Colonial Discourse and Post-Colonial Theory,* ed. Patrick Williams and Laura Chrisman. New York: Columbia University Press, 1994.

Sharpley-Whiting, T. D. "Anti-Black Femininity and Mixed-Race Identity: Engaging Fanon to Reread Capécia." In *Fanon: A Critical Reader,* ed. Lewis R. Gordon and T. D. Sharpley-Whiting. Cambridge, Mass.: Blackwell, 1996.

Smith, Sidonie, and Julia Watson, eds. *De/Colonizing the Subject: The Politics of Gender in Women's Autobiography.* Minneapolis: University of Minnesota Press, 1992.

Spivak, Gayatri C. "French Feminism Revisited: Ethics and Politics." In *Feminists Theorize the Political,* ed. Judith Butler and Joan Scott. New York: Routledge, 1992.

———. *In Other Worlds: Essays in Cultural Politics.* New York: Routledge, 1988.

———. *The Post-Colonial Critic: Interviews, Strategies, Dialogues.* Edited by Sarah Harasym. New York: Routledge, 1990.

Stora, Benjamin. "Algérie: absence et surabondance de mémoire." *Esprit,* January 1995: 62–67.

————. *La gangrène et l'oubli: La mémoire de la guerre d'Algérie.* Paris: La Découverte, 1991.

Tcheho, I. C. "Lahsen Mouzouni et la réception critique du roman marocain de langue française." *Esprit créateur* 26.1 (Spring 1986): 86–93.

Todorov, Tzvetan. "Bilinguisme, dialogisme et schizophrénie." In *Du bilinguisme,* ed. Jalil Bennani et al., 11–26. Paris: Denoël, 1985.

Turk, Nada. *"L'amour, la fantasia* d'Assia Djebar: Chronique de guerre, voix des femmes." *Celfan Review* 7.1–2 (1987–88): 21–24.

Westermarck, Edward. *Ritual and Belief in Morocco.* 2 vols. New York: University Books, 1968.

Wood, David, ed. *Derrida: A Critical Reader.* Cambridge, Mass.: Blackwell, 1992.

Woodhull, Winifred. "Exile." *Yale French Studies* 82 (1993): 7–24

————. *Transfigurations of the Maghreb: Feminism, Decolonization, and Literatures.* Minneapolis: University of Minnesota Press, 1993.

Yacine, Kateb. *Nedjma: Roman.* Paris: Seuil, 1956.

Yetiv, Isaac. "La dimension juive dans l'oeuvre d'Albert Memmi." In *Albert Memmi: écrivain et sociologue,* ed. Jeanyves Guérin, 79–89. Paris: L'Harmattan, 1990.

————. "Du *Scorpion* au *Désert,* Albert Memmi Revisited." *Studies in Twentieth-Century Literature* 7.1 (Fall 1982): 77–87.

Zimra, Clarisse. "Disorienting the Subject in Djebar's *L'amour, la fantasia." Yale French Studies* 87 (1995): 149–70.

————. "Writing Woman: The Novels of Assia Djebar." *Substance* 69 (1992): 68–84.

Index

Ábd-al-Qādir, 1, 182
acentered, 195; margins, 202
affects, 97, 98
Africa, 26, 165, 172
African-American, 69, 175
agency, 10, 15, 21, 70, 72, 73, 139, 204;
    active, 6, 13, 73, 145, 191; collec-
    tive, 122; enunciative, 132; femi-
    nine, 17, 20, 56, 149; feminine-
    communitarian, 32, 139; modes
    of, 20; new boundaries of, 50;
    outside, 131; platform of, 151,
    191; public, 11, 18, 192; and
    women, 17, 19
ahistorical, 28, 30
Algeria(n), 8, 15, 24, 31, 32, 37, 40, 42,
    43, 44, 47, 72, 114, 118, 120, 121,
    123, 124, 125, 126, 128, 132, 133,
    135, 137, 140, 142, 144, 146, 147,
    149, 150, 155, 156, 157, 160, 164,
    168, 171, 176, 177, 181, 189, 190,
    199–202; authors, 40, 133, 186,
    197; conquest and colonization
    of, 1, 113, 116, 122, 130; feminin-
    ity, 120; first writings in French
    34; France's archives on, 111, 113;
    heritage, 184; history, 16, 18, 36,
    115, 116, 118, 136, 141, 201; inde-
    pendence, 25, 35, 40, 42, 116; na-
    tion, 45; people, 35, 41, 42, 44, 46,
    121, 135, 144, 163, 202; and the
    modern world, 36; postrevolu-
    tionary, 133, 135; rebels, 1; revo-
    lution, 41, 45, 52; war, 12, 39, 40,
    43, 47, 168; women, 20, 112, 113,
    115, 116, 117, 118, 119, 122, 127,
    128, 129, 130, 131, 132, 138, 139,
    144, 198, 201, 203
Algerianness, 159, 183
Algiers, 59, 122, 139, 178
Alloula, Malek, 124

Les Alouettes naïves 39, 40
alterity, 4, 7, 21, 30, 72, 110, 186
Amour bilingue, 65
L'Amour, la fantasia, 18. *See* chapter 3
androgyny, in *L'enfant de sable*, 79
animalization of the colonized, 24
Une année dans le Sahel, 125, 126
anomal, 59, 60, 155; state, 60
anomalous, 59, 75, 153, 203; space, 83.
    See also chapter 2
an-Other, 76, 167
anticolonial, 34; agendas, 35; discourse,
    35
Arab, 44, 47, 49, 52, 55, 62, 65, 66, 68,
    119, 122, 128, 157, 158, 159, 167,
    177, 178; culture, 38, 43, 53, 79,
    173; folktale, 85; in France, 25,
    34; heritage, 21, 31, 156, 164;
    history, 165; identity, 57, 164;
    nations, 193; -Other, 176 ; tradi-
    tionalism, 5, 157; women, 126,
    127, 144; worker in France, 46;
    world, 194, 200
Arabic, 51, 55, 80, 84, 95, 97, 116, 117,
    139, 163, 165, 166, 174, 200
Arabization, 33, 48
Arabized, 150
asexual and androgynous, 65
assemblage(s), 59, 60, 76
au-delà, 60
autobiographical, 136, 146; details, 131;
    time, 118
autobiography, 16, 131, 137, 199; ap-
    propriated, 117; collective, 118,
    121; and Djebar, 112, 141; femi-
    nine, 18, 119
autosufficiency, 59
awakening of feminine, 12, 16

Bakhtin, Mikhail, 140
Barthes, Roland, 119

Index

Index

Index

interstitial space, 5
intersubjective, 56, 61, 64, 68, 72;
   space, 6
intersubjectivity, 6
Iraq. *See* the Epilogue
Irigaray, Luce, 70
Islam, 62, 110
Islamic, 200; fanaticism, 134, 143; tra-
   ditionalism, 80, 164
Islamism, 8

Jeune Afrique, 77, 93
Jewish, 49, 172, 199

Khatibi, Abdelkabir, 5, 32, 52, 55, 59, 65

Lacanian, 29
Laronde, Michel, 182
Lettres parisiennes: Autopsie de l'exil, 50
Libération, 174
line of flight, 4, 5, 20, 76; in *L'enfant de
   sable*, 88, 91, 110
linguistic field. *See* Bourdieu, Pierre
Lionnet, François, 142
logocentrism, 17; Western, 19
logoi, 17
Loti, Pierre, 158, 159
lutteuse in *Shérazade*, 163
Luxemburg, Rosa, 181, 182
Lyotard, François, 12

Maghreb, 12, 13, 25, 31, 32, 33, 34, 37,
   43, 44, 49, 52, 53, 55, 56, 57, 64,
   68, 71, 72, 76, 85, 95, 124, 130,
   132, 133, 135, 144, 153, 183, 189,
   190, 191, 193, 203; and the postcolonial, 22, 38; and women, 24,
   112, 200, 202
Maghrebian, 2, 44, 48, 49, 50, 52, 56,
   62, 70, 81 124, 156, 163, 176, 183,
   199; consciousness, 5, 9; countries, 33, 189; Francophone author, 2–3, 5, 15, 26, 32, 33, 38, 43,
   51, 53, 54, 66, 69, 77, 154; feminine protagonist, 72; feminism,
   71; French, 21, 45; ideology, 43;
   literature, 22, 55; narratives in
   French, 25, 35, 51; women, 18, 21
   19, 20, 32, 43, 50, 71, 72, 73, 118,

124, 155, 170, 177, 190, 191, 201,
   202, 204
Maghreb pluriel, 55
majoritarian position, 67
majority, 68, 69
Mammeri, Mouloud, 34
map(s), 156, 172; of identity, 171
mapping, 90
maquis, 177, 203
Marche des Beurs, 170
marginal(ity), 10, 12; and Ben Jelloun,
   76, 77, 78, 87, 92; position, 17
marginalization, 11, 20, 43; process, 51
marginalized, 50, 63, 153, 168, 181;
   groups, 24, 46, 48, 75, 93, 122,
   157, 167
margins, 47, 51, 53, 61, 145, 156
marriage, 44; mixed, 33; Arab-French
   metaphor, 33, 44; as destruction
   of the household, 45
master and slave, 5, 125
materialism, 70
Matisse, Henri, 160
Mauresque, 124, 125, 126
McClintock, Anne, 27–28
Meddeb, Abdelwahab, 142
Memmi, Albert, 24, 25, 33, 38, 40, 43,
   48, 51, 125
Mémoire de l'absent, 47
Mernissi, Fatima, 9, 71, 80, 144, 190,
   201
Messaoudi, Khalida, 201–4
metaphysical philosophy, 17
métissage, 199
microfemininity, 67
militancy, 37, 38
militant, 41; discourses, 23; -national-
   ist, 23, 34, 37
mimetic, 56, 125, 155
mimeticism, 34, 105
mimicry, 29, 34, 126
minoritarian, 67
minorities, 18, 28, 53
minority, 59, 67, 68
modernism, 44
Mokeddem, Malika, 7, 11, 13, 21, 25, 32,
   55, 72. *See also* the Epilogue
molecular, 66; groups, 66; woman, 67
mondialisme, 57

Index

Index

About the Author

Valérie Orlando completed her Ph.D. in French Studies at Brown University in 1996. She has taught Francophone literature, nineteenth- and twentieth-century French literature, French philosophy, cultural studies, and film studies at Eastern Mediterranean University in the Turkish Republic of Northern Cyprus. She has published articles on Francophone literature of the Maghreb and French philosophy and literature. Presently she is working on a second book on recent thematic developments in Francophone literature of Africa and the Caribbean. Professor Orlando is an assistant professor in the department of modern and classical languages at Illinois Wesleyan University.